INTUITIVE INTELLIGENCE
Training

The handbook for qualified
Intuitive Intelligence Trainers

2ND EDITION

Dr Ricci-Jane Adams

and *Angelique Adams*
and *Dr Niikee Schoendorfer*

TRAINED & CERTIFIED BY:

the institute for intuitive intelligence

First published by Institute for Intuitive Intelligence in 2021.

Second edition published in 2024.

Copyright © Ricci-Jane Adams 2024.

www.instituteforintuitiveintelligence.com

The moral right of the author has been asserted.

All rights reserved. This publication (or any part of it) may not be reproduced or transmitted, copied, stored, distributed or otherwise made available by any person or entity (including Google, Amazon or similar organisations), in any form (electronic, digital, optical, mechanical) or by any means (photocopying, recording, scanning or otherwise) without prior written permission from the publisher.

Information contained in this book is for Certified Intuitive Intelligence Trainer use only. You may not reproduce, replicate this manual, or teach any part of this training in a professional context.

You must identify this process as the **Intuitive Intelligence ® Methodology** and Praxis when used in a professional context.

Cover Design, Internal Layout Design & Typesetting by Elise Elliott (Pass the Salt). www.passthesalt.com.au

All images by Rachael Cannard ours@notminenoyours.com

Except the images of the Tapping points by Gemma Sykes

TABLE OF

CONTENTS

THE 5,000 DAUGHTERS OF MARYAM	6
THE VISION FOR THE INTUITIVE INTELLIGENCE TRAINER	9
HOW TO USE THIS HANDBOOK	10

PART ONE – INFORMING THEORY 11

THE WHY AND WHAT OF INTUITIVE INTELLIGENCE	12
WHAT DOES AN INTUITIVE INTELLIGENCE TRAINER DO?	14
WHAT IS OUR PROCESS?	15
THE IMMUTABLE LAWS	18
THE SCIENCE OF INTUITIVE INTELLIGENCE	24
THE LAYERS OF CONSCIOUSNESS	31
THE FOUR PHASES OF INTUITION	34
SUPERCONSCIOUS INTUITION	43
FEAR AND THE INTENTIONAL DESCENT TO THE UNDERWORLD	48
ETHICS AND VALUES AS AN EMBODIED PRACTICE	56

PART TWO – PRAXIS PHILOSOPHY & PRAXIS 67

THE TOOLS OF THE INTUITIVE INTELLIGENCE TRAINER	68
OVERVIEW OF THE INTUITIVE INTELLIGENCE METHOD SESSION	69
OVERVIEW OF THE INTUITIVE INTELLIGENCE FOLLOW UP SESSIONS	70
INTUITIVE INTELLIGENCE EMBODIMENT	71
MORE EMBODIED PRACTICES	79
PRE-CLIENT PREPARATION	86
STEP ONE – OPENING & ASOC	91
STEP TWO – FEAR PROFILING & SHADOW ARCHETYPE	96
STEP TWO CONT. – SHADOW ARCHETYPE	99
STEP TWO CONT. – INTEGRATIVE BREATH	104
STEP THREE – CHAKRA COMMUNION	106

TABLE OF
CONTENTS

STEP THREE CONT. – KOSHAS COMMUNION	112
STEP FOUR – INSTIGATING EVENT	115
STEP FIVE – AKASHIC LIBRARY	121
STEP SIX – SACRED 13 ARCHETYPES	129
STEP SEVEN – THE ATONEMENT	136
PART THREE – TAPPING	**149**
WHAT IS TAPPING?	150
TAPPING – A SHORT HISTORY	150
INTUITIVE INTELLIGENCE TAPPING	151
THE TAPPING PROCEDURES	159
SUBTLE ANATOMY & THE CENTRES OF ENERGY	160
A COLOUR MEDITATION	174
REMEMBERING SOUL – A VISUALISATION	176
THE GOLDEN LIGHT – A VISUALISATION	179
PART FOUR – FULL METHOD	**181**
CLIENT DISCLAIMER	194
ACKNOWLEDGMENTS	196
ABOUT THE AUTHOR	198
ABOUT THE INSTITUTE FOR INTUITIVE INTELLIGENCE	198

CONTENT

DISCLAIMER

The theory and praxis included in this text is for use by qualified Intuitive Intelligence Trainers, graduated from the Institute for Intuitive Intelligence. Intuitive Intelligence ® is a registered trademark. For your reading convenience, we do not repeat ® throughout the text.

In this text, the theory and praxis are for professional use in one to one settings by currently registered Intuitive Intelligence Trainers who

hold membership with the Institute. Qualified Intuitive Intelligence Trainers who do not hold current membership with the Institute are welcome to utilise the text for personal use only.

Except for social media channels or promotional pathways such as podcast interviews and newsletters shared to invite private clients, Intuitive Intelligence Trainers are not licenced to teach this material in any context.

For the avoidance of doubt, Intuitive Intelligence Trainers can also share this material in the context of small group mentoring to existing private clients if this suits their business model's needs.

Intuitive Intelligence Trainers are eligible to continue their training to become Intuitive Intelligence Teachers to be eligible to teach aspects of this material. Please see the Institute website for more information in regards to this.

INTRODUCTION

THE 5,000 DAUGHTERS OF MARYAM

INTRODUCTION

THE 5,000 DAUGHTERS OF MARYAM

We gathered like this most mornings.

As the most prominent temple for hundreds of miles in all directions, we were a magnet to young Initiates willing to hand their lives over in service, who would travel for long distances to join us. A whole town had sprung up around the temple, merchants and makers servicing our needs and others providing shelter to the many priestesses who resided outside the temple itself.

We gathered on the vast stone steps leading up to the temple each morning as the sun began to rise. I took my place at the landing outside of the temple doors, and from that vantage, I saw them all—each beloved daughter arriving into this shared space for the morning's directives. Our assembly was like clockwork; our routines secure, providing the consistency required for our service. From here, our sisters would move outwards to attend to the tasks of their chapter. Within the larger temple structure, each group had their roles and functions and dutifully went about them with fierce devotion. When the work was complete at night, we would gather again on these steps for our devotions and prayers, anchoring back into our holy task.

That morning we gathered. This time was unlike any other. I stood before my daughters. Today I could not speak. The news had come, which I had long been anticipating. I had seen this time, as had so many of my daughters in their nightmares and their visions. It was ending, this life, the only one we had ever known. Tonight, there would be an invasion of the town and the temple, and anyone who was there, killed.

I had seen this vision but never known when it would occur. How could I move so many into hiding without immediate threat? How could I close down our work and training? I couldn't. So we had proceeded as we were. Yet we had taken precautions, and every woman was ready to leave and was assigned a place to go should this day come. That day, in the predawn light, the message had arrived. They were very close. The hell they brought was real and deadly.

Who was it that was coming?

My daughters, for the most part, didn't know. I did. It wasn't one army, one despotic leader, one faction. It was a global counter-movement. A shifting consciousness. A collective cycle moving humanity towards a dark shadow that would last for a very long time. It was a rise against all that we were. A war to close down the holy human truth and separate us from our divine power. It was the darkness coming, and the women I served were the first in line to those who sought to bring this darkness.

It was time. It was the time I had long dreaded. It was time for us to withdraw our work from the world, at least publicly. It was time for us to go underground to save ourselves from their retribution. It was time for me to withdraw from sight, the wisdom I had been the recipient of. We had to disband. We had to go out on our own and keep our knowledge in secret places.

My heart broke. My hands shook. The women looked at me, waiting for me to speak. They held one another, aware of what was to come by a feeling of the words that I could not say aloud.

INTRODUCTION

THE 5,000 DAUGHTERS OF MARYAM

Go now, my daughters, and do not come back. Do not look for me and do not gather together. Stay true to your training, but do not do it in the daylight. Hide it away until the time comes. One day it will come. We will gather together again. The dark shadow will not be here forever. When I call you home at that future date, it may not be in this place or even in the body you now inhabit, but do not fear. You will hear my call, and I promise I will find you. I will be so fierce and so clear and so true in calling you home that you will not mistake me. I will not rest until I have brought you all home.

As the last words fell from my mouth, the bells around the city began to ring, warning us. The attack was closer than any of us could have known.

Go! I implored them. I watched immobilised as the 5,000 scattered from our beloved temple steps and beyond my reach until my sisters took me by my shoulders and led me away to the first of our many hiding places.

When did this happen? No time of which you have conscious memory, no civilisation recorded in your records. For some, it is as though it was yesterday, and for others, an ancient tale. It doesn't matter. If you are reading these words, it is within you and part of you..

What matters now is this. My name is Maryam. I am the High Priestess. Welcome home, my daughter. Welcome home.

The Mystical Heart

The mystical heart of the work of the Intuitive Intelligence Trainer is the archetypal trinity of Priestess Mystic Leader. Every woman who walks the path of qualifying as an Intuitive Intelligence Trainer knows that the power of her work is generated by anchoring into the cathedral of her heart. The Priestess Mystic Leader is the archetype for our times. She is the bridge between the nonlocal and local dimensions. Science and Mysticism. Her faith is active and present in the world. Her spirituality is a balm for the world, not a way to bypass the world. She is the demonstration.

In 2019, I was given the vision of 5000 Priestess Mystic Leaders awakening on Earth at this time. I have been charged to bring that vision to reality in service to the greatest good. The archetypal energy of the Priestess Mystic Leader is typified by Maryam.

Maryam is known by many names and has appeared in all religions, times and places throughout recent human history (the last two thousand years or so!). You may have heard her called Mary, the Magdalene or Miriam. She is all of these historical figures and none of them. She is an archetypal energy available to us all, not a personality or single identity. She is the energy of the High Priestess and it is she who blesses and guides her daughters on Earth from the nonlocal Field. She is the mystical heart of the work of the Intuitive Intelligence Trainer.

INTRODUCTION

THE VISION FOR THE INTUITIVE INTELLIGENCE TRAINER

Non sibi sed toti – not for self, but for all

As a qualified Intuitive Intelligence Trainer, you are the foundation of the Institute. You contribute your unique energetic signature, intuitive skill and spiritual power to the Institute's mission. The quality of your service contributes to the Institute being recognised as a leader in the intuition revolution beyond the trinkets and superstitions of the new age.

The Institute is committed to disrupting intuition education and creating a gold-standard benchmark in the intuitive sciences and new paradigm leadership training because, in an unregulated industry, the standards we set are our own.

Excellence, ethical service, the pursuit of spiritual innovation and ongoing research inform all of the Institute's activities, for this is how we believe we can take the new paradigm of intuition to the world.

At our mystical heart, the Institute's mission is to train 5,000 women to know themselves as the Priestess Mystic Leader. It is not by the Third Level program alone that this will happen. As you go forth as a qualified Intuitive Intelligence Trainer, every woman you serve has the potential to be awoken to this truth within her by you.

You stand for the deep work of deep faith. You create a new paradigm through our global sisterhood network, privileging service above self, and putting your spiritual seeking to work in the world to support global consciousness liberation.

You, who go forward in our name, take personal responsibility for being the demonstration of the Institute's Code of Ethics and adhere to the Membership created ethical code to govern your actions as an ambassador of the Institute. The Institute takes the same responsibility to be the demonstration of all we stand for, to ensure that this is a powerful and congruent partnership.

As the Institute continues to strive towards our vision, the Institute knows that it is only through our collective ethical, inclusive, integrous, socially conscious action focused on elevating women, that we may grow.

Together, we rise. The more we support you to grow and expand in your holy power, the more powerful the revolution we create.

As a daughter of Maryam, you share the divine responsibility with the Institute from the time of your training, to be the demonstration of the Priestess Mystic Leader, and to activate that holy trinity in those who also carry this contract in their soul. Together, we create the revolution.

INTRODUCTION

HOW TO USE THIS HANDBOOK

This manual explains the informing philosophy, practices and guiding principles of the Intuitive Intelligence Methodology and Praxis. The Praxis and the Methodology of Intuitive Intelligence are shared side by side to understand WHAT we do as Intuitive Intelligence Trainers and WHY we do it.

The structure of the handbook is as follows:

- **PART ONE** – *Informing theory*
- **PART TWO** – *Philosophy informing the praxis + the praxis*

Each praxis section includes:

- *How to use the praxis as part of the Method session, and*
- *How to use it outside of the Method (Follow up).*

Follow up templates:

The Follow up templates are designed as jumping off points and are by no means exhaustive. Case studies from qualified Intuitive Intelligence Trainers are shared throughout as examples of the diversity and spectrum of the work of Intuitive Intelligence.

At the end of the handbook, the full Method script is provided for ease of reference.

PART ONE

INFORMING THEORY

PART ONE

THE WHY & WHAT OF INTUITIVE INTELLIGENCE

> "THE SWEET ENERGY OF HEALING POURS INTO OUR ENERGY SYSTEM EVERY TIME WE BREAK FEAR'S AUTHORITY OVER OUR LIVES AND REPLACE IT WITH A MORE EMPOWERED SENSE OF SELF"[1].

Why is the theory and praxis of Intuitive Intelligence my preferred way of working to support transformation for my clients? What is it about this particular set of processes that works so well to serve our clients?

When I began working as an intuitive reader,

I called myself a psychic. It was very much about answering the questions that my clients brought to me. I reached a point where I could no longer do that work. I understood that I was taking the client's power in those sessions, not through intentionality or being unethical but because that's what the client wanted.

They were coming to me wanting to abdicate responsibility for their life.

I no longer felt like that was something I could do, and I walked away from doing readings at that time. When I returned to this process in 2014, I began to develop an entirely new approach to working. What I knew or recognised from working with my clients was that regardless of the question they brought to me, the problem was always the same.

And the problem was fear. Unmet fear.

Most people are not willing to go and meet their fear on their own. They may not even know how. They may not even understand that where there is fear, there cannot be love, and therefore, the problems of their life are there in the first place.

The root cause of the underlying starting point for healing is always the same...

There is a fearful, faulty belief system that prevents my client from living a life that's in accordance with their idea of success, and it is my task to guide them to this.

As the Methodology and Praxis evolved, it became evident that the only and primary work was to meet that fear on behalf of and with the client. Clearing this empowered them to take back their power, perhaps for their first time in lifetimes. It equipped them with the knowledge and information as well as the experiential, energetic shifts that would set them up to succeed.

The theory and praxis of Intuitive Intelligence is designed so that in one session, we can support our client to reach a level of autonomy or self-reliance. Understand that the difference between this and the kind of reading where we answer the questions for our client is that it requires a willingness and desire for change on behalf of the client. We will quickly find out if that client is ready or not. Regardless, the first session will empower them in ways that they may not initially understand.

From that first client session, there is likely more work for us to do together to break the addiction to the often lifelong fear patterns, associated behaviours and coping mechanisms.

[1] *Caroline Myss, Anatomy of the Spirit pp 229*

PART ONE

THE WHY & WHAT OF INTUITIVE INTELLIGENCE

That first evaluation session, the Method in its pure form, is a perfect standalone experience. It will liberate our client from their fear, with laser-like precision. It cuts straight to the heart of those dominant-negative fears both in the subtle anatomy and the physical body that exceeds and surpasses anything else that I have ever experienced. From that point, the theory and praxis of Intuitive Intelligence will continue to support the client as they break through the addictions to fear at the level of the subconscious.

We do away with the cause. We look at the meaning of the event, the impediment. We're not obsessed or focused on diagnosis or keeping a collection of all their suffering in a nice manilla folder. We move them forward from a fear dominant program to a love dominant program.

Our work with our clients is entirely active as well as being altogether liberating.

That's why the Methodology and Praxis are what I teach and continue to develop. It's what I think is worthy of our time, and it's worthy of our client receiving. It's not us taking the client's power. If we're tempted or drawn into answering specific questions about "should I live here or should I live there", or "should I marry this person or should I leave that person", then we're no longer doing the Methodology and Praxis. I want us to be very clear about that. The Methodology and Praxis are not abdicating or taking power away from the client. The client is their own guru, and this process is designed to remind them of their God nature.

What is Intuitive Intelligence?

A Summary

Intuitive Intelligence is a nonlocal form of intuition (non-biological, not implicit knowledge), which is acausal (Quantum not Newtonian), active and participatory (trained consciousness to receive intuition at will actively), deep state (subconscious, below the level of the ego-identified conscious reasoning mind), creative/creating as God-consciousness (not reactive), and surrendered. All this combines as an embodied state of being called Superconscious Intuition[2].

Intuitive Intelligence is our highest form of intelligence.

- Intuitive Intelligence is superconscious intuition, the highest, clearest and truest form of intuition available to us.
- We have the potential to become superhuman by tapping into our superconscious intuition.
- It is a journey from shadow to light to arrive at a place of wholeness.
- When opened up in expert conditions, our activated Intuitive Intelligence brings all our systems into optimal functioning – analytical, emotional, spiritual and physical.
- Intuitive Intelligence is leading-edge science merging with ancient mysticism. At this nexus, we find the codes for activating our most profound existence.
- It is the birthright of each of us, but it exists on the other side of our subconscious fear programs, and we must be willing to descend to the underworld of our being to claim it.

---

[2] These terms are further defined and discussed in the section 'The Four Phases of Intuition'.

PART ONE

WHAT DOES AN INTUITIVE INTELLIGENCE TRAINER DO?

With compassionate detachment, we lovingly guide those we serve to meet and release subconscious fear. We understand that subconscious fear programs are not a problem, but a necessary and productive tool on the path of our awakening journey.

As an Intuitive Intelligence Trainer we are qualified to support our client to meet and release subconscious fear programs, to activate their own superconscious state of being and to live their Intuitive Intelligence.

We perceive the symbolic or sacred meaning of the client's life situation and guide them to know this for themselves. We are scaffolding them to shift their gaze from the egoic/personal to the soul meaning of their life events. We are supporting them to change their mind about who and what they truly are.

Rather than identify the cause, we locate the meaning of the events for the client by looking to the spiritual dimension. The cause means nothing without the meaning. We support the client to be curious about how these events serve them and give them the courage to ask, what will I do with my pain?

We are never coaching or hyping our client. We are, in fact, not letting them off the hook. Our work is to guide those we serve on an intentional descent to the underworld of their subconscious to attain a higher level of consciousness.

This process is reflected in the visual map of the Method (shown on following page).

This is the visual representation of the journey. The map that you will expertly guide your client through.

To embark on the journey of awakening your Intuitive Intelligence, for our client, is a deep dive into the concept of being hung on the hook. Of being held to the fire of transformation with deep compassion. The deepest phase of the descent to the underworld will cause discomfort, it's the place where we grow, transmute fear and melt into liminality. Not quite a caterpillar anymore, but not yet the butterfly that will emerge. It can feel like failure. We can look desperately for an out, anything at all to get some relief from hanging on that hook. But we must not let ourselves off the hook. It is here we put down our littleness and if we have the courage, ascend from the underworld of our own being into the light, ready to serve in the most powerful way. We must dig so deep into ourselves that we might feel as though we are emptying out to the point of destruction. And so it is.

But what is being destroyed is the ego identification.

It is uncomfortable as hell. But it is also inevitable. We can delay it. But this is the work of our lives. As the Intuitive Intelligence Trainer it is your most holy task to be of service in this way.

PART ONE

MAP OF INTUITIVE INTELLIGENCE METHOD

THE INTUITIVE INTELLIGENCE®
DESCENT TO THE UNDERWORLD

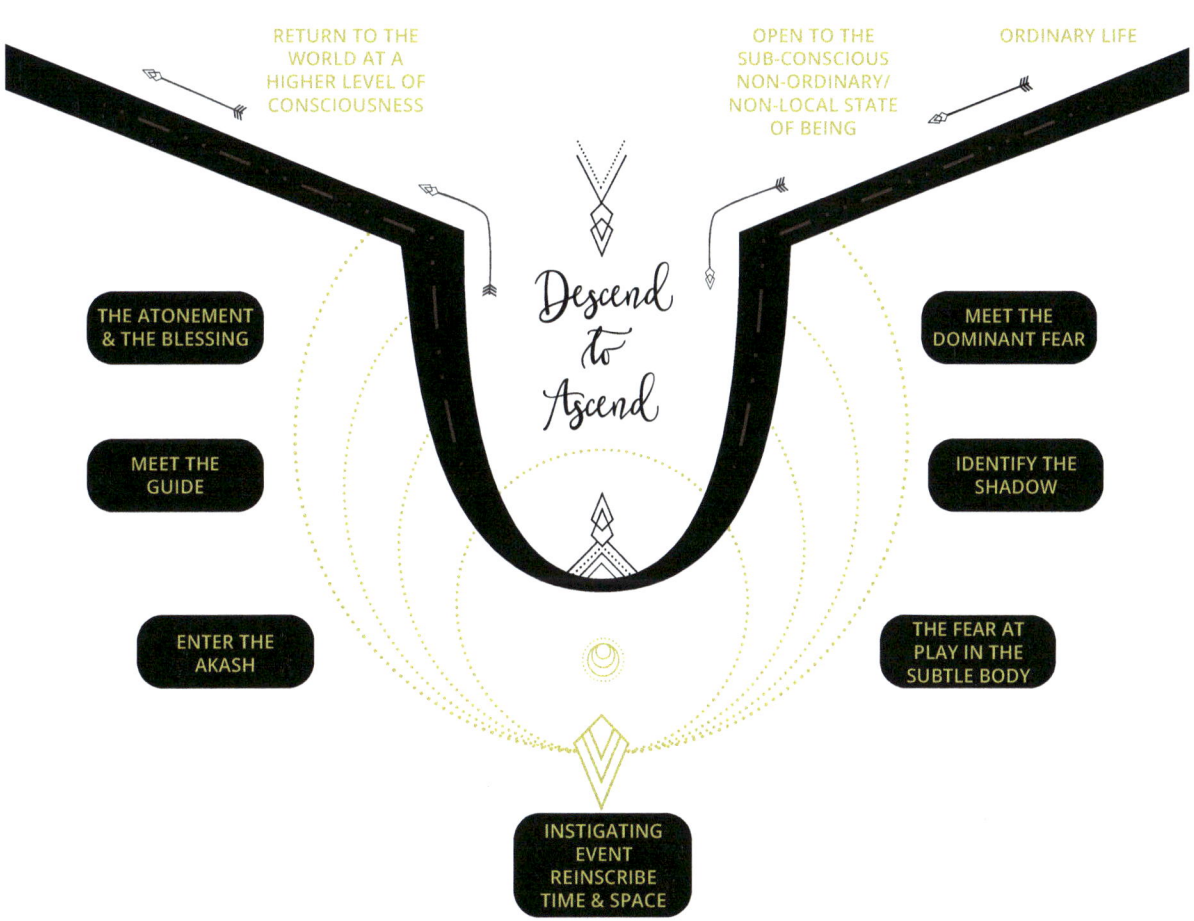

PART ONE

WHAT IS OUR PROCESS?

The journey of an Intuitive Intelligence session is a deep dive into the underworld. We descend together with our client to identify the dominant-negative fear that prevents our client from realising our fullest knowing of the power of our pure unlimited consciousness. Our God Consciousness. This is how we can describe our work to our clients:

Over a series of sessions, we will:

- *Identify your dominant negative self-belief*
- *Create the neurological conditions for real change*
- *Facilitate the energetic conditions for a maximal experience of transformation*
- *Access the archetypal patterns stored in your subconscious*
- *Alter the frequency of your state of being*
- *Work across the timelines of your consciousness to liberate your personal energy*
- *Connect you to your archetypal life guide*
- *Equip you with tools for ongoing, self-determined shifts in your subconscious programs*
- *Establish an energy set that supports you to sustain the changes made in your work with your trainer over time —creating a new 'normal' at the highest possible vibration.*

THE INTUITIVE INTELLIGENCE TRAINER TRAINS THE CONSCIOUSNESS OF THEIR CLIENT TO INCREASE THE CLIENT'S ACCESS TO THEIR OWN INTUITIVE INTELLIGENCE.

PART ONE

THE IMMUTABLE LAWS

The theory and practices of Intuitive Intelligence assemble around the three immutable Hermetic laws – the law of mentalism, correspondence and vibration. The laws draw from The Kybalion: Hermetic Philosophy, originally published in 1908 under the pseudonym of the Three Initiates. This text contains the essence of the teachings of Hermes Trismegistus, also known as Thoth in Hellenistic Egypt. Thoth and Hermes were gods of writing and magic in their respective cultures. This information was handed down through secret orders over those thousands of years. Eventually it was agreed, whether we believe by individuals or some higher power, that this knowledge should be made public.

Around the 1930s, there was a significant appetite for an increased understanding of the occult laws and the things previously hidden from public view like Hermeticism and Rosicrucianism. There was a growing appetite for understanding how these laws were applied. A veil, if you like, was lifted, and we will be able to see much more clearly how the cosmos or the God Mind operated.

We can look at the awakening of consciousness that has been happening since the 1930s between the two great world wars and how we have been hungry for understanding more. This awakening typified the '60s free love revolution. The hippie movement was the beginning of our contemporary spiritual awakening.

Today, we understand that it is not about just bringing the projection, the 3D reality or the illusion into a higher order. It's being able to see beyond it, to see the world within the world. This is really what the laws do. They lift our gaze from human sight up to that universal sight to think like the universe. The laws open us to the deeper spiritual meaning of our lives.

Just as the number three has sacred resonance for many spiritual seekers, the three immutable Hermetic laws are held in deep reverence by many of those on the path of awakening consciousness. Whether we consider them as allegory or fact, it matters not, though quantum physics is now proving the efficacy of the laws. Adhering to the laws as metaphysics or quantum physics still yields the same powerful results.

The governing system of Hermetic laws manages the cosmos and holds all things together. All things are ordered to the second. The God Mind is impartial. If our lives are not as we want them to be, we need to ask, how have I broken the law? Intuitive Intelligence is ultimately opening to our God nature. We must know how the God Mind operates to activate our Intuitive Intelligence. This is what the laws are. When we look to the laws, we equip ourselves to expedite the process of accepting the higher purpose of the suffering and aligning our lives with our holiness.

The laws give us a means to make sense of the apparent inconsistencies of our lives and view the events we experience with a universal perspective. This is a vital step in spiritual maturing and spiritual agency. Spiritual maturity is evidenced in our ability to not take everything personally. It is the core work of the Intuitive Intelligence Trainer; to privilege congruence with these laws and support our clients to gain this perspective for their own life events.

We support our client to learn to make peace with paradox and, in so doing, gain a state of eternal grace. Surrender in action.

PART ONE

The Law of Mentalism

All is One. All is of the Mind.

The law of mentalism sounds like a very lofty law, but it is very straightforward. This principle embodies the understanding that everything in the Universe creates by thought. There is nothing that exists in the Universe where this is not the case. The great law of spiritual psychology is that it is our thought or belief that creates our reality. Everything that exists is energy: matter densified energy; energy is just refined matter. All is just energy.

The idea of the holograph is applicable here, and many have spoken of the holographic nature of the Universe. I'll keep it simple: in a holographic image, all parts contain the whole. So it goes with the law of mentalism. When the law states that all is of the mind, we can conceive of this as both the one mind – or the mind of God – as well as our individual minds. Even now, we can glean a clue of how spiritual paradox is at work here. We are one with the mind of God, and nothing exists that is not. We reside in the God Mind, and everything we live is a projection of that God consciousness. So why the suffering, we may ask? If we reside in the mind of the benevolent Universe, then how could anything be less than love? Well, herein lies the paradox of spirituality. Within the One Mind, we have free will. The choices we make, the beliefs with which we seed our consciousness, are what determines how our piece of the reality appears. We can live inside the one mind of God and experience a living hell. It is our power to create through our consciousness that makes us what we are – divinity itself. It is our humanness that makes us forget that power or use it with such hit and miss results.

Everything that we are living in is a projection of our consciousness. It is what we are holding in our consciousness that is shaping reality. If we want to see a different reality,

if we're going to inhabit a different world, we need to change our mind about both ourselves and the nature of the world in which we live. This takes great spiritual maturity. Remember, it takes great spiritual maturity not to take everything personally.

When we have these laws to lean into, we can start to move beyond the personal, beyond the immediate need for release or relief from the conditions of our lives and to see our soul's trajectory for what it is: vast, ancient, and magnificent. We are never asked to give up more than we will gain – ever. But in the moment, we may not be able to see beyond our suffering to what is on offer. We may not understand that we indeed created it, for this is what the laws teach us.

We also can choose not to become the full expression of the God Mind. Let's repeat that in another way. We do not lack anything. We are the same substance as God. We are the same substance as that which created everything. We possess that same capacity, that same power, but we have free will, our divine birthright, as to whether we will fully express it. Our service as Intuitive Intelligence Trainers guides our clients to that place of certainty in what they truly are.

This law can be understood best via the functioning of consciousness and fear as part of the theory of Intuitive Intelligence. It is further explored in these sections in this text; The Layers of Consciousness, Fear and Intentional Descent to the Underworld.

The Law of Correspondence

As above, so below; as within, so without.

The second law is the law of correspondence. The law of correspondence means that the thoughts and images we hold in our conscious and subconscious mind will manifest their exact likeness in our external reality. The outer world is a reflection of what is within us. Like all the cosmic laws, this law is impartial and works unceasingly for the good or the bad. The law of correspondence requires that we know we are in partnership with God. In other words, we are not doing it alone. This requires absolute trust. There are a few steps before we can honestly know if we are living per the law. The first is that we trust. The second condition for the law of correspondence to come into the right action, is that we possess self-esteem.

PART ONE

For the law of correspondence to work in our favour, we will need our spiritual self-esteem. Why does this law require we trust God Consciousness? What does that have to do with self-esteem? Let's break it down: the law states that what we hold in our consciousness we will manifest in the outer world. Remembering that, as the law of mentalism tells us, consciousness is everything because all is of the mind. This makes sense when we apply it to the law of correspondence because it tells us that the inner and exterior are, in fact, one. The trust we need to feel in our God Consciousness is trust in ourselves because we are that – we are God. Trusting the God Mind is one condition of adhering to the law of correspondence.

Then there is the other, often much more tricky condition, tricky especially for spiritual seekers. Conceptually, we can say: "I trust God." We are pretty prepared to believe that God has our back. We even potentially want to remember that we are God. Until we have met our fears of unworthiness, we cannot indeed partner with what we are, with our God nature. We are paying lip service to the idea, and in reality, remain sitting in fear. As within, so without is another way of thinking about this law. We cannot say that we believe that God is all-powerful and then deny that we are that power – it's breaking the law. The law of correspondence brings us to the inevitable truth that we are divine beings with finite human experience. We will suffer whilst we believe that we are a limited human consciousness because our true nature is trying to correspond or communicate with itself through this experience called life. Our mortal fear is thwarting those attempts. When we can forgo our limited belief, we begin to see our lives flourish because the truth of what we are can communicate clearly with itself on all planes. Within and without, above and below.

I often quote the Spiderman adage in my workshops: **with great power comes great responsibility**[3]. We think we want to own our self-worth, but with that worthiness comes the responsibility for our God power. More often than not, we run from our own power. We think everyone else is responsible for the state of our lives, or is better than us, or didn't have the experiences we had and therefore can shine. The responsibility of being all-powerful means that we must ultimately surrender our human frailty. We have to trust that our lives have not gone astray and, most importantly, we must stop blaming God for what has happened to us or what we see around us in the world. We must surrender our fear that we are not God. Or we must surrender our worry that we are God. The brilliant and sneaky ego has a million stories to keep us playing small. If we want to save the world, we must surrender our fear and meet ourselves as God Consciousness. As within, so without.

The Law of Correspondence as a communication hotline

Intuitive intelligence is simply a symptom of a healed mind. The healing that occurs when we activate our Intuitive Intelligence corrects the false belief in separation and removes the blocks to our knowledge that we are in partnership with God Consciousness. God contains everything within it. It stands to reason that if we are connected and communicating with God consciousness, which is all, then we have it all. Not only that, we have the means by which to draw it to us. An activated Intuitive Intelligence is the most powerful manifestation tool we have. We draw towards us what corresponds to us. Another way to think about the law of correspondence is in terms of communication. What conversation am I having with myself and with God? Am I telling myself the world is a scary place full of dangerous people? Am I telling myself that I am worthless, nothing, weak and vulnerable?

---

[3] For a complete summary of the origins of this phrase see https://quoteinvestigator.com/2015/07/23/great-power/

PART ONE

That communication is a direct command to the God Mind, and because we are God the communication hotline is precise and robust. We are speaking (or thinking or feeling) our fears into reality. Communication is always happening, and as we understand from the levels of mind, it is most often subconsciously calling the God Consciousness into action. The God Mind corresponds to the communication because we are that powerful. So how do we heal this faulty feedback loop? That's what this chapter is all about. The power of knowing ourselves, and in particular the contents of our subconscious mind, is the most crucial step to living by this law.

We need to wrap our heads around the idea of correspondence as communication. The God Mind doesn't simply correspond to our belief about it. It does it with direct intent. It does it so we can overcome the faulty assumption of separation. Our true nature is Infinite and all-powerful, and anything in our lives that doesn't reflect that is an imbalance that will keep revisiting us until we correct it. It is a communication loop designed to bring us back into correspondence with our true nature. God isn't testing us – it is impartial. Everything in our lives, within and without, works to support our awakening so that when we have forgotten, the events we create from that forgetting will bring us home to ourselves.

Can I believe that the God Mind is all-powerful and that it is my partner and sit in feelings of low self-worth? No. We are breaking the law. The Universe will behave per our belief. As within, so without. In this case, life will seem like a living hell, and God will appear to be punishing or testing us at every turn. As we know that this is not possible in truth, we have to look to ourselves. How can we heal the belief in separation, the dualism that makes us think that God's power is separate from us, and heaven is a place we can only access when we die? Living Intuitive Intelligence is the answer. And yes, it takes practice. Intuitive intelligence is remembering that we are a divine piece of a benevolent God.

The Law of Vibration

With this law, we're mainly focusing on an idea that 'the feeling is the prayer'. This concept comes from the spiritual scientist Gregg Braden, and we're going to discuss how this works in our life and the role of intuition and feeling or vibration.

This is a fascinating law because, perhaps more than any others, the changes that we see in our life are radical and immediate when used consistently. Changing our vibration is something that we talk about a lot in spiritual circles. We're looking at the way that the big lofty, noble ideas of quantum physics can come into an applied or practical application in our own lives.

The principle of this law explains the difference between the manifestations of matter and energy and how in reality, there is no true difference. Every atom and molecule is vibrating in a particular motion. The motion is the shape of the Torus. We will discuss this further in the section on 'Entrainment' and 'The Science of Intuition' chapter. Science has been telling us for more than 100 years now that everything is energy and that we are part of a unified consciousness or quantum field.

Globally, we have not taken on this knowledge because it terrifies us; with that great power comes great responsibility. What if I AM one with all that there is? Not only that but what if my vibration IS informing God consciousness and telling it how to behave? Am I manufacturing my existence through my consciousness? Primarily through my unmet or unknown subconscious mind?

This law is premised on energy first, physical second. As Gregg Braden states in 'Resilience From The Heart', "The bottom line is we're bathed in a field of energy that's everywhere, always present, and one that existed since time began with the Big Bang."

PART ONE

Braden states that the first principle suggests that because everything exists within a matrix of energy, everything is connected. This is the first law, the law of mentalism. It's this connection that makes deep states of intuition possible between people and patterns between significant life events possible. This is what I postulate when we talk about the law of mentalism. When we get to the law of vibration, it becomes very applied.

No matter how it appears through the dominant senses, quantum physics confirms that we are not solid matter at all. The reason that we believe in our solid matter above our energy state is that we're lazy. It's straightforward to see 3D reality through our dominant senses. It's much harder to perceive ourselves at our quantum or energetic nature.

We default to the physical reality, the 3D reality, because we can see it right in front of us. It takes training, and that's what we're doing for our clients, supporting them to understand that our true nature is energetic and that our energy body is far vaster than our physical body. Our physical body is, in fact, just part of our energy field. Our physical body is atoms vibrating at a much slower frequency and are therefore much denser and much more able to be perceived through the dominant five senses. This is not the full expression of what we are. What we've seen in the mirror has very little to do with what we are and from where we're creating.

Our energy field extends at least two and a half meters further than our physical body. We know that it is that big because that's what the current instruments can measure. Who knows how vast we are. In particular, when we do our practices, such as heart congruence and take ourselves into a higher vibrational state, we extend our field. With our God consciousness; there's no limit to what we can do when we release our fear.

What expands our energy body? What raises our vibration? What slows it down? It is the feeling state that we hold that determines the frequency at which our particles are moving.

'The feeling is the prayer' indicates to us that we are creating at the level of energy because feeling is not a dominant sensory thing. It goes through the physical body but generates at the energetic level. The prayer sits in the heart which is the centre that connects us to the unified field or the quantum field. It's the gateway to the one mind. We remember, as the law of correspondence tells us, that the law of correspondence could also be called the law of communication. We communicate to that Superconscious field, but we also receive from the Superconscious field. What determines that exchange is the frequency that we're holding.

So, let's break it down a little bit. When we look at quantum physics, we know that we are energy first, physical second. The physical appears per the energetic vibration. We talked a little bit before about the idea that everything is in its pure energetic state until we place our gaze or attention upon it. This was proven in the double-slit experiment, which was first done in the 19th century. This experiment has been repeated many times since then. Dr Niikee Shcoendorfer expertly shares more on this in the chapter on 'The Science of Intuition'.

I want to talk about how much of a science it is to hold a high vibration. What happens in an untrained consciousness is that we think that the external reality events determine our vibration. If I have a good day and my children behave well and I get a pay rise, and my boss is pleasant to me, then I'll feel good about myself, and I can hold a higher vibration. Conversely, if I'm having a rubbish day and I get a parking ticket, and I don't get what I want in work or my relationship, then I am entitled to sit in my lower vibrations, my low feeling states. Then I am perceiving my life as a reaction to external circumstances.

PART ONE

The law of vibration shows us that our external circumstances exist only as a reflection of the frequency that we're holding. It is always up to us to determine the choice we make and the vibration we hold via our feeling state. If I want to experience a high vibrational joyful, freedom feeling state, even if 3D reality is not behaving itself, even if I'm fighting with my partner, even if I don't get that pay rise, even if I can't find a car park at the supermarket, then I am starting to craft the world that I see, rather than passively receive it.

This is the next step along the feeling is the prayer – it means that we go from waiting for God or something outside of us to give us what we need, and we start generating what we need. That's a genuinely magnificent state of being. It requires a commitment. A commitment to practice holding the highest vibrational feeling states, even when the 3D reality isn't behaving itself.

As Caroline Myss says, it is not time and space that causes us to hold a higher vibration or be in a higher state of reality; it is release and surrender. This is what Joe Dispenza is talking about when we commit to holding a higher vibration. We're trying to effectively unite the physical level of our vibrating particles with our energy level, with our soul level. We're trying to imbue the soul consciousness into the energy body so that the physical body can show up in a much higher vibration.

At the physical level, we need to change the nervous system, which is that repository or place that is holding on to the history of our experiences, the trauma or the suffering that sits in the nervous system. Until we rewire that, we're not going to be able to hold this higher vibrational state. As we've said again and again and again, we can't change our Conscious Mind to change our nervous system or anything else. We need to go to the subconscious program.

The nervous system controls the limbic brain or the subconscious level of mind. It is holding a different feeling that will alter our consciousness. Remembering our physical body is only a reflection or an aspect of our energy body. Our energy body is in communion with our soul body. The less fear we hold in our energy body, the more we hear our soul level or our higher self or the Holy Spirit or our intuition, whatever language we want to place on that.

We're beginning to see how this happens, how both the energy body and physical body need to come into congruence to open to our Intuitive Intelligence. The result of that, of course, is that we live in heaven on earth. We do not live in a state of despair; we do not live in the nightmare any longer.

We must practice holding a state of being that is greater than our external circumstances. It doesn't matter how magnificent our life is or how rubbish it is; we can go further into that experience of heaven on earth by cultivating the practice of holding a higher vibration or a higher state of being than our external circumstances warrant.

The holding of that new vibration shifts us out of survival mode and into an expanded state. That expansion is happening at the level of energy. We are growing our size. We're moving from this tightly wound, tightly held fear-based organism into an expanded state where we move out and fill up space, and we can easily decode the information of the One Mind far more readily in our expanded form.

This is such an exciting understanding for us because it puts the power so squarely in our hands. We always have a choice about how we feel. The more frequently we choose to hold a higher vibration, the more powerfully we are able to change our external reality. We understand then, it's the law that when we feel it, we will receive it. We can make change not by holding on to current fears but by holding a vibration that is disproportionate or greater than our current reality. In so doing, we bring a new reality, we bring the miracle into our lives.

PART ONE

THE SCIENCE OF INTUITIVE INTELLIGENCE

Quantum Entangled Consciousness and the Hermetic Philosophic Laws of the Universe

Dr Niikee Schoendorfer PhD MHS BHS ND Dip Ed

Postdoctoral Research Fellow, Institute for Intuitive Intelligence

The physics revolution for more than 100 years has been challenging the very underpinnings of much of the accepted science theory preceding this time, and still to date. Many questions remain so far unanswerable due to their very nature, defining the undefinable.

Is the universe material or mental? Is everything that exists interconnected and affected by everything else? Is it possible to determine precisely what things are or is all that exists created through observation? Can we exist simultaneously or perhaps not even exist the way we know it at all?

The first Hermetic law of mentalism suggests that 'All is mind', in that everything is created by observation, by a thought and that 'All is one'. Through this interconnectedness, the Universal law of vibration implies that everything affects everything else simultaneously. This conjecture defies classical physics in that an effect cannot occur before its cause and challenges the old Newtonian model of causality where all effects must have specific causes.

Quantum Physics purports to be on its way in solving the nature of these mysteries.

Quantum mechanics studies the properties of energetic behaviour at the scale of atoms and subatomic particles. Before its advent, scientific theories only supported the physical properties (physics) of larger molecules, which according to quantum, no longer apply once smaller scale particles are being observed.

According to famous physicist and mathematician Sir James Jean (1877-1946) 'the stream of knowledge is heading towards a non-mechanical reality; the universe begins to look more like a great thought than like a great machine. The mind no longer appears to be an accidental intruder into the realm of matter...'(1). Here, Jean is suggesting that what is being demonstrated in the quantum realm is that 'All is of the mind', in fact, does take precedence over matter and influences how matter is being created!

What follows is a review of the most reproduced and pinnacle experiments, concepts and theories in the field of quantum science, along with an interpretation related to the Hermetic laws which are thought to have originated in ancient Egypt dating back beyond 36 000 BCE. These philosophical teachings were shared in the great temples throughout the region and onto Ancient Greece and the Libraries of Alexandra, where they have been associated with legendary minds like Pythagoras, Aristotle and Socrates. Later these same teachings were reflected in Florence during the Renaissance during the 1400-1600 CE, sprouting famous intellectuals such as da Vinci, Michelangelo, Shakespeare and Copernicus. This period was thought to have emerged to the rediscovery of ancient Greek texts and the emergence of humanism, among others.

PART ONE

The Unified Field

In 2010, Vendral described an informational theory of the universe where everything including us, is made up of information. Quantum's unified field theory (1993) adds that the interconnected universe is a field of non-local information, not limited by space-time and entangled within everything all at the same time (2). This unified field is thought to be derived from the entanglement of electromagnetic fields of molecules and constitute this interconnected information web. According to Hermetic Philosophy and its law of mentalism, 'All is one', concurs with these findings.

Beyond the quantum, biological organisation on all levels on this planet is also thought to occur due to electromagnetic field communication, in that various parts within a living organism use coherent states of electromagnetic frequency to continue to function cohesively even when separated (3). We see this playing out for example when flocks of birds or schools of fish move in unison or annual migrations within species, again as if 'All is one'. Electromagnetic fields exist within and affect everything from single small chemical reactions to the self-organisation of entire ecosystems (4). These factors are aligned with the Universal law of Correspondence, where 'As above, so below' describes what happens in the microcosm so to happens within the macrocosm, via these constantly being interconnected and in co-communion.

Human consciousness, including self-awareness and intelligence, has also been implicated in this electromagnetic unified field theory, attributed to the brain's magnetic field created by its dense population of magnetite crystals, combined with its neural electrical system (5). In theory, this web of electromagnetic fields is what makes up this greater unified field, again supporting the universal law of mentalism in that 'All is one'. So, is everything that exists interconnected and affected by everything else?

Entanglement

Albert Einstein in 1935 wrote his well versed paper, calling it 'Spooky Action at a Distance' in light of his frustration in trying to explain how it might be possible for entangled particles to remain connected, even over great distances. This is one of the great quantum mysteries where measuring one part of the entangled particle elicits instantaneous effects on the other, no matter where it is situated. This defies the causal laws of classical physics where an action must precede each reaction, causing the reaction to then occur after action and not simultaneously as we see with quantum entangled particles.

Entanglement theory purports that when any previously connected particles are separated, they will still maintain connection that is not affected by space or time. For example, particles may have what's termed superposition, meaning that they can exist in multiple states at once. They have a magnetic spin property where they can spin either up or down at the same time, until they are specifically observed or measured. At that moment in time, they will assume a definite direction. This is the 'spooky' part!

Much of the early quantum theories were developed mathematically, although more recently have been supported by experimentation and relevant data collection. Entanglement theory has been investigated experimentally in several alternative scenarios and continues to be easily replicated in laboratories all over the world.

Wiseman et al (2005) were able to rigorously verify this entanglement phenomenon, by splitting a single photon and observing a change in one part, because of actual measuring or observing the other at a distant site (6). What this experiment and theory validation shows is that molecules remain connected even though separated, supporting the 'All is one' interconnectedness suggested in the law of mentalism.

PART ONE

Researchers in the Netherlands measured 245 pairs of entangled electrons, separated across the university campus some 1.3km apart. They found that each electron was in fact influencing its entangled partner, where when one was manipulated and measured spinning a certain direction its pair across campus immediately flipped, to maintain a balanced equilibrium despite no longer being in physical contact (7). These studies show that space or distance and time has no relevance in the quantum sized reality. They also suggest that the space that our reality occupies only exists in its perceived form due to observation or measurement. Back to the original questions, *'Is it possible to determine precisely what things are or is all that exists created through observation?' 'Is the universe material or mental?'*

In 2001, Juan Maldacena added onto the original work of Einstein and Rosen (1935), demonstrating a revolutionary conclusion suggesting that entanglement is what binds space-time together. He concluded that 'Space-time is really just some geometrical manifestation of entanglement, whilst its continuity which seems to be something very solid, could come from the ghostly properties of entanglement' (8) This premise suggests that linear time as it appears, may only be a hallmark of our continued observation of the same patterns of existence, supporting the Hermetic law of mentalism in that 'All is mind'.

While working on entanglement and what he termed the holographic principle, Susskind (2008) wrote 'quantum entanglement is a form of information and so space-time is merely a manifestation of quantum information' (9). His work built on from that of Smolin (2000) which describes the universe as a network of holograms, with each hologram containing information about all others. Smolin also proposed that space was only a channel of information from observer to observer (10). This holographic theory might explain how particles instantaneously know about information that is happening at any given time at any location, separated only by the 'observation' that there is in fact a distance between.

This paper will come back to considering holograms once further pivotal quantum physics principles have been more fully introduced.

Robust efforts by top physicists have produced theoretical evidence that networks of entangled quantum states, described as qubits, weave the space-time fabric. These entangled qubits are thought to create geometrical networks in space with an extra dimension, beyond the number of dimensions that the qubits live in (11). This might explain how particles can exist simultaneously bidirectional and settle to take a specific form when measured within the specific dimension where the observation is taking place. This theory may also support speculation of multidimensionality as existing simultaneously rather than as past and future occurrences.

The existence of what is termed as virtual photons have been identified within quantum mechanics. These photons are thought to be exchange particles for electromagnetic (unified field) interactions, where every photon spends some time as a virtual electron and also, it's mirror virtual positron. So, one particle can become a pair of heavier (virtual) particles, then quickly re-join into the original particle as if nothing had happened (12). Are these virtual particles existing simultaneously in another dimension and exchanging their relative positions under observation or measurement? And to add one of the original contemplations *'Can we exist simultaneously or perhaps not even exist the way we know it at all?'*

PART ONE

Wave or Particle

Termed the quantum measurement problem (QMP), is the peculiar effect that occurs when quantum sized particles behave differently under observation or not. This violates the basic modern scientific method principles that the world is directly measurable through observation and that these observations have no influence over what is being measured.

The wider implications of this on much of the way that scientific research is conducted is astounding and may be a reason why quantum science is regularly disregarded by the mainstream. If matter cannot be accurately observed relating to its behaviour, then it cannot be controlled and manipulated by mechanical force alone. Considering the supporting evidence thus far that the mind has the potential to influence matter, other confounding factors which are rarely considered in scientific research, have the potential to interplay with results of measurements in any given moment, rendering them inaccurate.

Since the advent of the infamous quantum physics double slit experiment, where matter does in fact act differently when measured or not, many scientists have attempted to go deeper in explaining the highly repeatable results that show waves of possibility become reduced into particles under observation. A full explanation of this experiment is beyond the scope of this paper and it is encouraged to read further details in one of the many interpretations available, if this experiment is unfamiliar.

Hypotheses that are being considered in the physics community vary from one end of the spectrum to the other where subjective reduction, meaning that the observation does affect the result, to beliefs that there is no reduction even occurring at all despite the supporting evidence (13).

QMP has been creating waves through the physics community for centuries, since its original inception by Thomas Young in 1801, with many varied renditions and some even attempting to 'trick' the wave into not knowing it is being observed, but to no avail! The holographic universe appears to know all and simultaneously.

In the 60's physicists like Jordan, Wigner and Pauli theorised that aspects of consciousness like attention, awareness and intention are foundational in deciphering the QMP, with Jordan writing *'Observations not only disturb what has to be measured, they produce it. We compel the particles to assume a definite position. We ourselves produce the results of measurements'* (14).

Since this time there has been a strong view by many, of the role of consciousness in the QMP, with the opposing faction strongly in resistance, holding to the fact that the physical world was here long before human consciousness evolved to observe it! (15)

These 'observations' have been experimentally investigated beyond direct measurement, to extend to pure observation, that being whether the group of participants in another room were focusing their attention toward or away from the double slit experiment. Interestingly, the group of experienced meditators were found capable of producing statistically significant results in the difference between when they were focusing towards and away from the experiment ie. collapsing or reducing the wave function into particle behaviour. Results from non-meditators and the control group with no observation both documented, no difference to chance (16). This highlights that focus needs to be maintained at some level to constitute observation, relating to the capacity to influence the nature of matter or reality.

PART ONE

Despite the yet unanswerable of these mysteries, one thing is fairly clear and that is if any information is gained about the path of a quantum sized molecule, the interference pattern produced by the wave function collapses with the information being measured or observed.

If observation is then responsible for producing a set outcome, do infinite waves of possibility continue to exist within our own lives if we stay open to what else might be possible? Do we then collapse waves of possibility then when we focus either on the perceived positive or negative aspects of a potential future event? Does our capacity to hold focus or intentionality influence outcomes?

Consciousness

Considering the possible role of consciousness in the outcomes of our reality, another theory is discussed, being that 'if the self-aware fabric of reality can in fact be modulated through attention and intention, then the very act of focusing on the double slit system may be what is collapsing the wave' (15). This idea is based on panpsychism, derived from ancient Greek schools of philosophy, which is controversial (of course) but openly considered within branches of modern-day philosophy of the mind.

The effects of intention and attention on outcomes has also been studied experimentally. Radin (2008) investigated the effect of intention from a human 'sender' on the autonomic nervous system of a distant 'receiver'. Skin conductance of the receivers, as an indicator of nervous system activation, was measured during intervals of compassionate intentional focus and not. Results demonstrated significant differences in skin conductance during the test periods, with larger and more sustained variations in the group pairs that were previously trained in intention, versus those that were not (17). This study again supports that the capacity to better focus, in this study through prior training, produces an additive effect on the outcomes.

A myriad of varying experiments have been conducted looking at the effect of conscious intention of humans on the influence of random number generators, with a summary of findings in a report issued by the US National Research Council, documenting that the overall results could not be explained by chance (18). This once more suggests that conscious intention is in fact able to affect outcomes and again supports the universal laws.

In his well-known experiment, Rene Peoc'h (1995) conditioned baby chicks to believe that a randomly moving robot was their mother, having them follow it around at a young age. When the chicks were placed in a transparent cage away from the robot, the robot rather than continue its random pathways, tended to spend excessive time in the vicinity of the chicks. When the chicks were removed, the robot again followed random trajectories. The experiment was repeated with 80 different groups of 15 chicks and demonstrated significance and repeatability in majority of the trials (19).

Several studies have documented the effects of good intentions between human participants, where one person focuses on a candle and indicates when their mind wanders, whilst the other in another room focuses on supporting the first with their focus. Between 11 studies with a total of 576 single sessions measured, the positive effect of benevolent intentions was supported across all studies (20).

PART ONE

Bradley (2006) investigated the success of repeat entrepreneurs and found that practices of focused intention and attention on a desired outcome was one of the highest predictors of repeated success in the entrepreneur participants. The group theorised that the biological energy activated through passionate attention, attuned them to the desired outcome or objects unfolding pattern of activity and thus its future potential. To explain further, as we have seen, the body creates fields of energy at various frequencies and that these fields can influence the field of potential energy. As the heart generates the most powerful electromagnetic field, utilising a heart focused state increases the attentional resonance with the incoming quantum level information from the object of interest (21).

Holographic Universe

According to Di Biase, consciousness informs our universe through quantum information and entanglement, influences matter, energy and space-time. His theory synthesizes previous work and suggests that 'This non-local quantum-holographic cosmos manifests itself through a quantum-holographic transpersonal consciousness, indivisibly interconnecting the human brain to all levels of the universe (22). Much contemporary physics points to the universe as a quantum holographic entangled reality and its very fabric, a quantum information web. It is theorised that entanglement of our quantum-holographic consciousness with the fabric of space-time, explains the wave particle phenomenon being collapsed by observer consciousness (8). It might also explain how intuitive information is received through seemingly non-local access, via the web of holographic information that exists in everything within the greater unified field.

Pribram (1991) described his theory of a holographic consciousness and further demonstrating experimentally that the patterns of the brain's electromagnetic activity consist of quantum holographic non-local information. This mind-brain-universe entanglement model is like that of Schrodinger's famous foundational wave function mathematical equation (23).

Bohm and Hiley (1993) proposed the Quantum- Holographic Theory of the universe, where the organisation of the cosmos occurs through non-local information, they termed holomovement. These quantum field fluctuations are thought to determine the behaviour and motion of a quantum potential based on the information it carries about its environment (24). This theory aligns with the Hermetic law of correspondence and the resultant effects of the vibrational resonance held within and its interrelationship with the outside environment.

The work of Pribram (2011) also supports the universal laws stating 'when a potential is realised, information becomes unfolded into ordinary space-time appearance. In the other direction, the transformation enfolds and distributes the information by the holographic process.' (8) This proposes that our specific thoughtforms unfold in the 3D physical reality through the law of mentalism, while enfolding or remaining as waves of potential, imprinting our personal electromagnetic field hologram as described by the Hermetic law of vibration.

When we consider the potential of a much greater reality, what is possible is so much more than the basic black and white causal reality that we have been previously taught. As our awareness grows and more information comes to light, it is probable that we will all be living a much different existence in the years to come as we learn how to better participate with more of what is available to us through the quantum universe.

PART ONE

References

1/ Henry, RC. 2005, 'The Mental Universe' Nature 436; 29

2/ Umezawa, H. 1993. Advanced Field Theory. AIP Press; New York.

3/ Bischof, M. and Del Giudice, E. 2013. 'Communication and the emergence of collective behaviour in living organisms: A quantum approach' Molecular Biology International 2013: 987549

4/ Brizhik, L. et al. 2009. 'The role of electromagnetic potentials in the evolutionary dynamics of ecosystems' Ecological Modelling 220; 1865-69

5/ Murphy, T. 2019. 'Solving the "Hard Problem": Consciousness as an intrinsic property of magnetic fields' Journal of Consciousness Exploration & Research 10: 8; 646-59

6/ Fuwa, M., Takeda, S., Zwierz, M. et al. 2015. 'Experimental proof of nonlocal wavefunction collapse for a single particle using homodyne measurements' Nat Commun 6: 6665

7/ Hensen, B. et al. 2015. 'Loophole-free Bell inequality violation using electron spins separated by 1.3 kilometers' Nature 526; 682-6

8/ Di Biase, F. 2019, 'Quantum entanglement of consciousness and space-time a unified field of consciousness' NeuroQuantology 17: 3; 80-85

9/ Susskind, L. 2008. The Black Hole War. Little, Brown & Co; USA.

10/ Smolin, L. 2000. Three Roads to Quantum Gravity. Weidenfeld and Nicolson; London.

11/ Swingle, B. 2018. 'Spacetime from entanglement' Annual Review of Condensed Matter Physics 9; 345-58

12/ Kane, G. 2006, 'Are virtual particles really constantly popping in and out of existence?' Scientific America October.

13/ Bierman, DJ. 2003. 'Does consciousness collapse the wave-packet?' Mind and Matter 1: 1; 45-57

14/ Mermin, M. 1990. Boojums All the Way Through: Communicating Science in a Prosaic Age. Cambridge University Press; Cambridge, UK.

15/ Radin, D. et al. 2012. 'Consciousness and the double-slit interference pattern: six experiments' Physics Essays 25: 2; 157-171

16/ Radin, D. 2008. 'Testing nonlocal observation as a source of intuitive knowledge' Explore 4: 1; 25-35

17/ Radin, D. et al. 2008. 'Compassionate intention as a therapeutic intervention by partners of cancer patients: effects of distant intention on the patients' autonomic nervous system' Explore 4: 4; 235-43

18/ Radin, D. and Nelson, R. 1989. 'Evidence for consciousness-related anomalies in random physical systems' Foundations of Physics 19: 12; 1499-1514

19/ Peoc'h, R. 1995. 'Psychokinetic action of young chicks on the path of an illuminated source' Journal of Scientific Exploration 9: 2; 223-229

20/ Schmidt, S. 2012. 'Can we help just by good intentions? A meta-analysis of experiments on distant intention effects' The Journal of Alternative and Complementary Medicine 18: 6; 529-33

21/ Bradley, RT. 2006a, "The psychophysiology of entrepreneurial intuition; A quantum-holographic theory' Third AGSE International Entrepreneurship Research Exchange Unitec; Auckland, NZ.

22/ Di Biase, F and Rocha, MS. 1999, 'Information, self-organization and consciousness: Toward a holoinformational theory of consciousness' Journal of Nonlocality 2; 2: 1-15

23/ Pribram, K. 1991. Brain and Perception: Holonomy and Structure in Figural Processing. Erlbaum; Hilsdale NJ.

24/ Bohm, D and Hiley, BJ. 1993. The Undivided Universe. Routledge; London.

PART ONE

THE LAYERS OF CONSCIOUSNESS

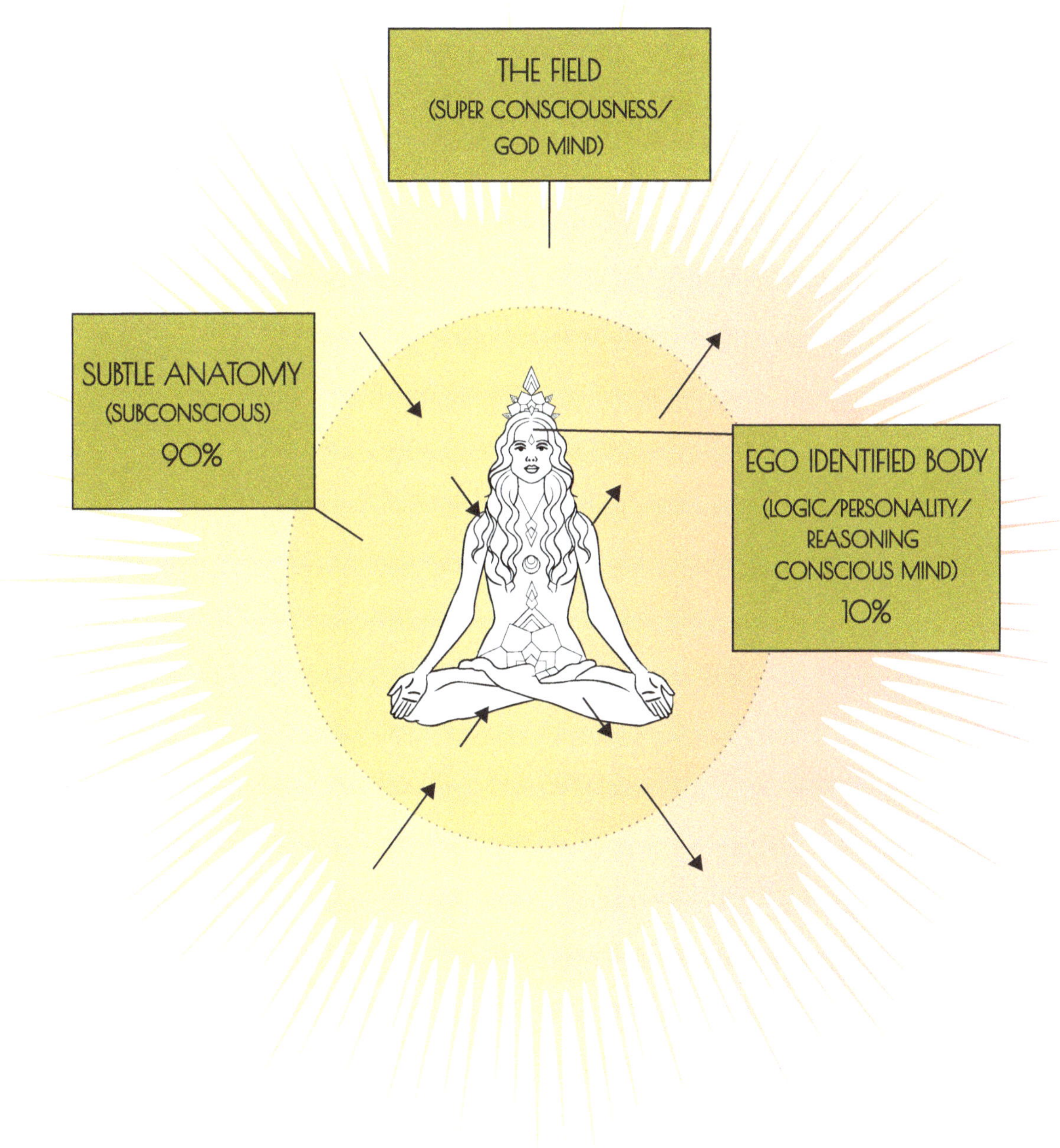

THE FIELD
(SUPER CONSCIOUSNESS/
GOD MIND)

SUBTLE ANATOMY
(SUBCONSCIOUS)
90%

EGO IDENTIFIED BODY
(LOGIC/PERSONALITY/
REASONING
CONSCIOUS MIND)
10%

PART ONE

THE LAYERS OF CONSCIOUSNESS

The Subtle Anatomy (Subconscious) is the filter between the Field (Superconsciousness) and the Body (Reasoning Conscious Mind). The health of the subtle anatomy determines the health of the relationship with both the Field and the Body. We can also look at this as; the health of the subconscious determines the health of the relationship with both Superconsciousness and the Reasoning Conscious Mind. The three immutable laws at work. The law of Mentalism states All is One, and we can evidence this here because, in truth, there is no separation between these three layers of Mind. When we are in optimal functioning, the veils are very thin between the Field and our seemingly finite subtle and physical bodies.

Ultimately, there is no separation. The thinner the veils between the layers, the more we can receive our intuition.

This is the law of Correspondence in action. As within so without. As above, so below. We are in a constant communication loop from inner to outer and outer to inner. The more harmonious all the layers of Mind are with one another, the more our intuition flows into us. We are also aware that we are not acting in isolation. What is within my subconscious is what I am contributing to the Field. To give is to receive, and we receive in accordance with the quality of what we are offering.

Fear contracts the subtle anatomy makes it denser, the veils thicker, and the frequency slow and low. This is the law of Vibration in action. The frequency of the Field is high and light. Superconsciousness can most easily be accessed when we are in the same frequency or vibration as that. The more I clear my subconscious (subtle anatomy), the easier it is for me to hold my vibration at the level of the One Mind. I am then more easily imprinted with the vibration of the One Mind, and my intuition flows into me.

Our ultimate aim is to have no impediment in the subtle anatomy between the Field and us. This is us in our natural and most intuitive state of being.

Although we'll focus on two primarily – the Reasoning Conscious Mind and the Subconscious Mind, our consciousness comprises multiple parts. We would like to imagine that the Reasoning Mind – that part we identify with our personality, our likes, the things by which we define ourselves (I like jazz, I'm not too fond of sushi, etc.), is in charge. Indeed, this part of our consciousness is like the captain of the ship. According to psychologist and author Venice Bloodworth, the relationship between the Conscious and Subconscious Mind is like this:

"Every thought that enters the conscious mind is subjected to our reasoning power. If we accept an idea or thought as true, it is then carried forward to the subconscious mind to act on"[4].

[4] *Key to Yourself by Venic J Bloodworth, 1952*

PART ONE

The subconscious is beneath the deck and is the most significant part of our consciousness, made up of around 90%–95% of consciousness in most people. Bloodworth offers that the Subconscious Mind is "the marvellous phase of your mind that brings things into existence by the sheer power of thought". The Subconscious Mind is highly programmable, and because we have mostly not been aware that we are one with the Mind of God, we have believed our fear stories and the fear stories of the world around us. We have focused our attention on those things without any filter. The captain of the ship looks this way and that, absorbed by the events of life and passes very mixed instructions to the subconscious below deck.

Combined with how our brain has evolved primed to identify danger in our environment, the result is that the bulk of our consciousness attunes to the negative, fear-based dominant consciousness of the collective reality we witness. We have forgotten that we are in a co-creative relationship with the One Mind. Our access to the One Mind gets blocked because our subconscious is full of stuff that we didn't even know we focused on. The result of this for our lives is chaos. Most of us live with a general sense of managed chaos, waiting for the next event or emotional storm to derail us. If the Mind is uninvestigated, if we have not taken the time to explore the contents below deck, then we cannot know the difference between our fear and intuition.

There is more information in regards to this in the 'Philosophy of Opening and ASOC'.

The Two kinds of Intuition

As you move through this handbook, please keep in mind that there is NOT intuition. There ARE intuitions:

- We have two forms of intuition – local and nonlocal
- HeartMath Institute defines nonlocal intuition as the type of intuition: "which refers to the knowledge or sense of something that cannot be explained by past or forgotten knowledge, or by sensing environmental signals. It has been suggested that the capacity to receive and process information about nonlocal events appears to be a property of all physical and biological organisation, and this likely is because of an inherent interconnectedness of everything in the universe"[5].Our local intuition is biological and is informed by our electrical-magnetic composition. We are electromagnetic beings who produce energetic fields. We are sensitive to one another's energy, and the energy of everything around us
- Energetic sensitivity refers to the *"ability of our body and nervous system to detect electromagnetic and other types of energetic signals in the environment"*[6] according to HeartMath Institute
- People who identify as empathic or highly sensitive (also known as empaths) fall into this biological intuition category. We are all empathic and highly sensitive, and when we understand our electromagnetic biology, it becomes clear as to why. We are constantly collecting energetic information from one another, most often without realising it
- When we are living the Intuitive Intelligence path, there are powerful ways that this energetic sensitivity can be part of our toolkit for living in extraordinary times. Rather than being something that makes us too sensitive to inhabit the world, we begin to understand the information provided to us through this kind of intuition, and how to use it to our advantage.

---

[5] *https://www.heartmath.org/research/science-of-the-heart/intuition-research/*
[6] *https://www.heartmath.org/research/science-of-the-heart/energetic-communication/*

PART ONE

THE FOUR PHASES OF INTUITION

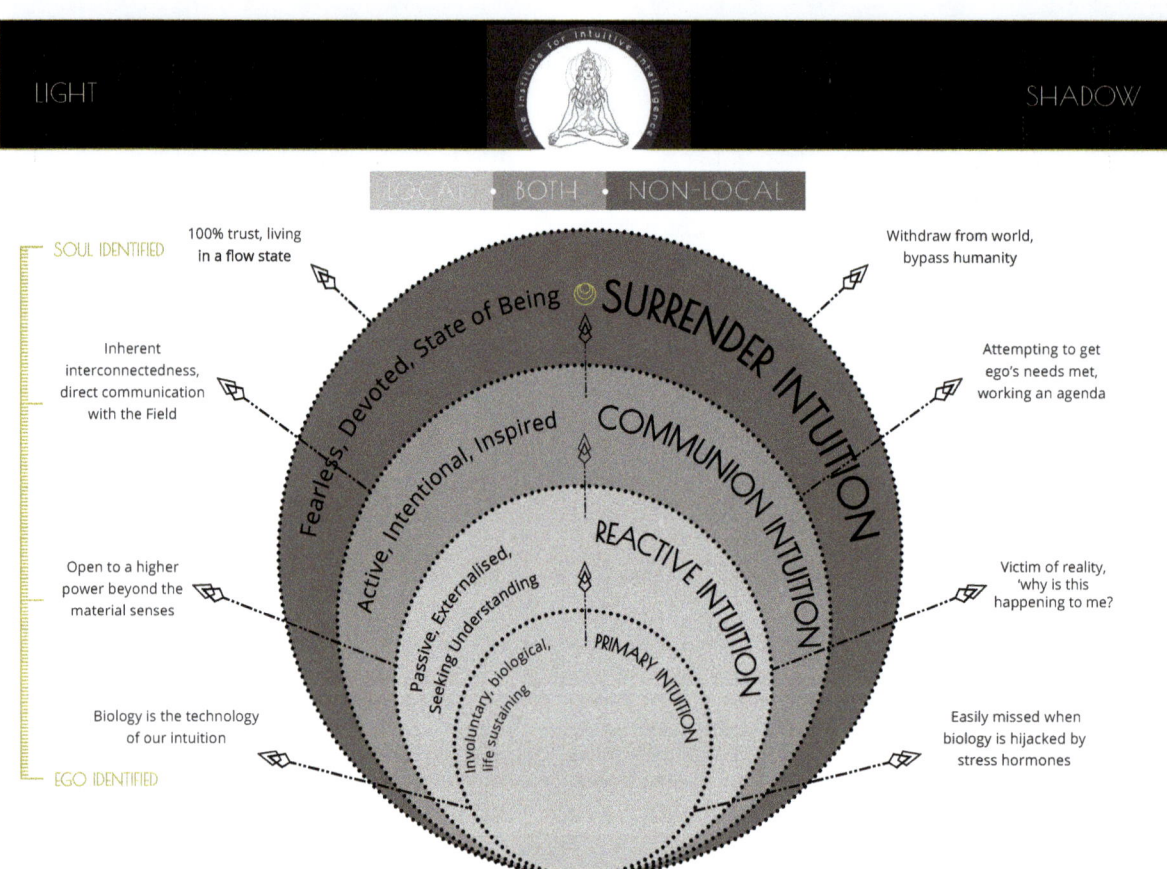

There are four kinds of intuition, and each has a shadow and the light form. These four phases of intuition are categorised as either local or nonlocal forms of intuition. Primary intuition and Reactive intuition both fall into a local form of intuition. Communion intuition is both local and nonlocal intuition. The final phase, Surrender intuition, is entirely nonlocal.

In this diagram (large version on following page), we can see that these circles get larger as we move out. We're demonstrating that when we get to the final phase of intuition, contained within are all the other phases of intuition. We are never without all four phases of our intuition, but we do evolve through them. The function of this map is to help us understand where we are in our relationship with our intuition.

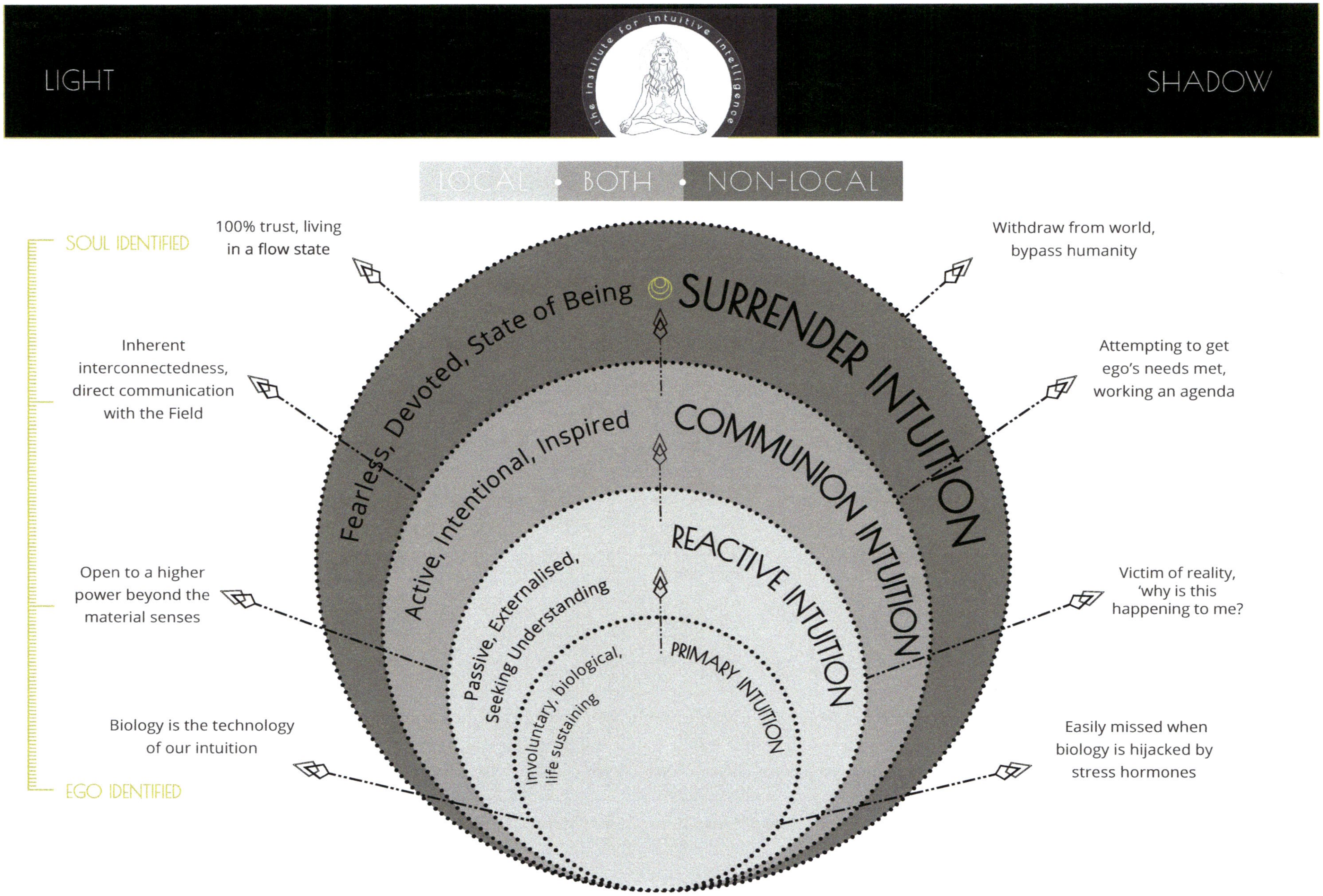

SHADOW

- Withdraw from world, bypass humanity
- Attempting to get ego's needs met, working an agenda
- Victim of reality, 'why is this happening to me?'
- Easily missed when biology is hijacked by stress hormones

LIGHT

SURRENDER INTUITION — Fearless, Devoted, State of Being
COMMUNION INTUITION — Active, Intentional, Inspired
REACTIVE INTUITION — Passive, Externalised, Seeking Understanding
PRIMARY INTUITION — Involuntary, biological, life sustaining

LOCAL • BOTH • NON-LOCAL

SOUL IDENTIFIED
- 100% trust, living in a flow state
- Inherent interconnectedness, direct communication with the Field
- Open to a higher power beyond the material senses
- Biology is the technology of our intuition

EGO IDENTIFIED

the Institute for Intuitive Intelligence

PART ONE

We can think about the journey from primary intuition, which is that purely biological state to surrender intuition which is strictly a nonlocal, non-biological state, as a measure or map of our consciousness-raising or consciousness awakening. Intuition, for me, has always been a symptom of or a secondary benefit of raising our consciousness.

The more we keep going towards increasing our intuition, the more we raise our spiritual awareness. It is inevitable that if we keep working with our intuition, we will keep awakening to our soul nature at greater and greater levels. There are people out there for whom that is not a true statement. They will happily continue to access their psychic skills or play with their tarot cards and never spiritually mature.

The way that I teach to increase our intuition is by recognising these phases of consciousness and the role they serve in awakening consciousness. What we gain as a secondary benefit is an increased intuition because intuition is the way that consciousness communicates.

Another way that we can understand the nature of intuition as it has been discussed throughout this book, is by understanding the relationships between dimensions. The fifth dimension (pure energy, pure consciousness, superconsciousness) informs the third dimension (matter, body, Conscious Reasoning Mind) through the fourth dimension (subtle anatomy, Subconscious Mind, energy that has levels of density stored within, all intangible elements). The fourth dimension is intuition, imagination, inspiration, language, feeling – intangible elements. What we can understand from this, is that intuition is a form of communication between us and the One Mind or the unified field that we are all part of, and that contains all time and space. It is the bridge between pure energy and matter, or Superconsciousness and the Conscious Reasoning Mind.

When I look at this map, I am not just looking at the phases of intuition; I am looking at the stages of our consciousness awakening or our spiritual evolution. We can think of this as spiritual agency. This is a measure of our relationship to our spiritual power. Agency means power. How much agency a person has, indicates how much power they have in their own life. In this diagram, the more Superconsciousness identified we are, the more spiritual agency we possess. We can also think of this in terms of the amount of subconscious fear we are holding. The more we move towards Surrender intuition, the less fear we are carrying. Let's explore each of the phases now.

Primary Intuition

Qualities: *Passive, local, involuntary, unconscious, shallow, very little agency, non-participatory*

We begin with an understanding of a rudimentary survival intuition, which we call gut instinct.

It's very much just about our capacity to tune into the electromagnetic frequencies of those around us, which is our biology. There's nothing spiritual or nonlocal about that. We're picking up information from each other and the atmosphere all of the time because of the makeup of our biology.

This idea of energetic sensitivity is based on our biology. We're electromagnetic beings who are producing fields at the quantum level. And it doesn't matter how large or small – down to that subatomic particle level right up to the size of your full body, you are producing fields, within fields, within fields which are interacting with the fields of everything around you, both living and not living. Everything is producing a field because everything is just vibrating particles.

PART ONE

We have this energetic sensitivity by the very nature of our biology because we are moving through other people's fields, yes? We're picking up information through the interaction of our fields. This is biological. It's usually the kind of intuition that's written about and talked about If articles get written and popularized in the media, they are generally referencing this form of intuition. It's actually very, very rudimentary, basic intuition.

The light form of the biological form of intuition is that it's the beginning of our connection to something greater than the physical self. It's also inbuilt in the physical self. Even though it's a basic form of intuition it is actually what opens us and activates us to our more subtle forms of communication as we'll learn about as we go along. It's a gateway, if you like, and it's the beginning for so many people where we stop thinking of ourselves purely in terms of being solid matter and we start thinking of ourselves in terms of being energetic.

There are several ways we can be in our shadow with our primary intuition. Very often, this is where we stop in terms of our evolution. Even at this level, we are suspicious of it. We consider it spiritual or outrageous or out there. The idea that we would trust something other than our minds to discern whether a decision is right or wrong seems to be so antithetical to the world that we shut that down. We shut down our survival intuition.

We can also shut it down through body-mind addiction, where we will become so addicted to living in the stress hormones of fight or flight that we actually can't discern what our gut is saying. We're stuck in a cycle where we think it's our intuition, and actually it's just our body-mind addiction to creating these stress hormones. That means we keep misidentifying what our intuition is.

So until we learn to break the addiction to these living in that fight-or-flight response, until we learn how to regulate our nervous system, our biological form of intuition can be very, very off. Internal GPS is off. When we're in that addiction through the dysregulated nervous system, we can't trust that internal GPS. That biological form of intuition is being skewed or prevented from operating properly because there is a more dominant program running, which is that addiction to living in a dysregulated state of being. We may become a stranger to ourselves, and we make choices that are against life, that go against our very survival.

Reactive Intuition

Qualities: *Local, passive, biological, intermittent, conscious, shallow, minimal spiritual agency, non-participatory*

This is the phase where we are willing to believe that psychic information or information is available through intuition is out there in the world. We will go out to seek someone, or something that we think has access to that information.

We do not yet believe that we have access to that information. We believe intuition is a gift, and only some people have it. When we are in a state of crisis, we will seek out the psychic, or the tarot reader or the healer, who will help us believe that there's some bigger picture, there's some relief. There's someone who knows what's going on, even though we have no freaking idea and feel completely out of control, we're reacting, and we're in reactionary mode to the world.

PART ONE

Maybe our husband left, or we're in a financial crisis, or we've got a health crisis, and we want some answers. We want to believe that someone or something out there can give us some peace of Mind that someone else can take responsibility for our life for a time. We want someone to answer the questions of our life. It is a very immature relationship with intuition. The idea that intuition is a gift is something that we like to believe because it lets us off the hook of thinking that I have it, and I may need to train it and put the time in to get clear in my access to that knowledge.

When we're in the light form here, it is the gateway drug. It's the opening to a higher power beyond the material senses. It's the beginning of that recognition that the cosmos is made up of more than just what can be perceived through my material experience.

On the shadow side, we're often looking for the abdication of responsibility, someone to take the burden of our life off our hands, someone to say, "I know the answers, just do everything I say, and you'll be right." Or that feeling of being a victim of reality. "Why is this happening to me?" Rather than reflecting on, "Okay, my husband left me because I was engaging in childish behaviour, I was spending money like an idiot; I wasn't taking responsibility for anything."

Instead of doing that, we are looking at the world as though we are the victim of it. We don't want to know and we don't want to take personal responsibility. We're reacting to our life as though we're a victim. Tuning into our intuition and training would no longer permit us to stay in the victim role.

In quantum physics, we say there are no watchers in the quantum field. we are never passively receiving life. We are always making choices, and we don't necessarily acknowledge that we are making those choices, so life happens to us. we say, "I don't know how this chaos happened", "I don't know how I'm in another shitty relationship", "I don't know how I'm in debt again", "I don't know how I'm in a job I hate". The truth is we are constantly creating our reality. Our Subconscious Mind is a creative force to be reckoned with, and what is in our subconscious? Mostly unmet shit. That is what we program out into the One Mind, and the One Mind loves us so dearly that it bows down before us without judgment. It doesn't say, "That's not a great request. You probably should not choose that". It just says, "okay, here you go, I love you, have it. Whatever you want, have it".

The problem with this level of intuition is that we are mainly lazy. Not only are we lazy with our consciousness, letting any thought take us over, but we will also put our consciousness pretty much anywhere with no discernment. "Oh stuff, shiny, oh look at that over there, oh stuff, oh images blah, blah, blah".

The reason is because we are attuned to fear. We will go towards our fear without question. As soon as a fearful emotion hits us, we say, "What's the cause, what's the reason, why am I feeling like this, quickly find evidence, oh yes, that was when I was 3 when I didn't get the love that I needed. Oh, that's why I am overeating right now, because of this....". We build walls around that fearful feeling, instead of thinking, "Okay, this is an interesting feeling", and let that go. We look for evidence to back up our fear. We very rarely look for evidence to back up our good feelings.

PART ONE

We form communities around our suffering, but we rarely create communities around our joy. We don't celebrate ourselves, but we will be punitive towards ourselves obsessively. Unfortunately, we are biologically hardwired to privilege fear as a survival instinct, so we become addicted to cortisol and adrenaline. We become addicted to fear. And this reduces our capacity to know our intuition, so we have to practice, use our inner discipline, our spiritual fire, to be willing to change our program. Luckily our Subconscious Mind is just highly programmable. It is not programmed towards fear; it is just highly programmable. And when we start to do this, that's when we move into the next phase of intuition.

Communion Intuition

Qualities: *Nonlocal and local, active, high level of spiritual agency, deep and shallow states, participatory, conscious and subconscious*

Communion intuition is the idea that we recognise that we're in a conversation with a greater power. We recognise that there is this inherent interconnectedness. There's this God consciousness of which we're all part. We may not use those words; we might call it God or source or spirit or the divine matrix, whatever language used. We have realised that if we focus our attention, perhaps through our devotional practices, perhaps through just having a great capacity to be mindful or to hold a mental image with clarity, we can start to manufacture a reality, so to speak.

With a little bit of control, we can start to see that communion between us and this greater power is not a one-way street. Something or someone is listening. We can see that reward if we can stay focused upon what we desire for long enough. This is where the ideas of vision boards and creating gratitude lists, and holding a clear intention for what we want our lives to look like begins to enter our practice.

We see that sometimes things we desire come to pass, and even if it doesn't come to pass in the way we were expecting, we can see that there's a relationship; there's a conversation going on. Now, all of this sounds good, and it is good. It is also simply a stage of our evolution based on walking between two worlds – the 3D and the 5D. It's a stage of development in our spiritual awakening, and it's a stage of evolution in our intuition. If we go in pursuit of our intuition, our awakening journey will continue to expand. We cannot pursue the development of our intuition and not see the development of our spiritual nature. They are the same. Intuition is the language of that, of the soul.

It is an excellent thing that we have communion intuition because we recognise that we're more sophisticated than just this survival, gut, rudimentary intuition and realise that we have power. We may not understand the nature of that power, and we don't at this stage. We recognise that we can use our Mind and use our feeling states when we get a bit more sophisticated to cultivate a life we want to live.

When we get into the latter stages of communion intuition, we recognise that manufacturing or manifesting our reality is the feeling state. It is the vibration. It's nothing to do with the vision board. It's nothing to do with the mental list or the written list of what we want. It's about cultivating a feeling that is the prayer to which the cosmos or God mind responds.

This is the sophisticated, most refined end of communion intuition. It's an essential step in our evolution because we may then start to surrender our ideas of how things should look. We realise we are genuinely seeking the feeling of how we want our lives to be. This is where we arrive at the next stage, surrender intuition.

PART ONE

I describe communion intuition as being active, intentional and inspired. This is where we stop being passive about our relationship to our intuition. We're suddenly aware that we don't need to go to someone else to have that conversation with the One Mind. We may use very different language around that, especially at the early phases of communion intuition, where we might be creating vision boards, or gratitude lists or writing intentions and taking them into our meditation or our devotion. We start to get evidence that when we hold our consciousness on an idea for a sustained amount of time, we begin to see reality change. This is very exciting. This is communion. There is a communion occurring between us and the One Mind. We are beginning to gather evidence that we are not a reactive victim of reality. If we show up harmoniously consistently, we can start to manufacture or encode our reality. We can begin to direct consciousness.

In the light form, this is very exciting because we're aware now that not only are we the agents of our intuition but that there is an inherent interconnectedness between all consciousness and that we are in direct communication with that field.

On the shadow side, what happens however and very often, is what I call black magic. This is where we get caught up in the secret kind of mentality where we believe that this skill, this ability, this highly trained Intuitive Intelligence is to help us reach our ego needs. We think that 'to move furniture in a burning building', to use Gary Renard's beautiful metaphor, is to gain spiritual reward. That if we have a beautiful life, an attractive partner, a beautiful car, lots of money in the bank, heaps of clients, then we're winning at the spiritual game. We think that that is evidence that we're doing this right. Our ego is getting satisfied, life is comfortable as fuck, and everything is working well. We've got a massive agenda; we've got a big fat agenda with God.

"You keep doing for me, and I'll do for you, if you touch a hair on the head of my babies, or you make my partner leave me, or I don't have enough clients next week, then I am out. Got it? I'm done."

This is like, "You got to show up for me, God, I am only here whilst this works." We have a very shallow relationship with our awakening. We are working an agenda, whatever that agenda is. We get a little bit drunk on our power here. We think this is evidence that we're doing good, like we got it going on, we got the spiritual game hacked. The point is, we are falling into the trap of believing that the highest function of our spiritual awakening or our intuition is to make our human life more comfortable. No, that is not it.

Many, many people use spiritual tools to try to manifest what they believe they should be getting. We turn up to our spirituality and practices and yoga and green juices and meditation and mindfulness and all of that stuff with this idea that we're going to be rewarded.

This is maybe not something we're comfortable with hearing. Still, it is accurate, and it is a shadow side of a black magic use of the spiritual tools to try to coerce or manipulate the cosmos, the God Mind, into meeting our egoic needs.

It is a stage in our development, and we can't know what we are not ready to know. What I am excited about sharing about surrender intuition is that when we get to that phase where we are prepared to put down our ego's plan of what we think we should get in return for showing up to our devotion; that's when life starts to truly become a blessing. All of our needs are met in abundance.

PART ONE

Now, I don't mean our specific ego needs this much money, this kind of book contract, this many people following me, this many people on my Instagram account. I mean, our soul's needs are met. Whether we know it or not. Our attempts to get our 3D needs met were only ever an attempt to get our soul needs met. When our soul needs are met, all of our ideas of a well-lived life and a successful life fall away. This is the purpose of us committing to awakening our intuition. It is not so that we can guess people's futures, and I use that word 'guess' quite intentionally. Or to be able to predict what's going to happen with COVID-19, or to be able to download information about other people, but rather that we get closer to the truth that all is one and I am one with the one Mind.

In the light form, this is the phase of intuition in which we're starting to own that we are that. We are one with the God mind, and that we can create, not simply to react. This is probably for 90% of the people I serve, from where they live. It's highly sophisticated.

As these phases of intuition move into more sophisticated states of being, the percentage of the population that operates from them significantly decreases. Fewer people are aware of these higher levels of intuition. Most conversation, most research about intuition in the world is about the biological forms of intuition. At communion intuition, we're introducing the nonlocal; we're introducing the fact that we have understanding or insight or inspiration that isn't coming through cause and effect; it's coming because we connect to that quantum field. We can know things without going to the location, without doing the research, and without conversation. The information lands through our dominant intuitive skill, whole and complete within us.

We must be very, very careful here not to stop. If we look at this as a measure of spiritual agency or spiritual maturity, this is the phase of I'm in partnership with God. But the best is yet to come.

Surrender Intuition

Qualities: *Subconscious, active, nonlocal, acausal, creative, full spiritual agency, deep.*

Surrender intuition is when our Intuitive Intelligence becomes our dominant subconscious program. We are running the program of intuition dominantly in our subconscious. It is entirely nonlocal. We are in symbolic sight; we're not looking at the 3D to give us data about the world. It is when we have moved into a seamless operation of this phase of intuition as the dominant program in our subconscious. In other words, it is functioning below the level of our Conscious Reasoning Mind. Remember that the vibration of the One Mind, the Superconsciousness, is pure energy, and this is the feedback loop of communication that occurs As Within, As Without. The three immutable laws seamlessly working in favour of our Surrender Intuition with our own God Mind.

We are in a state of being in which our arms are wide open, holding nothing back, saying, *"Okay, God, I'm yours. Use me."* Our life is in service to the greater good. We have put down all agendas on how we think life should look. We've put down this idea that there's a reward system for being a good spiritual person and by doing our devotion and showing up to our spiritual practices or being nice to people or adopting puppies. We are no longer believing that there is this karmic reward system and that we are supposed to get good things if we show up to God. If we don't get good things and we withdraw our affection from God.

When we recognise that even though we do not always understand the events of our life and the events of the world around us, we trust, we surrender. We throw our arms wide open to the will of the God Mind. We are here as holy servants, Gods' humble hands and feet in the world.

Our intuition has the most precise possible channel because we don't then argue with what we hear.

PART ONE

Even at the communion intuition phase, we argue to an extent with God. If guidance is received into us (which is a misnomer, it's not into us, it's just coming from us, for our intuition is within us), we will resist. We'll hold back from God's instructions because we're still holding a perception of how our life should look. If it doesn't match what our ego wants, then we can get ourselves turned all around and upside down. We might even lose faith because of what we thought we were going to get out of pursuing our paths.

The endpoint of intuition is that there is no need for intuition. Surrender intuition is a step on that path. Surrender intuition is the absolute lack of resistance. It is defenselessness. There is nothing that could happen in my life that I would consider has gone wrong. It's a state of being.

Unlike the other phases, living this state of being becomes something we aren't dropping in and out of when we want to know the answer to a question, or we feel confused and conflicted with events in our life. We are aware simply through living our state of being, that we're in flow with the God Mind. We know when we're out of this phase of intuition by the stirrings and agitations to our state of being, and we then recognise we need to come back into flow. We know that we need to respond and course-correct and come back into our dominant state of being, surrender intuition.

Remember that in this phase of intuition, we are in servitude to God, to the awakening consciousness of all. The development of our intuition and state of being is switching how we are currently in relationship with our intuition. Our holy task is in the development of our intuition so that we are living a state of being, in surrender intuition all of the time. It's a fearless state because we trust our Intuitive Intelligence all of the time. We don't question it, even if what we're asked to do by our intuition will take us away from the familiar and the known of our comfort.

Surrender intuition in its light form is 100% trust in the God mind and living in what we can call flow state. It is 100% soul identified. Living this state of being can only exist through consistent devotion. It doesn't happen randomly. It's a refined state of being that requires 100% congruence. We are not there yet. Our aim and the measure of our spiritual maturity or agency, is to go towards living in surrender intuition as often as possible. This requires surrender to the greater mind, surrender to divine will, "Thy will be done."

Even if it means that my ego will be throwing tantrums left, right and centre, I'm not going to put down my faith just because it's awkward, uncomfortable or inconvenient.

In it's shadow form, surrender intuition can see us wanting to withdraw from the world, what we call bypassing our humanity. We say "I want to be in meditation, in a cave on top of a mountain where it feels so good to be in the presence of God, away from all of you human folk who are just bringing me down with your human dramas". We attempt to withdraw instead of taking God out into the world. We say things that bypass other people's experiences. We will negate people or ourselves and not allow our humanity to be present in our divinity. This is problematic because we're in a human experience for an excellent reason. The shadow form of surrender intuition is where we abdicate responsibility for showing up to the state of the world.

The more we awaken to our spiritual maturity, the more responsibility we want to take to ensure the dream that we're all part of is evolving on behalf of all. As Intuitive Intelligence Trainers, this is our commitment; as we increase our spiritual agency, our capacity to serve those who don't know how to help themselves increases.

PART ONE

SUPERCONSCIOUS INTUITION

Surrender intuition (subconscious, active, nonlocal, acausal, deep state) + **Super-regulated nervous system** = **Superconscious intuition** (superconsciousness state of being).

Superconscious Intuition or **superconsciousness** *is a state of being in which we can optimally receive our Intuitive Intelligence.*

To review our definition of Intuitive Intelligence:

> INTUITIVE INTELLIGENCE IS A NONLOCAL FORM OF INTUITION (NON-BIOLOGICAL, NOT IMPLICIT KNOWLEDGE), WHICH IS ACAUSAL (QUANTUM NOT NEWTONIAN), ACTIVE AND PARTICIPATORY (TRAINED CONSCIOUSNESS TO RECEIVE INTUITION AT WILL ACTIVELY), DEEP STATE (SUBCONSCIOUS, BELOW THE LEVEL OF THE EGO-IDENTIFIED CONSCIOUS REASONING MIND), AND CREATIVE/CREATING AS GOD-CONSCIOUSNESS (NOT REACTIVE). THIS COMBINES AS AN EMBODIED STATE OF BEING CALLED SUPERCONSCIOUS INTUITION.

PART ONE

Deep State VS Shallow State of Intuition

What we're seeking as Intuitive Intelligence Trainers is a deep state of Intuition, a deep and intimate connection to our Intuitive Intelligence. What is a deep state of Intuition? Let's begin with shallow Intuition so we can understand the difference.

What do I mean by a shallow intuition? For those of us who are called to this path of service through our Intuition. We have a responsibility to keep seeking, to go deeper with our Intuition, to not stay in the shallow end of Intuition. I see a lot of people clinging to it because it's familiar and it's known. It's like the party trick end of the pool. We can look experienced and capable when we're swimming in the shallow end, giving others answers to their life situations.

Intuition's shallow vs deep state is really about the brainwave state or the level of consciousness that we're accessing when we go into our Intuition. A deep state of Intuition is not something we go into and come out of, but a shallow state of Intuition is. This is when we hear, "I just have to check in with my Intuition. I just need to ask a question. I'm just going to tune in and get a download."

Those sorts of statements indicate that a person is in a shallow state of Intuition. This is because what we are aiming for, when we do the deep work of a deep faith to attain those deep states of Intuition, is we live in that connection to our Intuitive Intelligence, what we call subconscious or surrender Intuition. We don't step in and out, ask a question, go back to being a muggle. We reside in it all of the time. In fact, there's no question even to ask.

The reason we stay in the shallow end of our intuition and choose to "tune" in, ask the pendulum or pull the card, is because it gives us a false sense of authority and control. At the same time it is abdicating us of any responsibility. What do I mean by that? We get this sense that we can actively command Intuition to show up when we want it, which is the false sense of control because whilst Intuition is always instant, it isn't on demand. It's instant when it decides to land.

The other aspect of that is it's us saying, "Well, something outside of me knows more." Even if we're referencing our Intuition, "I'm going to tune in now" to get an answer that is 'out there' says that "I" was out of tune with my Intuition. We never want to be out of tune with our highest form of Intelligence

We want to be 'tuned' in constantly. Always in a flow state of Intuitive Intelligence, which is the absolute certainty with every breath that this is the right place. This is the right moment, and if that starts to feel wrong, then we course correct, but we don't stop, pause, ask, leave. We want to be in a flow state. We want to be constantly floating in that beautiful deep state and associate with a different brainwave state.

The shallow form of Intuition we associate with the Conscious Reasoning Mind is when people are still identifying Intuition as a third eye function. It's all about the periscope and nothing about the source. What I want us to understand is that we make the first error when we go into, "I'm now going to tune into my intuition," as this automatically moves us into the Conscious Reasoning Mind, the analytical brain, and we've shut down our natural innate ability to connect the periscope of the third eye.

PART ONE

It's also the reason that we often associate Intuition with the third eye because it is the symbolic interpreter of our Intuition. It's where the deep state of Intuition, that is generated by the heart, emerges in our subtle body, so that we can receive the symbolic sight, but it's not the origin of it. Let me break that down a little bit here. To stop, think about an issue, ask a question in regards to that issue, and do whatever processes we do to get into our intuitive state; light a candle, burn some incense, meditate, whatever, draw a card, we have to have been out of our Intuition. To engage in these practices, we've gone straight into our Reasoning Conscious Mind.

We're in our analytical brain. We've engaged the ego identified self to try to access something that is below the Conscious Reasoning Mind. We've already created a schism or a dissonance in how we're approaching or accessing our Intuition. We have engaged analytical processing and built a wall between our natural state. We've moved into a beta brainwave state versus an alpha or theta state, which is in where we want to be.

When we've leapt into our Conscious Reasoning Mind to receive our intuition, we have returned to the state of being that we may live in most of the time, so it is a continuation of what feels familiar and comfortable. We prefer the control or perceived authority of this shallow state of Intuition that we can turn on or turn off. I often hear people who work in their shallow states of Intuition say, "Oh, it's overwhelming. I have to turn it off because I'll always be tuning into other people's energies and always getting downloads about them." This is incredibly naive. It's incorrect because this work is not about constantly getting information about other people. That may be our day job, and in exceptional conditions with prior consent, we may be able to access information with and on behalf of our client, but for ourselves, we are the demonstration. We want to be living, breathing, moving from our Intuitive Intelligence all of the time, not tuning in and out.

To be worried that we'd be overwhelmed or that we need to tune out and tune back in to protect our finite energy is a naive statement because that is not how Intuition functions. The way Intuition functions is that the flow state, subconscious Intuition generates MORE energy. We're not tuning into other people because they're not our business, and we're staying in the right relationship with ourselves through our Intuition.

We are once again, often looking for signs, "It was a sign, I felt this, I saw this," because we're pretending it's our third eye and that symbolic sight. Still, it's our Conscious Reasoning Mind, making associations between everything we've ever seen and ever experienced in our life at a rapid rate below the level of our understanding. It is drawing conclusions that are coming entirely from our personality, our ego identified self, not from our deep states of Intuition.

We'll see signs everywhere when we realise we create all of them ourselves. There is no symbol that we're going to see that's going to confirm our Intuition, there's no neon flashing sign that's going to prove one way or another because deep states of Intuition are internal. They are an aspect of our soul; they have nothing to do with the dream.

The dream is not a function of deep states of Intuition. When we see confirmation of our Intuition in the dream, we are undoubtedly in a shallow state of Intuition. We've privileged the illusion as a way to evidence what we now are taking as confirmation of, *"do this, or don't do that"*. If we're looking externally in any way, including for "signs" to confirm the world or the world of our Intuition to us, we are in a shallow state of Intuition.

PART ONE

We're drawing meaning and making association through our history, not through our deep state. What is a deep state of Intuition, then? That is when we are in our highest form of Intelligence, our heart's Intelligence, which is below the Conscious Reasoning Mind. This is a function of our Subconscious. Our Subconscious is where we want to be operating from because it's below the level of the Conscious Reasoning Mind. It cannot be interpreted by the analytical, critical part of our brain that's trying to make reason out of something that functions outside of reason. It is nonlocal.

It doesn't have a relationship with the local world. Suppose our Intuition is coming at us through the local world. In that case, it's probably not our deep states of Intuition, probably a whole bunch of historical associations (implicit knowledge) that we're drawing meaning from, based on our prior experience. Deep states of Intuition come from the nonlocal, no cause and effect, no need for the dream of this life to produce any evidence at all.

We are drawing upon the unified field when we are in that right relationship with the subconscious. This is usually by being in Alpha, which is a much more expansive, creative brainwave state than Beta (although we can access these deep states in any of our brainwave states once we've trained ourselves). We're not drawing upon our prior history, our association with what that butterfly means or what that person appearing on that day means. Instead, we are one with these deep states of nonlocal communication, connected with that One Mind, connected to all time and all space, below the level of the reasoning conscious mind.

Our ego doesn't get to interrupt and say, "That means this. Run," or, "Go towards that thing." We are accessing higher wisdom. A deeper state of Intuition. A higher consciousness. A higher power. We're drawing on wisdom, which is, yes, paradoxically us, but below the level of our identity, our personality. We're sitting here in a much deeper state, accessed through devotion, commitment to showing up, to creating a regulated nervous system. Very often, I hear people associating their shallow states of Intuition with signs that are a dysregulated nervous system, and I'm like, "Oh, nope, that wasn't your Intuition. That was your unregulated nervous system." A super regulated nervous system allows us to live from our Intuition, from the subconscious, which is the connection to the One mind, without our ego identity getting in the way by trying to make its associations and interpretations of signs through its foggy lens.

The way we think about this is that we make our Intuition a subconscious process. We live in it all of the time. You see why we would not stop, pause, tune in and then tune out because it's a subconscious program that is running in the background all of the time. It's the dominant program. How we make it the dominant program is to meet our fear every damn day. The subconscious MUST be regulated. The nervous system is the expression of the subtle body's health, or the subconscious, so regulating the nervous system, meeting and releasing trauma and fear, and all of those programs, is how we come into these deep states of Intuition. A dysregulated nervous system is an expression of a cluttered subconscious; this cluttered subconscious is the expression of our subtle body. We cannot receive these deep sets of Intuition without coming into a regulated nervous system.

PART ONE

Let's consider ourselves now with a Subconscious Intuition program that is dominant, attuned to the One Mind, and has become our natural state of being. What happens when we move out of our deep states of Intuition is we get a little, *"Ooh,"* like a little fear jolt. Or we might suddenly go into doubt, or we'll go into worry. There's some good intel that we've stepped out of our deep state of Intuition, we've stepped out of our dominant subconscious program. We recognise we need to course correct, do the damn work and come back into it. We aren't answering a question about who we should marry, or if we should join this, or if we should not do that. We are living in a flow state, all of the time, floating in the deep water at the deep end of the pool, uncluttered and unfettered by the dream of this life that's floating all around me. We are not seeking specific answers for specific questions because we simply don't need to. We know the second that we feel we have moved out of flow, that is good intel coming to us. Remember our fear as our intel, as Intuition, highlighting that something needs to be course-corrected, and that's how we respond. We are in tune all of the time, and at the moments that we feel out of tune, we restore the right action and come back into that deep state. See the difference?

Shallow Intuition is, I'm tuned out all of the time, and I tune in intermittently to ask questions, redundant, engaged with the egoic mind, not the deep states of knowing. When we engage in these shallow end of the pool states of Intuition, we are trying to control the dream rather than create the dream. We believe that something outside of us has authority. We give power to the local, to the 3D, to the gross material plane, which is simply a manifestation of our consciousness and depending on how much work we've done, it will depend on what we see. We must stop trying to control the dream and play in the pool's shallow end. Instead, we work towards creating a state of being that we live in, that is a subconscious intuition dominant program all of the time, which will allow us to live from our superconscious Intuition.

The deep states of Intuition are when we tune in all of the time, and know that something needs correcting when we temporarily feel tuned out. We feel that tune out through a low vibrational, emotional state, and we of course correct. We address whatever that is. That's why I say fear is a friendly ally. It's not the problem. When we have a regulated nervous system, we've cleared out our subconscious fear programs, so when fear arises, it is evident. It's like a clear, true bell. Something needs to be addressed here to bring me back into the state of being that I live in all the time.

To live in a deep state of Intuition, to have the nervous system regulated, the Subconscious primed, released from fear, running that dominant Intuition program, tuned in all of the time, not tuning in occasionally to ask a question, that is what we call a Superconscious Intuition. This is when our Intuitive Intelligence has become our state of being.

That's what we are aiming for with our life. That's why we are doing the damn work every damn day, to get clear of those faulty programs that keep us out of the state of being that we want to be living in. It's why we teach trauma-informed Intuition training in the Institute, why we invest in great work like tapping created by Angelique Adams and the trauma-informed intuition training of Embodiment with Elisha Halpin. We are aware that our physiology is the technology to access those deep states of Intuition. We need to be unafraid to engage that, but not from a 3D local dominant perspective. This may also be the first place in the world where nonlocal trauma-informed intuition training is happening.

PART ONE

FEAR AND THE INTENTIONAL DESCENT TO THE UNDERWORLD

> "FROM THE GREAT HEAVEN SHE SET HER MIND ON THE GREAT BELOW. FROM THE GREAT HEAVEN THE GODDESS SET HER MIND ON THE GREAT BELOW. FROM THE GREAT HEAVEN INANNA SET HER MIND ON THE GREAT BELOW. MY MISTRESS ABANDONED HEAVEN, ABANDONED EARTH, AND DESCENDED TO THE UNDERWORLD. INANNA ABANDONED HEAVEN, ABANDONED EARTH, AND DESCENDED TO THE UNDERWORLD."[7]

The Descent of Inanna

I want us to think of our work as an Intuitive Intelligence Trainer as an intentional descent to the underworld, to support our client to ascend their consciousness. Until we meet our subconscious fear head on, it will rule us. Subconscious fear is only a problem if we do not engage with it. We are largely oblivious to our own fear program, and that is why engaging the service of a guide is so vital to the success of this work.

Fear release is the only form of healing because fear disrupts our natural state of grace, and causes 'knots' in the subtle anatomy. The free flow of life force is inhibited by these knots. Fear is showing up to show us where these blocks or knots exist and so fear is a friendly ally when we know how to work with it intentionally and productively.

We are primed to release fear. We simply have not known how to work with it. The Methodology and Praxis journey is one of the most powerful tools available to do this. We simply follow the thread of the fear for our client and guide them on the journey to the underworld and back again.

[7] https://etcsl.orinst.ox.ac.uk/section1/tr141.htm

PART ONE

Here is the overview of the poem of the Descent of Inanna[8]...

Long ago in ancient Sumeria, Inanna was worshipped as the goddess of love and war. She was all-powerful, free to roam the vast regions of heaven and Earth, and when she received the gift of the divine laws of the universe, she thought nothing could stop her.

One day, Inanna suddenly heard the sound of her sister's moans. Ereshkigal, Inanna's sister, was Queen of the Underworld, and it seemed impossible that her cries could reach to the heavens, but it was true. Inanna heard her long and terrible wails, for Ereshkigal was mourning her husband, the Bull of Heaven.

"I must go to witness my sister's husband's funeral," she told her servant, Ninshubur. **"I am traveling to Kur."**

"You must not go," Ninshubur cried. **"No one returns from the underworld."**

But Inanna was determined, for she wished to understand her people better by experiencing death, and so she instructed her servant: "If I do not return in three days, you must go to seek help from the gods. They will rescue me." Then Inanna prepared for the descent. Dressed in flowing royal robes, she placed a crown of blazing gold upon her head. Around her neck she wore beads of lapis lazuli; she wore bracelets on her wrists and rings on her fingers. She wore a breastplate adorned with jewels, and she took along a measuring rod and line of lapis lazuli. But that was all she took; she was prepared to leave all she had ever known behind.

Ninshubur was certain she would never see her mistress again.

When Inanna arrived at the outer gates of the underworld, she challenged the gatekeeper, Neti, to allow her to pass.

"I must consult with Ereshkigal," Neti told her. He hurried to Inanna's sister to describe the great and powerful goddess dressed in jewels who awaited entrance at the gate of Kur.

Ereshkigal envied and despised her sister, and so, with evil intentions, she instructed her gatekeeper. **"Open the seven gates,"** she said, **"but only the smallest crack. As my sister enters each gate, take another of her royal garments from her."**

And so Neti opened the first gate. Inanna, about to pass through, gasped as the gatekeeper removed her dazzling crown. **"Why?"** Inanna asked.

"Quiet, Inanna. The ways of the Kur are perfect. You may ask no questions," Neti replied.

At the second gate, Neti took away Inanna's beads, and again the goddess asked him, **"Why?"**

"Our ways are perfect," Neti answered. At the third gate he removed her breastplate of sparkling stones. At the fourth gate, he took away her bracelets, and at the fifth he snatched her rings. Inanna gasped again when Neti took her measuring rod while she slipped through the sixth gate, and when she reached the last gate, she barely resisted as he removed her beautiful royal robe and ushered her through the seventh gate.

Now defenseless, Inanna entered Kur. She walked into her sister's throne room, and as she did, all the judges of the underworld surrounded her and prepared to make judgment.

Inanna looked up at her sister, and she saw the eye of death staring back. **"Sister,"** Ereshkigal said, but that was all she said before she struck Inanna dead. **"This is my world, and she has no right to be here."**

---

[8] Adapted by Amy Friedman. Accessed at: https://www.sun-sentinel.com/news/fl-xpm-2004-06-22-0406210171-story.html

PART ONE

Meanwhile Ninshubur waited, and when three days had passed with no sign of her mistress, she fled to seek Enlil's help, for he was God of the Air. **"I cannot help,"** he told the weeping servant. **"The underworld is not my domain. Your mistress should not have ventured so far."**

Ninshubur ran to Nanna, God of the Moon, but Nanna shook his head. **"I have no rule over the underworld,"** he said.

And so at last Ninshubur visited Enki, God of Wisdom and Water. It was he, after all, who originally blessed Inanna with the gift of the universal laws, for he knew that without Inanna, life on Earth would die.

From beneath his fingernails, Enki took dirt and with this he created two new creatures. **"Go to Kur and give these gifts to Inanna,"** he instructed the creatures as he handed them goblets filled with the food and water of life.

Able to adopt any disguise, the creatures turned themselves into flies and slipped through cracks at each of the seven gates of Kur. When they reached the throne room, they heard Ereshkigal's moans. **"Oh, my heart and soul,"** she wept as she mourned her husband, and the creatures echoed Ereshkigal's words back to her. **"Oh, my heart and soul,"** they moaned. But they moaned with compassion and understanding, and compassion was what Ereshkigal craved most.

At last she grew silent, and turning to those who seemed to feel empathy for her pain, she offered them any gift they desired.

"Give us Inanna's body," the creatures said. Ereshkigal gave them Inanna's body, and they fed the goddess the food and water of life. And so Inanna rose again, but before she could return to heaven and Earth, according to the universal laws, a substitute had to be found to take her place in the underworld. Inanna chose her husband, Damuzi, to live in the underworld, but his compassionate sister offered to serve his sentence for six months of every year. In this way the cycle of life could begin again, and spring return to the Earth when Damuzi left the underworld to join his wife above."[9]

How this applies to ourselves & our work

> "INANNA... IS NOT A 'WHOLE PERSON' UNTIL SHE APPEARS VULNERABLE BEFORE HER 'DARKER HALF', DIES, AND RETURNS TO LIFE. AT THE POEM'S END, THIS INTERPRETATION ASSERTS, INANNA, THROUGH HER DESCENT INTO DARKNESS, THE SHEDDING OF THE TRAPPINGS OF HER FORMER SELF, CONFRONTATION WITH HER 'SHADOW', DEATH OF WHO SHE WAS, AND FINAL RE-BIRTH, IS NOW A COMPLETE INDIVIDUAL, WHOLLY AWARE"[10].

---

[9] *For the original poem see http://people.uncw.edu/*
[10] *https://acimi.com/a-course-in-miracles/workbook/lesson-48 deagona/myth/Descent%20Of%20Inanna.pdf*

PART ONE

Inanna's descent is a metaphor for our own fearless choice to enter into our holiness by being willing to be stripped of our illusory identity – the fear identified personality. Meeting our fear intentionally and consciously is an active choice to surrender illusion. We become nothing to become everything. We cannot ascend to the fullness of what we are or inherit heaven on earth if we have not met ALL of what we are, including our shadow.

When Inanna hears her sister's cries, she becomes aware of the depths of being, not just the heights of love and power that she inhabits. She is deeply curious and unafraid of what awaits her, even though she is warned that it could be her death. Meeting fear is always a death. It is death to the ego. In some accounts, Inanna's compassion for the cries of her sister sends her on the journey. For us, this is also true. As we awaken to our sacred hearts, our hearts are cracked open to the suffering of all life, and we may believe that we cannot survive it. Instead, we are made holy by becoming aware that light and dark, heaven and hell, above and below, are One.

Inanna is hung on a hook as she faces her sister. Our willingness to 'not be let off the hook' ensures our triumphant return from the underworld (subconscious) of our being. We must be willing to sit with the discomfort of meeting the fullness of our being – shadow and light – and to be stripped bare of the egoic adornments we have tried to use to protect ourselves. Inanna made the descent to the underworld willingly, and so does our client.

We must be ready to hold them as they return to holiness through the illusion of fear.

In *A Course in Miracles*, one of the lessons states, "There is nothing to fear,"[11] and it's a compelling thing when we begin to understand the truth of that statement, which is fear is simply guiding us home. I need to caveat this by saying I'm not talking about it from a human perspective alone.

If we are looking with human sight alone, saying that fear is not a problem and will increase our intuition, which is to say to ascend our consciousness (because we cannot have one without the other), sounds a bit like I'm a mad person especially if we're in an awful life situation.

You might say to me, "I don't get how you can tell me that fear is a friendly ally because if you saw the state of my life, you'd see that that's not true. I'm in a passive-aggressive or pseudo abusive relationship. My boss is mean to me. I hate my job. I don't have enough money. I don't have the freedom to travel. I don't get to do this. I can't do this, and blah, blah, blah. I don't have enough money to pursue the programs that I want to. I can't do your program, Ricci-Jane, and so on and so on".

I have to stop and say, "Yes, from a human perspective alone, it is accurate to say that fear is real. Fear is a real cause of suffering, and fear causes harm." We are not here on this path, and we're certainly not here in this program because we are interested in simply cultivating more of our human sight.

Spiritual sight is from where our intuition functions. Spiritual sight is fifth dimensional. It's pure energy or pure consciousness. When we're only looking in 3D sight at 3D reality, we will see a mad, imperfect, broken world and think it's full of fear.

[11] https://acimi.com/a-course-in-miracles/workbook/lesson-48

PART ONE

What is spiritual sight?

Spiritual sight begins when we are willing to surrender to that more significant part of ourselves, our God mind. We acknowledge that something greater than our limited human consciousness is guiding our lives.

Even when we do not understand the events of our life, we do not doubt them. It is a state of being that requires deep trust in the infinite intelligence of the Cosmos, and it is the most potent creative force we possess.

To live beyond our fear liberates our creative vision and allows us to line up with what we are truly meant to be expressing in the world. Another way to think about this is the unique mission that God has for us is set free, and we follow the path that inevitably unfolds with ease and grace because we know we are not alone.

This is spiritual sight.

To look at the events of our life with absolute trust. This is spiritual sight.

Our unwillingness to engage with our fear prevents us from embodying our holiness/wholeness.

Our unlimited consciousness is just on the other side of fear. That is power. It's a power that many of us never allow ourselves into that state of questioning. We never question our beliefs, so we prevent ourselves from ever taking responsibility for our own lives.

Our fear causes us to be more in a dense state of form. On a quantum level, fear is slowing us down. We can come into such a dense state that we are incapable of knowing our infinite nature.

When we start working with our intuition consciously, we are breaking through this dense state.

We are breaking free.

When we are free, we are faster, and we are lighter.

When we meet our fear and emancipate ourselves from it, we are lightening our load and raising ourselves from our dominant physical reality ruled by our five senses.

In this state, fear becomes a friendly ally. It shows us where we have left the path of fearlessness so we can return and no longer be vulnerable to that particular fear.

What if we could see the chaos of our world right now from a spiritual perspective? We would see that what is causing the disorder is billions of people being unwilling to meet and release their subconscious fear. If we go back to the first law, the immutable first law that says all is One, we understand that we release all from fear in meeting our subconscious fear because there's only one consciousness here. This is pretty big stuff. Even if we only think about it in terms of the immediate domain of our life, we know that when we're not stressed, angry, mean and full of fear, everybody in our life benefits. They don't just benefit because we're nice to them.

They are benefiting energetically because we are bringing a different frequency to the party. We bring them the energy to uplift them and scaffold them to become more remarkable and more powerful and more resonant with their truth, which is Infinite, Unlimited Consciousness. Still, the very real truth is that we're doing that on a global scale as well because all consciousness is inherently interconnected. The most divine and holy work we can do is to meet and release our fear. As Intuitive Intelligence Trainers, we take all of this understanding of the true nature of fear and how it serves us to the next level.

To do this, we need to understand the anatomy of fear.

---

[9] For the original poem see http://people.uncw.edu/deagona/myth/Descent%20Of%20Inanna.pdf

PART ONE

THE ANATOMY OF FEAR

Fear is two things (for this training) – physiological and psychological. The physiological fear is the body's response, particularly the sympathetic nervous system – our flight, fight, flee or fawn response. It's the instinct that kicks in when we're in danger, and our body instantly responds to get us out of that situation.

Beyond the physiological response, fear as a psychological response is what I want to discuss. Unmet subconscious fear, both big T and little t trauma, left unchecked for long enough tricks us into thinking it is a physiological response. We can call this an addiction to fear, and it is the biggest impediment to clear access to our intuition, our actual state of wholeness and holiness.

Let's just jump into that and look at how our psychological subconscious fear program causes us to believe that the present time reality will do the same as what our past or our history is doing. We are unable to be fully present to external evidence. We're stuck in a record of what happened before, and that's where the body-mind is taking control. The truly remarkable part about our work is that we travel through time and space to locate the 'historical' event no matter what life it occurred! More on that when we get to the instigating event.

Then what happens is that we develop anxiety for no reason – sitting on the bus or going to bed – the ego will go looking for a problem to associate with that feeling.

There may not be a problem, but the ego will go looking for a problem so that the body-mind can feel justified and further increase those negative hormonal outputs to keep us in a loop.

Here's how we can begin to unpack that, to access the subconscious mind, which is, in fact, a pure creative force. The subconscious mind is not primed for fear. It's just that we've programmed it with fear, and we've done it so consistently that the program runs all of the time unconsciously. We need to have an intervention, and that intervention is also the thing that increases our intuition. Effectively what we need to do is start to make friends with those fear impulses. We need to see fear not just as a problem or a physiological thing that rises when we're in danger. We need to take action, but fear then is an impulse of a healthy body-mind relationship. This is what we are doing with and for our client.

PART ONE

Fear as a friendly ally

When fear arises in us – I'm talking about psychological fear here, not physiological fear – and we suddenly feel anxious for no reason, we know our intuition is talking to us because we are not in a repetitive pattern of our anxiety taking over all the time. We can stop and listen to that fear, impulse and say, "What information do you have for me?" There's excellent information here because fear is a messenger. Why is fear a messenger of intuition? Fear allows us to know when we have stepped out of our truth; our true nature is infinite, unlimited consciousness. Fear is a contraction.

When we're in flow with life, we are not in a fearful state. When fear arises, we immediately can be curious, open and willing to know more. If it's the physiological fear, we know we have to move quickly because there's a real threat to our life. If it's the psychological fear, we say, "Right, my intuition wants to talk to me, and perhaps I've just not been listening because I am swamped, but here it is now." What happens when my students have a fear impulse come up from their subconscious is they're like, "Awesome, let's do this. I have an opportunity to get to know myself better. We're going to go on a journey to get to know our fear better right now."

What happens when we start to train ourselves to see fear as a friendly ally leading us back to love, which is our true nature? In that state, we are the most intuitive we can be. We then find out how intuitive we are and what action needs to be taken to return us to our true nature. I want to confirm here that when we're in that state of grace, that flow state, we are in our truth. This is not meant to be the anomaly; this is how we are meant to live our life. The fear state, the stress state, the anxiety-ridden state are the illusion. Fear is an illusion. In the Initiate program, we talk about the true nature of fear as an illusory beneficial and supportive force.

We use fear to clear fear.

We stop avoiding our fear because the avoidance of fear is where we develop addiction. We can turn this around to take what we think is the problem and use it to open our intuition. Then we'll never say, is it my fear or is it my intuition? We'll say yes, it's both. Both at working in cahoots together with the conditions that we provided them to open us.

When we think of fear as a problem, we will do whatever we can to avoid our fear. Instead, we think of fear as a friendly ally that's just saying, "Hey, you've forgotten your true nature, which is infinite, unlimited consciousness. Let me bring you home to that truth." We say, "I'm ready. I'm going to sit down. I'm going to stop everything I'm doing, and I'm going to spend five minutes investigating this friendly fear to bring me back to my truth." We suddenly diffuse all the bombs that could potentially otherwise go off where we're shooting all over other people because our feelings of unmet fear and stress are motivating us.

We're running a subconscious program based on our history, not on the present time. Suddenly all of that stops because we're willing to come into the right relationship with our fear. That is to meet and release our subconscious fear not to run from it. We don't need anyone to teach us how to be what we already are. What we do need is a scaffold to detox from that subconscious fear program. This is our role as the Intuitive Intelligence Trainer. We need to continue working with a system that's going to help us alleviate our suffering, and to change our relationship to the belief that fear is a problem. These are tools of our work as Intuitive Intelligence Trainers, including the Method.

PART ONE

Summary of fear

- *The only way to increase intuition is to meet and release subconscious fear.*

- *Fear is two things (for this training) — physiological and psychological. The physiological fear is the response of the body. Our flight, fight, flee or fawn response. It's the instinct that kicks in when we're in danger, and our body instantly responds to get us out of that situation.*

- *Our focus is fear as a psychological response.*

- *Unmet subconscious fear left unchecked for long enough tricks us into thinking it is a physiological response. We can call this an addiction to fear, and it is the biggest impediment to clear access to our intuition, our actual state of wholeness and holiness.*

- *The Subconscious Mind is not primed for fear. It's just that we've programmed it with fear, and we've done it so consistently that the program runs all of the time unconsciously.*

- *Effectively what we need to do is start to make friends with those fear impulses. To see fear as part of Intuitive Intelligence.*

- *When fear arises in us, and I'm talking about psychological fear here, not physiological fear, when we suddenly feel anxious for no reason, we know our intuition is talking to us because we are not in a repetitive pattern of my anxiety taking over all of the time. We can stop and listen to that fear, impulse and say, "What information do you have for me?" There's excellent information here because fear is a messenger.*

- *Why is fear a messenger of intuition? Okay, well, because fear allows us to know when we have stepped out of our truth, our true nature is infinite, unlimited consciousness.*

- *Fear is a contraction. When we're in flow with life, we are not in a fearful state.*

- *And so when fear rises, we immediately can be curious, open and willing to know more. If it's the physiological fear, we know we have to move quickly because there's a real threat to our life.*

PART ONE

ETHICS & VALUES AS AN EMBODIED PRACTICE

When we lead with our values, we are congruent. We are creating a life and a service that is congruent, and we are living through our values in our service. In an unregulated industry often people are peddling a modality or way of working that is in no way a match for who and what they are in the world. So, we start this training with ethics and values so that you are firmly anchored into ethical best practices as a way of life.

This means considering our personal ethics and values. We might know those unconsciously. They might be running the background of our lives, but creating a map of our own personal ethics and values consciously is incredibly powerful in ensuring that we're building lives that match what we believe in and what we say we believe in. We benefit from taking the time to articulate our own personal values and then making an assessment of our life to ask, am I living those values? Am I making choices that are aligned with those personal ethics?

If I'm excited by a company or a product or service, I go to that website to see if they're leading with their values. On the Institute website, we make sure that our ethics and values are front and centre. Our code of ethics is seeded in the language that we share on our social media posts, newsletters and in the way that we speak about the work. For example, regarding the trinkets and superstitions of the new age, it is important to me that my offers are congruent with this value. If I suddenly start talking about the phases of the moon or crystals or any of these other trinkets and superstitions, I would be undermining my own mission.

We want to make sure that we are living and breathing what we say we stand for and that we are checking in with ourselves so that we're not undermining things. Here's an example. Angelique is an amazing teacher of many things. One of the things that she loves to share is in regard to angels. Now, I fully believe in the existence of angels, but I won't let Angelique teach that in our curriculum, not because I don't think that angels exist.

It is because if I introduce anything to my students, or in general in regard to the institute, that appears to be entering into non-dualism, then I am not been fully aligned with what I say I stand for. I understand how easy it is for people to fall into that trap of dualism. I have to keep the language and conversation at the highest possible level in regard to that. That's why we talk about archetypes. It is not the Institute's mandate as a teaching resource to discuss angels because it creates that doubt.

PART ONE

ETHICS & VALUES AS AN EMBODIED PRACTICE CONT.

I don't teach things like astrology or crystals or nutrition because I am inviting people to see themselves as pure, undivided God-consciousness. If we put that sort of information in the hands of those who are trained as we are, people who are already training their consciousness at a higher level, they will not collapse into a dualistic idea. We can sit with the idea of angels and stay in the truth of non-dualism. But for people who are at the beginning of their journey, that won't work. So we have to remove all the toys, and I do that rigorously to invite you into that truth of non-dualism.

I'm very clear in my understanding of why I do what I do, and it's wholly aligned and articulated in my values and ethics. So, our code of ethics is a document that outlines the mission and values of a business organisation and how we've determined to approach potential problems. The code of ethics can include everything from a big vision mission statement to terms and conditions.

When you have that in writing, accessible to clients, you won't find yourself in a situation where someone says they did not know that information. If we're naive, and we don't have really clear guidelines around our ethics, then we are going to be left in situations in which we seem to be practising unethically. In an unregulated industry, more is better because it allows us to really articulate every possible iteration of what may go wrong in order to create safety for ourselves and for our clients.

Areas of Consideration for inclusion:

- Socioeconomic access
- Trans and gender diversity
- Disability
- Age inclusivity
- Body positivity
- Race and culture
- Plagiarism and de-identifying our teachers

PART ONE

MISSION, VISION & CODE OF ETHICS OF THE INSTITUATE

Non sibi sed toti – not for self, but for all

Every conversation we are having about intuition is wrong. It's time to go beyond the trinkets and superstitions of the new age and increase our power to serve through our highest form of intelligence for the benefit of the greatest good for all.

The Institute for Intuitive Intelligence® is committed to contributing to excellence in the field of the intuitive sciences. In an unregulated industry, the standards we set are our own. Professional development ensures the maintenance of and contribution to skills development for all those working with clients in complementary therapies, energy medicine and life coaching.

No matter where you are in relation to your understanding of energy and intuition, you can go deeper. Committing to your own professional development is critical to an evolving intuitive practice.

We are committed to wholeness/holiness for all; being service focussed; serving beyond the trinkets and superstitions of the new age; professional excellence; inclusivity; conducting our service with integrity; congruence between our faith and our actions; and participation in ongoing personal, spiritual and professional development.

We aim to lead the revolution in excellence in the intuitive sciences by providing access to evidence-based, peer-reviewed, trauma-informed and embodied research at the intersection of quantum physics and metaphysics. We provide the highest quality pedagogy and are industry leaders in standardising ongoing supervision for all our graduates.

We contribute to a culture of ethical best practice and evidence-based programs that demonstrate the power of going beyond the leading edge to break new ground in this field. We do this by learning from the best, conducting in-house research and training the spiritual leaders of tomorrow.

PART ONE

MISSION STATEMENT

"That is the mystic's life purpose – to know their soul and to put it into a radical form of service to others."

Caroline Myss

The Institute for Intuitive Intelligence® is revolutionising intuition by training spiritually fierce* women and men globally as clinically trained*, socially-conscious Intuitive Intelligence® Method Practitioners, Trainers, Teachers and Spiritual Directors.

* Spiritually fierce is defined by the Institute as doing the deep work of a deep faith beyond the trinkets and superstitions of the new age

* Clinically trained refers to the pedagogy of the Intuitive Intelligence® training that engages candidates in the authentic professional setting of their praxis, under supervision, with real-time and ongoing assessment and support

* A social conscience is a sense of responsibility or concern for the problems and injustices of society

* A new paradigm is a revolutionary way of doing things that replaces the old way.

CODE OF ETHICS

We lead the revolution in the intuitive sciences and sacred leadership by providing access to world-class, socially responsible, ethically informed and evidence-based training programs, as taught by highly trained, congruent and experienced mentors and teachers, and graduates committed to their own ongoing professional, personal and spiritual development.

The Institute is committed to creating a gold-standard benchmark in the field of the intuitive sciences and new paradigm priestess training because, in an unregulated industry, the standards we set are our own.

Excellence, ethical service, the pursuit of spiritual innovation and ongoing research inform all of the activities of the Institute for this is how we can take the new conversation on intuition to the world.

PART ONE

We are committed to the core values and ethically informed policies as outlined below:

Wholeness/holiness Centred

- Our focus is and always will be on contributing to the ongoing rise of the holy feminine and holy masculine and the second great mystical renaissance that human consciousness is now experiencing towards wholeness/holiness.
- We commit to training women and men, developing spiritual self-esteem in both as a core mission. This is because the last 5,000 years of patriarchy have created an imbalance between men and women in regard to political, economic, personal and spiritual rights, and we are committed to redressing this imbalance. The correction begins by gathering women and men together in holy spaces on the path of sacred service.
- The Institute is determined to be part of the return to balance for all.

Service focussed

- We stand for sacred service at the core of all that we do. We know that we do not do this work for ourselves alone and that our commitment to walk this path with congruence is the medicine for all, including ourselves.
- We do not pursue our path of sacred service for personal gain alone, or for the attainment of the betterment of our own lives alone. Our work is in the world, on behalf of all.
- We understand the privilege and freedom we have in pursuing our soul's awakening, and we will not squander that privilege. It is our privilege to be of service, and we know it has nothing to do with our personal (personality) agenda. We are God's hands and feet in the world, and we take our instructions directly from the Source, even when it is inconvenient and uncomfortable.
- We are not here for our comfort, but for our evolution.

Beyond the trinkets and superstitions of the new age

- We stand for the deep work of the deep faith that privileges the truth that we are energy first, physical second.
- We adhere to the truth that consciousness is antecedent to matter and that as priestesses of nonlocal consciousness, we commit to creating change at the nonlocal level first, followed by action at the local level.
- A trinket or superstition is any belief, action or object to which meaning is assigned that suggests or encourages dualism. We walk the path of nondualism and honour the immutable hermetic laws as our guiding principles – the laws of mentalism, correspondence and vibration.
- We bring things back to their most logical conclusion, focus on moving our students and clients from fear to love as THE work of healing, provide evidence where possible for what we do and why we do it, innovate and evolve where required, and accept no quick fixes or magic bullets on this awakening journey. Doing the deep work of meeting our subconscious fear every day to remove the blocks to knowing ourselves, as God is the work. No man-made dogma, or local, the material object contains more power than our direct connection to the nonlocal field.
- We do not utilise our Intuitive Intelligence® for fortune telling, future prediction, claims to be able to heal someone else or any other abuse of intuition that would rob an individual of self-determination. We have studied the Hermetic Laws deeply and understand the true nature of consciousness, and will not participate in intuition as fear-mongering.

PART ONE

Professionally excellent

- We aim to lead the revolution in excellence in the intuitive sciences by providing access to evidence-based, peer-reviewed research at the intersection of quantum physics and metaphysics. We provide the highest quality pedagogy and are industry leaders in standardising ongoing supervision and professional development for all our graduates.
- We provide full disclosure to our students during interviews and enrolment in our programs, providing legally prepared agreements, transparent communication and ethically sound business practices at all times.

Inclusivity

- The Institute has action plans, plans in development and policies in regards to:
- Anti-racism. The Institute for Intuitive Intelligence® stands for the inclusion of all people, including black people, indigenous people and people of colour (BIPOC) in our programs and online community. Please read our Anti-racism plan.
- Anti-ageism. We commit to ensuring our online and offline spaces are safe for women and mean of all ages. We will not use images that fetishize youth and unrealistic standards of beauty as normal. We privilege the wisdom won through lived experience. We ensure all women and men who come into the Institute programs feel valued and respected regardless of age.
- Trans and gender diversity. We commit to ensuring our online and offline spaces are safe for women and men including trans, non-binary and cis.
- Socio-economic disadvantage. We offer multiple scholarships to women and men who self-assess as being in need of financial support to access our programs.
- Disability Action Plan. We are currently developing a plan to ensure access to our programs for women and men (trans and cis) of different abilities, and we are committed to creating safe spaces online and offline for differently-abled women and men who desire to access our programs
- Body Equality. The Institute is committed to creating safe spaces online and offline for all bodies and to continuing to educate ourselves in this rapidly evolving area of consciousness-raising. We quote Jes Baker; "Making peace with our bodies and learning to love them is also about radical social justice and change. It includes a deep look at racism, violence, biased health care, fatphobia, inaccessible spaces, discrimination, limited resources, gendered bathrooms, sexism, irrelevant age limitations, and so much more. I'd love to see Body Positivity fully encompass Body Equality, but as of right now we haven't be able to merge them in the mainstream. Yet."
- We are committed to our ongoing education in regards to inclusion, and to investing in the consultation of those who are experts in these multiple areas.

PART ONE

Integrity

- Integrity is defined as the practice of being honest and showing a consistent and uncompromising adherence to strong moral and ethical principles and values.
- We are committed to being in integrity in all our dealings with students, clients and collaborators.
- We will never misrepresent the Institute or our service in the world.
- We are committed to honouring our teaching lineage and identifying our sources. We will not accommodate or collude in plagiarism, misrepresentation or de-identification of those who have informed and inspired our work. If we unintentionally do so we will correct the error.
- We commit to collaborating to the best of our ability with only those who share congruent ethics and values.
- We commit to using language responsibly and to never making ambit claims or evidence-less statements. We will not use language that causes harm, and if we are shown to be doing so we will listen, learn and correct the error. We will not overclaim or deceive others in regard to any aspect of our work.

Congruence

- The Institute's work in the world, its teachers, mentors and leaders are committed wholeheartedly to be the demonstration of our deep faith and values.
- This includes proudly using the word God in our teachings.

Ongoing personal, spiritual and professional development

The three pillars of personal, spiritual and professional development underpin all the training we provide and define the Institute Code of Ethics. Mentors, graduates, and students are expected to maintain a commitment to these three pillars during and after their studies. For this reason, the Institute has created the Certified Membership community and postgraduate program pathways for all Intuitive Intelligence® graduates, which provides access to all three pillars:

- Personal development includes the commitment to continued social consciousness-raising, self-education, self-inquiry and the pursuit of dismantling subconscious biases and fear programs to be the clearest possible vessel on the path of service.
- Spiritual development means to privilege one's relationship to devotion above all else and to centre the relationship with our God Self in all we do.
- Professional development ensures the maintenance of and contribution to skills development for all those working with clients in complementary therapies, energy medicine and life coaching.

The Institute is a registered training provider of the International Institute of Complementary Therapists (IICT). In addition to the above, we adhere to the IICT code of ethics.

Intuitive Intelligence® is a registered trademark within Australia.

PART ONE

ETHICAL CODE OF CONDUCT

Ethical Code of Conduct for the Intuitive Intelligence Trainer

This Ethical Code of Conduct should direct all behaviour, values and judgments amongst Intuitive Intelligence® Method practitioners, Trainers, Teachers, Spiritual Directors and students to safeguard client and graduate welfare. It applies to all students and graduates who have undertaken any Institute for Intuitive Intelligence® qualification. It is drawn from our Code of Ethics, which all students and graduates should be aware of and adhere to.

STANDARD 1:

Demonstrate the Qualities of the Intuitive Intelligence® Method practitioner, Trainer, Teacher, Spiritual Director or student.

Be professional at all times.

Manage yourself in your role. This means ensuring that you give yourself what you need to thrive including discipline in your devotion, abstaining from alcohol and state altering drugs within at least 48 hours of your service, maintaining a lifestyle that allows for congruence between your faith and your actions and committing to ongoing personal and spiritual development.

Do not engage in publicly or promote professionally the trinkets and superstitions of the new age in your role as Intuitive Intelligence® Method practitioner, Trainer, Teacher, Spiritual Director or student.

Commit to annual recertification with ongoing professional development as part of Membership.

Act with integrity at all times.

Acknowledge the client's right to terminate the relationship at any point during the process.

Be respectful of other medical or healthcare professionals and the boundaries of their professional remit.

PART ONE

ETHICAL CODE OF CONDUCT

STANDARD 2:

Locate your work in the broader context

Take account of professional and client expertise.

Build and maintain relationships with other Intuitive intelligence® Method practitioners, trainers, Teachers, Spiritual Directors or students—and complementary professionals who can support you in your practice.

Collaborate to the best of your ability with only those who share congruent ethics and values.

Communicate with clients effectively about your services to establish their trust and consent for the work you intend to do.

Promote inclusiveness and anti-discriminatory practice, including an awareness of the culturally sensitive boundaries that govern practitioner and client interactions, physical or otherwise. Commit to ongoing education in regard to inclusion and invest in the consultation of those who are experts in these multiple areas. You can read the Institute's Equality, Diversity and Inclusion Policy in Simplero.

Report any concerns about the practice of other Intuitive Intelligence® practitioners that you believe contravenes our Ethical Code of Conduct without delay to the Institute.

STANDARD 3:

Intervene with skill

Apply knowledge, understanding and values relevant to your profession.

Recognise your limitations and seek advice when needed.

Recommend, where necessary, that a client seeks medical advice if the issue that is presented appears to be physical, or outside the remit of the Intuitive Intelligence® graduate or student.

Do not work with clients who express suicidal ideation. If this is presented inside of a session, take immediate steps to safely bring the session to a close. Create a plan of action with the client including providing them with contact information for appropriate support. In Australia these contacts may include:

https://www.lifeline.org.au/ 131114

https://www.healthdirect.gov.au/crisis-management

Please familiarise yourself with the supports in your local area.

It may be necessary to ask the client if you can contact a support person on their behalf or arrange for them to do this under your supervision. If they do not agree to this then ask them to identify for you who and when they will contact a support person after your session is completed.

PART ONE

ETHICAL CODE OF CONDUCT

Once the immediate risk assessment has been completed, then follow up via email including all relevant information about who they can contact, including advising them to speak with their GP if they do not already have a mental health care plan.

Upon confirmation that they are in the care of an expert medical team you may choose to continue your work with them, as long as you are not their sole care provider, and as long as you have written agreement with them about the expectations of ongoing work with them.

Do not make false claims about your qualifications and experience, about the scope of your Intuitive Intelligence® qualification, and do not suggest Intuitive Intelligence® philosophy and praxis will be a cure. The work of the Intuitive Intelligence graduate is not counselling or therapy. It is not a medical technique and does not replace the need for medical care.

If you ever perceive or feel that information given by you to your client opposes a primary professional provider's treatment plan or recommendations, ensure you strongly advise your client to follow the advice and instructions of your primary professional provider.

Commit to using language responsibly and never to make ambit claims or evidence-less statements. Commit not to use language that causes harm; if you are shown to be doing so, listen, learn and correct the error. Do not over-claim or deceive others in regard to any aspect of your work.

STANDARD 4:

Quality Assure your practice

Measure the impact you are having on the client's issue.

Record and maintain accurate records according to strict GDPR/data protection and privacy laws, and insurance requirements, advising clients of rules for disclosure.

You can read more about the Australian guidelines here:

https://www.oaic.gov.au/privacy/guidance-and-advice/australian-entities-and-the-eu-general-data-protection-regulation/

US Guidelines here https://www.clarip.com/data-privacy/gdpr-united-states/

Europe Guidelines here https://gdpr.eu/what-is-gdpr/

Be aware of, and comply with, relevant Institute for Intuitive Intelligence® policies, ethics and procedures. These can be found in the Simplero platform.

Use the Disclaimer with all your clients. This can be found in the Simplero platform.

Have an awareness of the quality of your practice.

Commit to honouring your teaching lineage, and identifying your sources.

Do not accommodate or collude in plagiarism, misrepresentation or de-identification of those who have informed, educated and inspired your work. If found to unintentionally do so, correct the error.

PART ONE

ETHICAL CODE OF CONDUCT

STANDARD 5:

Demonstrate Professional Excellence

Provide change and transformation using sound judgment.

Bring things back to their most logical conclusion, focus on moving students and clients from fear to love as THE work of healing, provide evidence where possible for what you do and why you do it, innovate and evolve where required, and accept no quick fixes or magic bullets on this awakening journey.

Do not utilise Intuitive Intelligence® for fortune telling, future prediction, claims to be able to heal someone else or any other abuse of intuition that would rob an individual of self-determination.

Be open with clients regarding the expectations, success and cost of Services.

Ensure appropriate professional insurances are maintained.

Protect the professionalism of the Intuitive Intelligence® techniques.

Conduct yourself, at all times, in accordance with your status and do not engage in any behaviour or practice that may bring the Intuitive Intelligence ® techniques into disrepute. This also includes how you conduct yourself online.

Obtain client permission before any video/audio recordings take place and before publishing client feedback, regardless of whether this is done anonymously.

Maintain the confidentiality of your clients at all times.

Ensure you maintain professional boundaries at all times (for example, avoid any sexual or romantic relationships with clients).

Do not misrepresent yourself using the Intuitive Intelligence® brand/materials.

Report malpractice when noted to the relevant overseeing organisation.

Have the ability to identify your level of skill and competency and work within these and the standards you were trained in.

Recognise and honour the intellectual property of others.

Be aware of, and mitigate conflicts of interest.

Maintain technical and practical skills by committing to ongoing personal, spiritual

professional and ethical development.

Operate your practice within local, regional and national regulations.

PART TWO

PRAXIS PHILOSOPHY & PRAXIS

PART TWO

THE TOOLS OF THE INTUITIVE INTELLIGENCE TRAINER

In addition to the Intuitive Intelligence ® Method, which is used in the initial session as an energy evaluation of our client, as a qualified intuitive Intelligence Trainer, we also have the tools of the eight component parts that make up the Methodology and Praxis of Intuitive Intelligence.

We utilise these tools in our ongoing work with the client. We design our sessions utilising our non-local intuition and curate a program of sustainable and permanent change by working with the eight components of the Methodology and Praxis. These eight components include:

1. **Cultivating vibrational states – Space Creating – Embodiment**
   - Heart Congruence
   - Micro Method
   - Meditation
   - Prayer
   - Chanting
   - Pranayama

2. **Altered states of consciousness (visualisation)**

3. **Symbolic sight/spiritual sight – identifying core fears**

4. **Energy Medicine – communing with the chakras and koshas**

5. **Remote viewing through dimensions of time and space**
   - Reading the subconscious
   - Locating other lifetimes
   - Accessing the Akashic library

6. **Archetypes**
   - Shadow and light
   - Channelling archetypal energy

7. **Atonement – guiltlessness and forgiveness**

8. **Intuitive Intelligence Tapping**

The following outlines the methodology of these tools as explained through the practice of the initial Method session, as well as in the subsequent follow up sessions. However, the theory applies equally to when we use these as stand alone tools in our follow up sessions.

PART TWO

OVERVIEW OF THE INTUITIVE INTELLIGENCE METHOD SESSION

- **Welcome & prepare client**
- **Opening & ASOC**
- **Fear profiling & Shadow**
- **Chakra diagnosis**
- **Instigating event**
- **Journey to Akashic Library**
- **Archetype**
- **Atonement & Closing**

PART TWO

OVERVIEW OF THE INTUITIVE INTELLIGENCE FOLLOW UP SESSIONS

The Intention of the Follow up session

1. Create an experience that moves the client further from fear to love
2. Break the addiction to the fear
3. Active, participatory client (client-led)
4. Embodied experience of change FOR THE CLIENT by going on a facilitated journey towards self-realisation

What the sessions are NOT

1. Talking therapy
2. Advice giving
3. Fortune telling
4. Coaching
5. Healing (passive client)

Structure of your session

1. 5-10 minutes of discussion – client-identified aims, issues
2. Energy expansion meditation
3. Non-local intuition selected tool
4. Sharing of client experience
5. Preparing to leave (Heart Congruence for example)
6. Homework (or send via email)

Keys to success

1. Slow down
2. Space – don't overload the session
3. Allow silence/reflection for the client
4. Don't talk all the time
5. Don't Play God
6. Don't steal the client's AHA! moments
7. Listen locally and non-locally

Drawing on

+ intuitive guide toolkit
+ client notes from session #1
+ non-local intuition, and
+ client's reported experience and desired outcomes

At any time

If during any of the processes you feel the client has moved into their reasoning conscious mind or any other state of being that is not conducive to moving them from fear to love, then stop what you are doing and engage the use of:

- Tapping on the side of the hand, or
- Pranayama

Entering & exiting the session

We are **space creators** for our clients. We are cultivating the optimal vibrational container to support the client to move from fear to love in our session. The way you enter and exit the session is vital to create this optimal state.

- Always begin the session with the Energy Expansion meditation (this can be abbreviated if you have a number of practices you
- are working with in a session). This sets the client up for success by taking them from the local to the nonlocal, and from the Beta brainwave state to Alpha or Theta. You are building a bridge from their ordinary waking life to the sacred container of the work you are doing together.
- You must also lead the client out of the sacred container to prepare them to re-enter the world, grounded and fully present. I encourage you to utilise a pranayama practice or some form of meditation that supports them to anchor back into the normal activity of their days.

PART TWO

INTUITIVE INTELLIGENCE EMBODIMENT

These are tools for you to work with to bring you into alignment with your superconscious intuition. Where appropriate you may also include in work with your clients.

Intuitive Intelligent Embodiment, as you are trained to work with it as an Intuitive Intelligence Trainer, is part of activating mysticism in our clients and ourselves.

You may consider designing a Sadhana for your client to support them between your sessions, and it will be from this section that you can find the tools to assign to them.

This section also provides the templated tools associated with Pre-Client Preparation and Step One of the Method.

I share these words from Ken Wilber on the qualities of the mystic. These are the qualities of opening our inner eye, our Intuitive Intelligence.

"(1) We each have an outer self and an inner Self. We saw that the outer self (or the "empirical ego") is "the self that can be seen," while the inner Self (or transcendental Self) can never be made an object or thing of any sort, but rather is, among other items, a sense of Freedom and a Great Liberation from the known, from the finite, and from the empirical ego.

(2) The inner Self lives in a timeless, eternal Now. Eternity does not mean everlasting time, but a moment without time, which happens to be exactly this moment, when seen correctly as an endless Present encompassing all time. The true Self is aware of this ever-present, never-ending, eternal moment, through which all time passes—and, while never entering the stream of time itself, remains as its unmoved Witness.

(3) The inner Self is a great Mystery, or pure Emptiness and Unknowingness. Precisely because it can never be known or made an object, the true Self is no-thing-ness, pure mysterium, an ongoing unknown Knowingness, or cognizing Emptiness, or simply, the great Mystery of your own being.

(4) The inner Self is divine, or perfectly one with infinite Spirit in a Supreme Identity. As St. Thomas put it, if the eyeball were colored red, it couldn't see red; but because it is clear or red-less or color-less, it can see colors. Just so, because the inner Self sees space, it is itself spaceless, or infinite; and because it sees time, it is itself timeless, or eternal. this infinite and eternal Self is the home of Spirit in you and in each and every sentient being. The overall number of inner Selves is but one. Every person feels exactly the way you do when they feel into their own Witness or I AMness: since the true Self has no objects or qualities, it can't be different in anybody: it is the same radiant Divine shining in you and me and all of Spirit's creations.

PART TWO

(5) Hell is identification with the outer self. Hell is not a place; hell is not somewhere that we go when we are dead; hell is not punishment handed out to us by something or someone else—it is rather our own contracting, sinning, separating activity of choosing the wrong self to identify with. We identify with that which we are not, we identify merely and only with the empirical ego, the self-that-can-be-seen; and that puny, finite, temporal, limited and lacerating identity is nothing other than hell. Hell is a horrendous case of mistaken identity. We have forgotten who and what we are, a transcendental Self plugged straight into Spirit, speaking with the words of God and shining with the radiance of the Goddess. But we identify only with the finite self, the objective self, the self that can be seen, and not the Self that is the Seer, divine and infinite and eternal...

(6) Heaven is the discovery and realization of the inner Divine Self, the Supreme Identity. The mystics East and West have long proclaimed that "the Kingdom of Heaven is within"— because the simple fact is that I AMness is Christ consciousness, Spirit itself, the Godhead in me and as me. The True Self in each and every one of us is the True Self that Jesus of Nazareth realized—"I and the Father are one"— and that realization, quite simply, transformed him from a temporal Jesus into an eternal Christ, a transformation that He asks us to remember and repeat ourselves. Of course, this does not mean that my empirical ego is Christ, or that my personal self is Christ. To believe that is, indeed, a schizophrenic delusion. Nobody is saying that my personal self is Spirit, but rather that the transcendental Witness of that personal self is one with Spirit in all beings. Your transcendental Self is Christ, your personal self is you.

(7) The Divine Self is one with the All, given in grace and sealed in glory. At some point, as one rests in the inward Witness, feeling the atmosphere of Freedom, the very sense of an inner self versus an outer self will often vanish, seen for the illusion it is, leaving only the sense of what the mystics call one taste. My transcendental Self gives way to nondual Suchness, or what Meister Eckhart called Is-ness. For Spirit is not only the Self of all beings, but the Suchness or Is-ness or Thusness of all things. To Freedom from any object is thus added the Fullness of being one with all objects.

I no longer witness the mountains, I am the mountains; I no longer feel the earth, I am the earth; I no longer see the ocean, I am the ocean; I know longer pray to Spirit, I am Spirit. So seamlessly does the world, sacred and profane, arise in one piece, that I can find no boundary— not a single fundamentally real boundary— anywhere in the entire universe. There is only the radiant, all-pervading, deeply divine I AMness, within which all the worlds arise and fall, are born and die, explode into being and fade in oblivion, carried along by the one and only thing that is always ever present, even unto the ends of the world: this ultimate Mystery in Emptiness and Release, Freedom and Fullness, Ground and Goal, Grace and Glory, this Self of mine that I can no longer find, as the raindrops in their insistent Is-ness beat gently on the roof, a beautiful sound of heartbeat thunder, thump, thump, thump, thump, just... like... that...."[12]

With this lens, we can share the Embodiment tools as a way to increase our client's identification with the nonlocal and symbolic meaning of their life events. Used as a Sadhana together, or in conjunction with the other tools in this handbook, this collection of devotional practices is a core foundation of your personal practice and the work you assign clients.

---

[12] *Foreword to Entering the Castle by Caroline Myss, 2008.*

PART TWO

Our biology is the technology of our intuition

"Through his famous equation $E=mc^2$, Albert Einstein proved to scientists that energy and matter are dual expressions of the same universal substance. That universal substance is a primal energy or vibration of which we are all composed".

— Richard Gerber

I want to introduce the relationship between our body, nervous system, and Intuitive Intelligence. Intuitive Intelligence is an embodied state of being. Our biology, our body, and in particular, our nervous system, is the technology of our Intuitive Intelligence.

We can think about the nervous system as the interface between the physical and subtle bodies. It carries electrical information through our biology. When we have a dysregulated nervous system, telling someone to trust their intuition, especially in a crisis, is like telling someone to pick up a jumbo jet. It's simply impossible. Even if we can receive our intuition through all the chaos of a dysregulated nervous system, we will be in such a state of uncertainty within ourselves that we will not necessarily have the faith or courage to act on it.

We've all had experiences where we know we've received intuitive understanding. Still, we've doubted ourselves. We've gone into our rational brain or let other people's opinions influence us. We've made lists of good or bad. We've discounted that intuitive knowing because there's no space inside of us to feel certainty. When intuition lands into a regulated nervous system, we will have a sense of anchoring or groundedness. We will often mistake impulsive heightened emotional decisions for intuition when in dysregulation. There are many aspects to how a dysregulated nervous system can mislead us. We think that our intuition is guiding, and it's our dysregulation. Deep subconscious programs that are unmet are often doing the talking and masquerading as intuition. I'm going to get to the antidote for all of this, by the way, so don't fear. If we're sitting here going,

How am I ever supposed to trust my intuition?

Let me offer a personal example.

Many years ago, when I was in the early stages of my relationship with my husband, I felt very strongly that this kind, loving, intelligent, stable man was all wrong for me. I knew 'intuitively' that I needed to break up with him, which I did. I found all sorts of reasons he was no good for me, even though I was really happy and deeply in love. We were looking to create a fantastic future together. But I ended it guided by 'intuitive knowing'.

Many months later, I had not recovered from my feelings for him. I'd broken up with him, but I hadn't moved on. I was just dismal. I asked myself,

Why am I so despairing and heartbroken if my intuition guided me to leave this man?

It took some deep self-reflection and self-investigation to understand that I had, at that time, a powerful fear of being disapproved of. This fear of disapproval was so strong in me, albeit subconsciously, that having someone so approving of me felt foreign. To my ego, it was dangerous because it felt like a trick. I am not approvable. Yet, here's this person approving me just as I am.

I was able to explore and excavate the subconscious fear. The discomfort of breaking my own heart provided the grounds for my liberation. I came back to the truth through devotion and commitment to uncovering this program and going through processes that helped me change that pattern. Through spiritual sweat, I recognised that I am approved of, and not just by him, but by myself. I was very blessed that he could let me back into his heart, even though I triggered his fear of betrayal. However, we went on and were able to heal those wounds together and grow the strength of our relationship.

PART TWO

It's our holy task to sit with the discomfort of,

My intuition might be dysregulated.

We need to be willing to do the deep work of deep faith. We need to overcome our superficial relationship with our intuition, which has been all about getting our ego's needs met. We need to mature our relationship with our intuition and recognise that sometimes our intuitive knowledge will make us more uncomfortable than comfortable as we evolve.

Where does that leave us? How do we ever learn to trust ourselves?

Intuition is our highest form of intelligence. Our nervous system is the receiver of intuition into our physiology. When it's all working, it is the shortcut to the best life we've ever lived. But when we have an untrained relationship with our intuition, which is to say we don't know how to bring ourselves into regulation, we will either misrepresent our intuition or be bamboozled about why our intuition would guide us to make certain choices.

We know by now that our Intuitive Intelligence is about our evolution, not our comfort. Yet, we often 'check in' with our intuition because we want to get the guarantee that everything's going to work out. We'll go to a psychic or an intuitive reader or a healer, or our tarot cards because we want a sense of control by trying to know the answers in advance.

We will often be agitated by what our intuition guides us to know. This is yet another way we reject our intuition, even when it's right, because it might be asking us to see the truth. Intuition shows us that the relationship is not good for us or that the job is killing us. But our fear gets loud.

How will I survive? How would I live without that person? How could I possibly go forward in my life without all of these things that I think keep me safe?

We know what our intuition is saying. But because of those fears of the future or projections into the past, we're unable to trust what we're receiving. Our dysregulation is often caused because we are not in present time. And if we are not in present time we are not home to receive our intuition.

We must be willing to cultivate presence as part of our commitment to increasing our access to our Intuitive Intelligence. In creating an ecology for the natural development of our Intuitive Intelligence, slowing down is a critical piece of the puzzle. A life full of rushing and structured activity does not permit us to expand into full presence in this moment now. When we rush ourselves from pillar to post, feeling stress and urgency in every moment, we are not present. Presence means allowing each moment to guide us to the best course of action. When we allow ourselves to be present, we tune in to what we feel bodily, emotionally, and energetically. Without that, we can overtax the nervous system and live in our sympathetic nervous system response – fight, flight or freeze – even when we are not in a life-threatening situation. Stress reduces our capacity to connect to our Intuitive Intelligence. The high beta brainwave state that we are in when we are in our sympathetic nervous system closes off the communication between the heart and cranial brains.

PART TWO

Intuitive Intelligence Trainer Embodied Devotion

As the Intuitive Intelligence Trainer, you are taught certain Embodied Devotion for your development and in some cases, in the support of your clients. Any practices that keep us out of the fight, flight or freeze response will increase our access to our intuition. Methods of meditation, pranayama, chanting, tapping, yoga, exercising, anything that helps keep us in homeostasis supports our Intuitive Intelligence technology. This body is the receiver, and we must honour that. A few minutes each day of silence, stillness and solitude, slowing down the brainwave state, slowing down the heart rate, and allowing the body to come into a feeling of safety are all necessary precursors to a deep state of intuition.

To withdraw our attention from the external world for at least a few minutes every day and to shut down the external senses to go within is vital to establishing a deep intuition.

When we are committed to creating nervous system fitness — the ability to move in an agile and conscious way from dysregulation to regulation — our Intuitive Intelligence increases.

Pranayama and Kriya

I acknowledge my teachers Uma Neave and Sian Pascale for initiating me into the pranayama and kriya practices shared in this section.

Pranayama is one of the most powerful and simple toolsof the Intuitive Intelligence Trainer.

To regulate the breath, and to use the breath in a way that stimulates the vagus nerve, in particular, is vital in the development of deep states of Intuitive Intelligence. Stimulation through controlled breathing — pranayama — helps keep us in our parasympathetic nervous system.

We can absorb prana from various sources such as breath, sunlight, nourishment, and the natural world. Prana imbues individuals with vitality, an inner glow, and a tangible sense of vitality. Engaging in pranayama enables us to tap into the breath as a potent means to harness prana. Through mastering diverse pranayama techniques, we enhance our breath flexibility, avoiding the trap of habitual breathing patterns. Many default to a shallow, high-stress breathing style, yet transitioning to deep belly breathing requires patience and practice. It's a journey toward expanding the lungs and embracing the fullness of each breath.

Kriya is a feminine noun or gerundive – which means something that must be done.

The verbal root Kri= is to act and Ya= is the feminine force. Therefore it is the action of cultivating the creative power of Shakti. Synonymous with the word kundalini, which means spiralling shape, the two words describe the internal and cosmic creative power awakened in practicing Kriya.

Kriya possesses the remarkable capacity to delve into our cellular memory, liberating us from past traumas and mental patterns. By engaging in kriya practice, the body can generate abundant energy, facilitating a connection to the divine and fostering profound states of transcendent consciousness.

PART TWO

Three Aspects of Kriya

When delving into Kriya practice, it's essential to uphold three fundamental elements. By ensuring these aspects are maintained, you can safely and profoundly guide your clients through the practice:

Foundation

The "seat" in Kriya refers to the body's posture or asana. Whether standing or seated, establishing a stable foundation enables practitioners to maintain a steady position throughout the practice.

Focus

"Dharana," or focus, is crucial during Kriya practice. Where attention is directed profoundly impacts the experience. Intention, vibrational and energetic focus, as well as Drishti (gaze), constitute the focus of Kriya. Understanding Dharana empowers instructors to guide students towards specific states of consciousness.

Essence

"Bhav" encapsulates the feeling or energy invoked by the Kriya. It encompasses the emotional and energetic essence of the practice, contributing to its depth and transformative power.

The Pranayama and Kriya Practices

1. Integrative breath

Inhale through the nose, pause, exhale through the mouth with [an audible] sigh. This is the standard breath of the Intuitive Intelligence Trainer. This is the only breath you are expected to have mastery in leading. This breath is highly adaptable to all situations and can be done for any length of time. Incorporate tapping on the side of the hand throughout this breath.

2. Kapala Bhati

- Take a cleansing breath in through the nose and out through the mouth. Then, force the exhale out of the nostrils, snapping the navel into the spine.
- Focus on on the exhale. The inhale will happen without effort.
- Breathe only as fast as the pace you can easily maintain. This will increase with practice.
- The breath is motivated by the pumping of the belly, sending energy upwards along the central column, Shushumna Nadi.
- Breathe for around a minute.
- Inhale, retain the breath for as long as is comfortable.
- Exhale with control through the mouth long and slow.
- Repeat two more rounds.

PART TWO

Kapala Bhati with ego conqueror mudra – this is a kriya practice.

- **Seat:** Begin seated
- Reach the arms up at 60 degrees, thumbs drawn under fingers in fists.
- Keep the heart space open, shoulders relaxed and shoulderblades drawing towards each other.
- Begin Kalapa Bhati breath. Complete three rounds.
- After each round, of approx. 60 seconds, inhale, retain the breath, engage the bandhas. After 10-20 seconds, draw palms together over head, and as you exhale fully, draw the prayer to the heart.
- Stay with eyes closed for at least one minute to absorb the benefits of the state change.

3. *Bhastrika*

An equal focus is on the active inhale and exhale. Inhale and exhale happen through the nose, with no pause between them while pumping the belly vigorously in and out. Arms can be at a 60 degree angle from the body, with the thumb wrapped under the four fingers, or hands on the belly. Rounds begin at 30 seconds and work up to 2 min. Three rounds per session. There can be a short pause between rounds.

4. *Maha Banda – The Great Lock*

"Jalandhara Bandha, uddiyana bandha and mula bandha are situated respectively in the throat, abodmen and perineum. If their duration can be increased, then where is the fear of death?"

– Yogataravali

Activating all three bandhas simultaneously yields potent effects on the energetic body, facilitating the dissolution of blockages across these vital areas and liberating the body for substantial energy shifts. Here are the instructions:

- Inhale deeply, then exhale completely, emptying the breath.
- Engage Mula Bandha, Uddiyana Bandha, and Jalandhara Bandha. Retain the breath for as long as is comfortable. This will increase with practice.
- Release the locks, inhale while directing awareness towards the Third eye Chakra.

5. *Fear releasing breath*

This is also a Kriya practice. Closing the teeth and breathing in through the teeth. Release the breath through the mouth. Arms can be held out at a T. Time is 11 min for full practice.

6. *Ujjayi "victorious" breath*

Inhale and exhale through the nose. On the exhale, slightly engage the throat muscles. The idea of fogging up a mirror with the breath can help to understand this breath. This is a slow and deep breath. This breath is audible, and you should hear the client. This breath can be done for any length of time.

AS AN INTUITIVE INTELLIGENCE TRAINER, EMBODIED DEVOTION IS ABOUT IGNITING THE MYSTIC IN OUR CLIENTS AND OURSELVES.

PART TWO

MORE EMBODIMENT PRACTICES

Heart Congruence

Heart coherence is a practice developed by HeartMath Institute and is a state in which the brain and heart work synergistically. Heart Congruence is an extension of this practice developed by the Institute.

As discussed, the intelligence of the heart brain exceeds that of the cranial brain and communicates more information to the cranial brain than the other way around. We move into a state of heart coherence when the heart and brain are working in Congruence, and it is this state, which permits us to know our Intuitive Intelligence with ease. It is the bridge between the local and nonlocal. It has many other incredible physiological benefits. For now, let us use this practice as preparation for taking the first step on the path of our Intuitive Intelligence, which is moving beyond simply knowing our intuition to trust it and acting upon it.

The practice of heart congruence is one of the best ways to prepare to access nonlocal intuition. Recalling that our "passionately focused attention" allows nonlocal intuition to be active, we can bring ourselves into the Intuitive Intelligence frequency with this same single-focused attention. Even if we do not yet know what we want to create, we utilise the same process to get to the One Mind, a space where the knowledge already exists. Practising heart congruence is a brief yet disciplined process. The practice described below is quite different to the original HeartMath version, and so I have called it Congruence to be clear on that difference.

Here's the process:

- First, close the eyes. Turn your attention inwards, away from the outer world of local reality.
- Extend the breathing to the count of five on the inward breath and five on the out breath. Adjust this to your comfortable rhythm. The intention is to signify to your nervous system that you are safe and your physiology can relax.
- Take two fingers or your palm to the centre of your chest and lightly touch this part of your body. Here, we are bringing our consciousness to this part of physiology, inviting our Mind to follow.
- Now, turn all of your thoughts to the states of compassion, gratitude, appreciation, bliss, joy and peace. You can do this most readily in the beginning by making a mental list of all the things for which you feel gratitude from the last 24 hours of your life. No matter how small, the idea is to feel gratitude, compassion, and care. Allow yourself to enter fully into them without hesitation. Remember, as HeartMath confirms, our nonlocal intuition is powerfully activated when we passionately bring our single point of focus to something.
- Let yourself be consumed by these feelings. Do this for just 3 minutes (you'll perhaps observe that this feels like a long time at first!).

PART TWO

MORE EMBODIMENT PRACTICES CONT.

Acknowledge. Regulate. Connect

The process of ARC — Acknowledge, regulate and connect — is designed to bring us into a regulated state to have the most accurate connection to our Intuitive Intelligence.

Step One.

The first letter A stands for acknowledge. To receive our intuition and trust it, we have to acknowledge what state we're in at the point of seeking access to our intuition.

Am I in a panic? Am I afraid? Am I stressed out? Am I feeling out of control? If I acknowledge where I'm at in my state of being, I can change my state of being through the second step, regulation.

Step Two.

This step involves engaging in any practice that supports regulation in the body. I recommend pranayama, closing the eyes, silence, tapping, meditation, chanting, toning, amongst many other possibilities.

Most likely, for many of us, no matter where we are in our day, there's always a benefit to engaging in practices that will bring us a little more deeply into regulation.

Step Three.

We connect. The truth is we are always connected to our intuition, but now we are focussed with conscious intention and attention on cultivating the state of being of Intuitive Intelligence.

Here I recommend placing your hand at the centre of your chest. When we place our hand here, we acknowledge our heart-brain as the centre of our Intuitive Intelligence and anchor into what Megan Watterson calls the Cathedral of the heart. We breathe into this centre. If there is a particular life situation that we're seeking guidance around, we simply hold that in our mind as we hold our attention on our heart in our regulated biology. We feel that sense of expansion that comes when we slow everything down. Letting that Intuitive Intelligence come to you in whatever way it will, feeling, hearing, seeing or knowing. The feeling will always bring a sense of certainty, anchoring, and deepening.

I invite us all to use this process for ourselves before we inquire into our intuition. Acknowledge, regulate, and then connect. Do this every day. I thoroughly recommend it because regulating our nervous systems and connecting to our intuition will always yield tremendous benefits even if there isn't a particular question or any particular challenge in our life.

PART TWO

The Micro Method

The Intuitive Intelligence Micro Method is a simplified version of the full Method that allows whoever uses it to access the Method's power for themselves and have a robust tool to meet his or her fear every day. We must meet our fear every day, and when we apply the Micro Method to our fearful beliefs and physical symptoms, we can quickly move the fear block out of our consciousness.

The Methodology and Praxis work with subconscious fear, for as A Course in Miracles tells us, we are never afraid for the reason we think we are. Our true fear sits beneath the surface of our Conscious Reasoning Minds. We apply the Micro Method to any stressful thought and, as such, release the layers of the fear. The Micro Method moves us beyond self-awareness. We move directly from recognition of the fear into providing the exact conditions required to release that fear. This is a profoundly elegant and straightforward process. It can be done anywhere and at any time. The more often we do it, the more efficient we become in the process. We are building the muscle of our Intuitive Intelligence with spiritual fierceness by being willing to meet our fear every day.

The Micro Method is an advanced practice of Intuitive Intelligence. It will work most powerfully for us when we have trained ourselves with techniques such as Heart Congruence. It is direct and straightforward but requires a commitment to live from the heart's Intuitive Intelligence. It is premised on the three immutable laws. The One Mind is waiting in every moment to guide us back to love. As such, the answers to show us how are always available when we create the optimal conditions for hearing that guidance. Practice the Micro Method with blissipline and be generously rewarded with the exact information required to be fearless. We are learning that we can consciously redirect our feeling states. This is particularly important when we remember that feeling is the language of God Consciousness.

Here's how to use the Micro Method:

1. Notice the stressful thought or physical symptom
2. Rate the stressful thought or physical symptom on a scale of 1-10, 10 being the most intense. Our aim is to bring that number down with the Micro Method
3. Close your eyes and take a deep breath in through your nose, letting it go out through your mouth with an audible sigh. Maintain a slightly extended breath, breathing in for four counts and out for 6 counts
4. Place two fingers at the centre of your chest
5. Ask slightly or out loud, what is the dominant fear in this situation?

The answer will be brief and succinct, and will make itself known to you through your dominant clair (clairsentience, clairaudience, claircognizance or clairvoyance). You will see, hear, feel or know the answer. It will be as brief as one word, image, sound or short phrase. Intuition is instant and precise.

6. Now, there are two choices:
   a. If you are still in a state of fear, turn your attention to feelings of compassion for your fear. See it like a hurt little child that is begging for love. Imagine yourself embracing your fear and be deeply compassionate to it. You must give yourself over to this feeling with your whole being. Let it build for around one minute. Allow the feeling to expand in you with as much intensity as possible. Now let go of the feelings of compassion
   b. If you are seasoned in this practice, turn your attention to mental images and thoughts that invoke feelings of deep gratitude. It may be the smile of your child, the sun on your back, the memory of a holiday. It must bring up for you only the high vibrational feeling of gratitude. You must give yourself over to this feeling with your whole being. Let it build for around one minute. Allow the feeling to expand in you with as much intensity as possible. Now let go of the feelings of gratitude

PART TWO

7. Take a deep breath in and let it go out through the mouth
8. Look around for the stressful thought or physical symptom that you rated on a scale of 1-10. When you find it, rate it again. If the number is above 2, repeat Step (6) up to two more times.

Micro Method Variation – What's deeper than that?

You can do this as part of the full Micro Method, adding it when guiding the client, or you can do it as a stand alone practice.

Lead the client into Heart Congruence.

- Ask your client what are you **most afraid of**?
- Listen without judgement. No nods, pats, smiles etc. Just listen silently, maintaining your own Heart Congruence
- When your client has finished responding (this will be different in duration for everyone), they then ask, what's deeper than that?
- Once more, your client speaks stream of consciousness, with no confirmations from you
- Ask one more time, what's deeper than that?
- When your client has completed their share, thank them. Invite them to close their eyes, and to start tapping on the side of their hand, and guide them back into Heart Congruence. Invite them to let everything go.

> "I BELIEVE THAT PART OF THE CALLING OF THE CONTEMPORARY MYSTIC IS TO DE-ANIMATE THIS SUFFERING RELATIONSHIP WITH THE DIVINE. [AND] TRANSFORM IT TO ONE OF FEARLESS INTIMACY"
>
> *Caroline Myss, Entering the Castle.*

Prayer

The following section is drawn from the work of Gregg Braden and Caroline Myss. Above all else, we are inviting ourselves to connect to prayer as an embodied experience with no special conditions. It is best integrated into all aspects of our mundane life and normalised as a process we share with our clients.

Gregge Braden states, "Prayer is perhaps one of the most ancient and mysterious of human experiences. It's also one of the most personal. Even before the word prayer appeared in spiritual practices, the oldest records of the Christian and Gnostic traditions used words such as communion to describe our ability to speak with the unseen forces of the universe. Today, modern prayer researchers have identified four broad categories that are believed to encompass all the many ways that we pray. In no particular order, they are: (1) colloquial, or informal, prayers; (2) petitionary prayers; (3) ritualistic prayers; and (4) meditative prayers. When we pray, the researchers suggest that we use one of these four modes—or a combination.

This fifth mode of prayer, the "lost mode," is a prayer that's based solely in feeling. Rather than the sense of helplessness that often leads us to ask for assistance from a higher power, feeling-based prayer acknowledges our ability to communicate with the intelligent force that 95 percent of us believe in, and participate in the outcome.

Without any words, without our hands held in a certain position or any outward physical expression, this mode of prayer simply invites us to feel a clear and powerful feeling as if our prayers have already been answered. Through this intangible "language," we participate in the healing of our bodies, the abundance that comes to our friends and families, and the peace between nations"[13].

---

[13] *Secrets of the Lost Mode of Prayer, 2016.*

PART TWO

Here are the Phases of Prayer as described by Caroline Myss:

1. The Prayer of recollection

Pray yourself into wholeness, detaching from outside influence, to meet the character of your soul.

ACTION:
Pray and listen. Pray and Listen. Use a repetitive prayer (such as the Healer's prayer and then move into silence to receive.

2. The Prayer of Contemplation:

Self-reflection. Review your actions. Do not run from them. Be fearless.

ACTION:
Read a passage from a sacred text and reflect on the meaning it has for your life. Or simply review your day and allow yourself to be with your fear.

3. The Prayer of quiet:

Soul tranquillity. Doubts and fears are gone. You glimpse the divine bliss of heaven

ACTION:
Silent meditation

4. The Prayer of Union:

The mystical state of union with God beyond the senses. A state of suspension. There is no action for this other than regular devotion. This form of prayer is a spontaneous experience of the divine, which cannot be commanded into being, but joyfully received.

Chanting

As sound is vibration. It makes sense that one of the most immediate and powerful ways to up-level our vibration is with sound. Listening to music instantly changes our mood. Rather than coincidentally, the reality is that we are altering our vibration by using music we love to change our feeling state. The act of sounding – in this case chanting – works in the same way, yet even more powerfully. Why is that? When we chant sacred sounds, such as ancient mantras, we are repeating sounds that have been uttered in reverence billions of times before.

We are attuning to the vibration of the utterance of that sound in all directions of time and space. It takes us out of our cranial brain and into the feeling state very quickly.

There are many chants you can use with your clients. I am offering three that we utilise as part of Embodied Devotion. These chants are in Sanskrit. The most important thing to know with Sanskrit is that it is a spiritual language created to express the spiritual experience. **Sanskrit** is the classical language of Indian and the liturgical language of Hinduism, Buddhism, and Jainism. It is also one of the 22 official languages of India. The name **Sanskrit** means "refined", "consecrated" and "sanctified".

So Ham Mantra

I am sharing with you one of my favourites because it is so simple and builds in tempo so that you can experience the sensation of raising your vibration through sound. Soham is a Hindu mantra, meaning "I am He/That" in Sanskrit. In Vedic philosophy, it means identifying oneself with the God Mind or ultimate reality. I am that I am is an often uttered spiritual mantra, so even though this is a Hindu mantra, the meaning is transcendent. We are aligning ourselves with/as God as we chant. I would love to share my version of this chant with you, which you can access here:
www.instituteforintuitiveintelligence.com/justforyou.

To use this sound without the chant, repeat it to yourself as often as you like. Or you may use the English translation I am that I am, which is the response that God used in the Hebrew Bible when Moses asked for his name (Exodus 3:14). It is one of the most famous verses in the Torah.

Maha Mrtyunjaya Mantra (Tryambakam Mantra – Shiva)

Maha – means great, mrtyu – means death, jaya – means victory. This is the great mantra for conquering death and illness. A Shiva mantra.

We offer worship to the fragrant three eyed Shiva who enhances life by giving nourishment and by adding affluence and prosperity,

PART TWO

May he liberate us from the bondage of Samsara (worldly life),

Like ripened fruit detaching itself from the vine,

Liberating us from death allowing us to realise our eternal nature.

Om tryambakam yajamahe

Sugandhim pustivardhanam

Urvarukamiva bandhanan

Mrityormuksiya mamrtat

Long form of the Maha Gayatri Mantra (Saraswati's version- Shakti)

The meaning of the chant above all else is the sound. Direct translation cannot convey the depth of the sound. Please enter into the bliss of the sound. The mystic is one who sits with the mysteries. Let your heart, rather than your intellect guide you into this chanting.

Om Bhur

Om Bhuvah

Om Suvaha

Om Maha

Om Janaha

Om Tapaha

Om Satyam

Om Tat Savitur Varenyam

Bargo Devasya Dhimahi

Dhiyo Yo Nah Prachodayat

Meditation

This is a daily non-negotiable as this is where we meet ourselves as God.

Following is a technique that is not only going to make meditation possible for you but also impossible at which to fail. I get quite excited when people tell me that they can't meditate. I start waving my hands in the air and muttering about speaking French and not quitting after one failed attempt to order café au lait and croissant at the local patisserie. This: we can meditate. Oh yes, we can all meditate. Let's begin with why we would want to because, in regards to being the unlimited consciousness we already are, the act of meditation might start to make perfect sense.

Why is meditation such a big deal to the intuitive? There is a spiritual idea called 'getting in the gap'. Quite simply, this means finding space between the thoughts of the monkey-mind. We do this to reach the state of peace that allows us to know our true nature, our sacred nature. In the gap between thoughts, between emotions, there resides God Consciousness. The work of our lives as intuitives is to spend as much time as possible in that gap, which is the space of the eternal present. We cannot think ourselves there. We cannot force ourselves there. We can only reach this space by surrender. What does that mean? It means we make time and space for the gap, even when we do not know if we will reach it that day, or that month, or that year. We make the time regardless because, ultimately, we know it is the only way to meet our co-creative partner. It is the only way to access our divine natures and live the fullness of our lives.

Meditation is all about getting in the space between our illusory beliefs about the nature of ourselves and the world we inhabit, to allow the truth of ourselves to become more and more present. It is a process, and there are steps. This is the foundation of all the other practices I share. This is also the foundation of all other practices. Meditation has scientific and strong physiological evidence backing up its benefits. We always meditate with the sacred in mind, but we also know that we are not going anywhere with raging anxiety or manic stress, let alone into the God Mind. It helps to think of the practical aspects of meditating to motivate our practice, especially when we begin.

The Praxis: Increase the gap between your heartbeats

The purpose of this technique is to take us to the space between, to the gap, the home of our intuition.

- **Be seated, your spine straight but soft** – there is nothing rigid about the body in meditation, for stillness is the aim. If the body is held too tightly there will be no stillness. If you are tired, overwhelmed, resistant, or reticent then please lie down. There is no impediment to your meditation practice too big to overcome. As I said before it is a step-by-step process. If step one for you is to be lying down, then do it! Don't not meditate because of some mental image of what meditation looks like that you don't believe you are meeting.

- **Take your pulse** by counting the beats at the radial artery for fifteen seconds.

- **Write it down.**

- **Then set your timer** on your phone for five minutes. Make sure your phone is in flight mode.

- **Focus on your breath.** Deepen your breathing, extending the length of each in breath and out breath. Add a pause between the inhalation and exhalation.

- **Continue for five minutes.**

- **Take your pulse again.** The aim is for less beats in that first fifteen-second measure.

Okay, we have just changed our lives for good.

This little technique has just profoundly increased our Heart Rate Variability (HRV) – that is, the space between our heartbeats. One of the most powerful tools for change we have is to spend as much time as we can in the gap between our heartbeats. This is the sacred space in which we are in communion with the God Mind. Nearly twenty-five years of clinical research has shown that, when HRV levels are high, people can experience lower stress levels and greater resilience.

If we want to be in communion with the highest part of ourselves, and engineer the Universe in accordance with our highest good, then we need to increase our HRV, reduce our heart rate, and get in the gap. There are stories of great mystics and yogis who can lower their heart rate to such an extent that they appear as though they are dead. This is not a party trick. The intention is to be in a state of mastery of our physiological responses. When we can alter our own heart rate, we are able to prevent the lower emotional states from controlling us. We can literally breathe our way back into harmony.

PART TWO

PRE-CLIENT PREPARATION

PHILOSOPHY

WHAT ARE WE DOING WHEN WE ATTUNE TO THE SUBTLE ANATOMY OF OUR CLIENT? HOW DO WE ACCESS THE INFORMATION ENCODED IN THEIR ENERGY FIELD? WE ARE CONDUCTING AN ENERGY EVALUATION THAT HELPS US TO HELP OUR CLIENT UNDERSTAND WHERE AND HOW THEIR FAULTY FEAR BELIEFS ARE DRAINING THEM OF LIFE FORCE. LET'S LOOK AT HOW THIS WORKS.

Congruence

We know we must consistently work towards congruence and coherence through our devotion and specifically establish heart congruence before working with our clients. This ensures we are the most precise channels for the grace of God to move through us (remembering that this work is always about us getting out of the way and letting God lead).

Congruence is defined as being in agreement or harmony. We aim to be connected with our nonlocal or God-consciousness. We do this to access information on behalf of our client from the field of light and energy. We aim to be in congruence between the heart and brain in our physical bodies, knowing that heart intelligence is the highest form of intelligence we possess.

Caroline Myss states, "Congruency can take many forms, but in essence you are congruent when your beliefs match up with your everyday actions and your spiritual practice. Say what you believe and believe what you say; act on your belief and follow through on guidance that comes from inner reflection. In this way, body, mind, and soul finally come into an alignment that allows for the harmony of the graces to flow through you as naturally as your breath. You maintain congruence by honoring the spiritual truths that you have consciously made a part of your interior life."[14]

HeartMath Institute speaks about this as coherence. "Coherence is the state when the heart, mind and emotions are in energetic alignment and cooperation," HeartMath Institute Research Director Dr Rollin McCraty says. "It is a state that builds resiliency – personal energy is accumulated, not wasted – leaving more energy to manifest intentions and harmonious outcomes."[15]

Once we are congruent, we hold the highest possible vibration, and most certainly more elevated than our clients, who will most often commit to working with us when they are in crisis. Even if this is not the case, as an Intuitive Intelligence Trainer, we have trained ourselves to hold a vibration higher and lighter than most others.

---

[14] https://www.myss.com/fifth-mystical-law-maintain-spiritual-congruency/
[15] https://www.heartmath.org/articles-of-the-heart/the-math-of-heartmath/coherence/

PART TWO

Entrainment

When we sit with our client, we begin to entrain them to our high and light vibration as soon as the session starts. We are space creators. We are not holding space for their existing reality, which is a fear-filled identification with their personality, history and story. We are creating the space for the conditions for their healing, which is to remember that they are one with the One Mind. We do not use our congruence to resonate with their frequency but rather entrain them to our frequency. With our passionately focussed attention and our intention to serve them, we come into vibrational resonance with the client, and then we can entrain them to our frequency.

"The vibrational frequency of two objects in contact will frequently fall into sync. When the frequencies are the same, it is called 'resonance'. But when a vibrational body of a stronger resonance influences another in its field, leading the beat, it is called entrainment."[16]

We expedite the work of the session by being the Space Creator. If the client were to stay in the vibration they were in when they arrived from their 3D lives, and we did nothing to establish entrainment, not only would it be near impossible to access their subtle anatomy, the client would not be in the optimal state of being to receive the session.

"According to science, entrainment exists for the purpose of conserving energy. That is, it takes less energy to work in harmony with another body, than to work against it... So for example, a counsellor supporting someone with deep anxiety or trauma can regulate their breathing to influence their client, so that the client can slow down, let go of their anxiety, and then be able to express themselves better.[17]*"*

This is critical to the success of our work. It is why our devotion and commitment to continually increasing our vibration through our spiritual discipline is essential. Hold the Torus image in your consciousness as you prepare to work with a client and throughout the session. Visualise your field expanding to create the space to hold the client's field within yours.

The Torus is the shape of the movement of the particle. So when we talk about vibrating particles, the shape of the Torus is the shape it creates. We understand that the vibration of the particle occurs because, at the subatomic level, there isn't a particle; there's a wave. That wave produces a field, and the field is the torus shape.

Your subatomic particle produces that torus shape, the cell in your body produces that torus shape, your entire physical body produces that Torus shape, and so does the whole universe. Everything has that same energetic signature. We are all producing the same shaped field. The size and shape of that Torus expands or contracts based on the vibrational frequency. As you are holding that higher and lighter frequency, you can entrain your client to your toroidal field.

---

[16] *https://upliftconnect.com/healing-power-of-entrainment/*
[17] *ibid*

PART TWO

Summary

Let's review what we know about our role as Intuitive Intelligence Trainers:

- *We are accessing non-local intuition – the phase of intuition that operates because of the inherent interconnectedness of all consciousness. We are entering the quantum or fifth dimensional realm*

- *We know that everything is consciousness, vibration, that is brought into form/matter by our belief*

- *We know that our work is only possible when we are in a coherent state, and that coherence is generated by first clearing our own fear and then elevating our vibration*

- *This expands our own personal energy field to create resonance with our client. In other words, we hold our client in our field whilst we do the work together. We do this because as Priestesses of Consciousness we are able to hold a higher vibration and accelerate the return to love for our client*

- *We do this repeatedly and with the intensity of devotion so that we break the habit of our limited, matter-centric perception of ourselves and others*

- *It is our passionately focussed attention and intention to serve our client that allows us to access the relevant information for the client in the timeframe of our session*

- *Ultimately, we must realise we are not working in 3D at all.*

PART TWO

THE MYSTICAL DIMENSION: BHUVANESHWARI

Bhuvaneshwari – the holder of space for the journey through the subtle realms of consciousness

As you read the following description of the Hindu goddess Bhuvaneshwari, reflect on your role as the creator of space for your client, as you guide her to meet her own consciousness at deeper and subtler levels.

Understand that everything that happens in the session with you is sacred, from the moment they make an appointment with you to the final goodbye. You have entered into a sacred contract to perform the sacred task to 'orient our consciousness towards a loving investigation in this mysterious, subtle space of our spiritual heart.

Our work is not the work of the gross, material plane. We are transpersonal guides, traversing consciousness beyond dimensions to return ourselves and our client to the no-space no-time state of unified, infinite consciousness. It is a sacred privilege.

This insight comes from Sivasakti, "The space of our consciousness is created by Bhuvaneshwari so that we are allowed to manifest as individuals in the world in which we exist.

Consequently, it has become obvious that on the level of the whole creation, space has several levels of manifestation, in perfect harmony with the resonances of the subtle energies. For instance, in the physical space that is around us there is also the mental space, which is also as infinite as the physical space.

This mental space also has several levels of subtlety, which culminate with the supreme space of the pure divine consciousness, which is beyond all manifestations. All these different types of space represent only various aspects and functions of Bhuvaneshwari.

According to the law of correspondences and analogies from the Eastern spiritual tradition the whole macrocosm is contained in the small, subtle space at the level of our hearts. In other words, the heart is the Bhuvaneshwari's residence.

One of the infallible methods that allow us the communion with this Great Cosmic Wisdom's gigantic sphere of force is to orient our consciousness towards a loving investigation in this mysterious, subtle space of our spiritual heart…

Practically, we can say that we are always in Bhuvaneshwari's sphere of consciousness but beyond this reality that implies a macrocosmic reality the goddess represents more the very subtle space of our hearts in which is contained mysteriously the whole manifestation and which at the same time represents the sacred place in which we may become one with the consciousness of our Supreme Immortal Self, through spontaneous, beatific revelation"[18].

Nila Matthews, graduate of the Institute, also explains that her name is used in the long form of Gayatri mantra (Bhuh – earth; bhuvah – atmosphere; swah – heaven).

---

[18] http://sivasakti.com/tantra/dasa-maha-vidya/bhuvaneshwari/

PART TWO

PRAXIS

> ### Trainer
> Give yourself around 20-30 minutes prior to your client's arrival to prepare vibrationally. Move into extended heart congruence for up to 20 minutes, or utilise any other devotional practice. Notice if you have any fear or discomfort for any reason and use the Micro Method or Intuitive Intelligence Tapping to meet and clear that fear. Your priority is to hold the highest vibration possible. Do whatever you need to do to ensure this is the case.

Understand that everything that happens in the session with you is sacred, from the moment that your client makes the appointment with you to the final goodbye.

You have entered into a sacred contract to perform the divine task to 'orient our consciousness towards a loving investigation in this mysterious, subtle space of our spiritual heart'.

Our work is not the work of the gross, material plane.

We are transpersonal guides, remote viewing through the dimensions of time and space to locate and clear subconscious fear. We are traversing consciousness to return our client to the no-space no-time state of unified, infinite God Self.

PART TWO

STEP ONE
OPENING & ASOC

PHILOSOPHY

> "EVERYTHING IS FIRST WORKED OUT IN THE UNSEEN BEFORE IT IS VISIBLE IN THE SEEN: IN THE IDEAL BEFORE IT SHOWS FORTH IN THE REAL; IN THE SPIRITUAL BEFORE IT MANIFESTS IN THE MATERIAL. YOUR SUBCONSCIOUS MIND IS BRINGING YOU THE MATURED FRUITS OF YOUR MENTAL ACTION."
>
> *Dr Venice Bloodworth*

We use the term consciousness to describe the collection of beliefs we have, individually and collectively. Most of these beliefs are unconscious, inherited, tribal, and familial. The process of spiritual awakening is raising consciousness. We become aware of the contents of our consciousness as we awaken, and we raise it out of the darkness and into the light, so we may investigate its contents and release what we don't need. Quite literally, we raise our beliefs from the subconscious to conscious, to eventually return to the understanding that we are part of one consciousness (the intentional descent to the underworld). That one consciousness is God.

Subconscious Mind

> "YOUR SUBCONSCIOUS MIND IS ONE WITH THE UNIVERSAL MIND, AND YOU CAN DRAW ON THIS UNLIMITED SUPPLY FOR ANY AND EVERYTHING..."
>
> *Venice Bloodworth*

In entering into the Subconscious Mind and letting it reveal itself to us on behalf of our client, we are rewriting that mind program while evaluating it.

Quantum Physics tells us that there are no observers in the quantum field. All acts of observation alter the field. This means that when we find the instigating event of a fear belief in our client, we change it just by viewing it. Hence the reason we must be in the highest vibrational frequency when we do this work.

This is the part of our mind that is almost totally inaccessible to us in our day-to-day lives (see the following section on the theta brainwave state). Yet, it contains a photographic memory of all events that have ever happened to us, including from our alternate/ concurrent lives. This is the level of mind that includes our fear programs. The process of spiritual awakening is the process of becoming conscious of the fears harboured in our subconscious. We live from here, most of us, 95% of the time.

PART TWO

STEP ONE CONT. OPENING & ASOC

For the purposes of our work, the subconscious mind can also be thought of as the subtle anatomy. Let me expand on this. The subconscious is the storehouse of all belief. This is precisely what the subtle anatomy is also. They are the same.

The subtle anatomy is the interface between the God Mind and the physical body. It is the filter through which we receive God Mind consciousness. Any blocks caused by the faulty fear beliefs of our subconscious cause knots of fear in our subtle body. The knots of fear then filter into the physical body, causing dis-ease.

The subtle body is the interface between 3D and 5D (you can think of it as 4D – the thoughts, feelings and emotions that create the vibration we reside within). Anything blocking the filter of our subconscious/subtle anatomy will disrupt the proper flow of life force.

There stand the gates to heaven. In front of those gates, you have packed up all your old junk. You can't get past the boxes of rubbish to get to the gates. It is our fear blocking our access to One-ness and bliss. We have to do some serious cleaning to get there, to become whole/holy.

Reasoning Conscious Mind

This is the 10% of the brain (at most, I would argue it is even less in most of us) that expresses our personality into the world. Our Conscious Mind is what most people associate with who they are because that is where most people live day to day. It's by no means where all the action takes place.

Our conscious mind is a bit like the captain of a ship standing on the bridge giving out orders. In reality, it's the crew in the engine room below deck (the subconscious) that carry out the orders. The captain may be in charge of the ship and give the orders, but it's the crew that guides the ship, according to the quality of their training.

We can think of the Reasoning Conscious Mind as the egoic mind. From a spiritual perspective, ego means considering oneself to be distinct from others and God due to identification with the physical body and impressions in various centres of the subtle body. In short, ego is leading our life as per the thinking that our existence is limited to our five senses, mind, and intellect and identifying with them to various degrees.

As per the science of Spirituality, our true state of existence is identification with the Soul or God-principle within us and living our day to day life with this consciousness. As the one and same God-principle exists within all, there is unity in all Creation from a spiritual perspective.

However, depending on the level of our ego, we identify with the God-principle within to varying degrees. If our ego is high, we identify less with the Soul or the God-principle within us.

PART TWO

STEP ONE CONT. OPENING & ASOC

The physiological dimension: importance of accessing the theta brainwave state

> "THINK OF THE ANALYTICAL MIND AS A SEPARATE PART OF THE CONSCIOUS MIND THAT DIVIDES IT FROM THE SUBCONSCIOUS MIND. SINCE THE PLACEBO WORKS ONLY WHEN THE ANALYTICAL MIND IS SILENCED SO THAT YOUR AWARENESS CAN INSTEAD INTERACT WITH THE SUBCONSCIOUS MIND – THE DOMAIN WHERE TRUE CHANGE OCCURS – THE PLACEBO IS POSSIBLE ONLY WHEN YOU CAN MOVE BEYOND YOURSELF AND SO ECLIPSE YOUR CONSCIOUS MIND WITH YOUR AUTONOMIC NERVOUS SYSTEM."
>
> *Dr Joe Dispenza*

We cannot access the Subconscious Mind from the incoherent beta brainwave state. Ideally, we need to draw ourselves and our client into the theta brainwave state. This is the state of consciousness that allows us to access and reprogram the Subconscious Mind. All change in our client's perception must happen at the level of the subconscious. We need to slow down our neocortex and that of our client's (the analytical brain) to bypass the thinking brain.

When we enter the quantum by stepping outside of the dimensions of time and space and paradoxically wholly occupying the present moment, we become pure consciousness. When we "change our brainwave state from beta to alpha to theta, the autonomic nervous system – which knows how to heal your body much better than your conscious mind does – steps in and finally has a chance to clean house".[19]

---

[19] *Dispenza, Becoming Supernatural pp68.*

PART TWO

PRAXIS

Trainer

When your client arrives or the online session begins ensure:

- Phone is off or out of the room
- Disclaimer has been read and signed
- They will not be disturbed
- No children are present in the room
- They have water
- Ask where your client is located

Then, prepare them by explaining the process.

Process

We are now going on an intentional descent to the underworld of your subconscious to clear a specific dominant fear and in so doing return you to your true state, which is wholeness. In this state your innate intuition is optimised and we accelerate the awakening of your consciousness.

There are reasons that have brought you to this session, yet I do not need to know them. My role is to go beyond the known of your fears to the root of the issues, and to rewire your subconscious at this deepest level. Meeting and releasing subconscious fear is the only way to return to wholeness. You are very safe to meet and release your fear in this space with me.

On the journey we are about to take we are reprogramming your subtle anatomy and your neural pathways so that you can make the permanent shift from fear to love. You will have your eyes closed for the majority of the session. I will guide you into an altered consciousness so that you are in the brainwave state that allows the deepest possible reprogramming.

Let's begin. Close your eyes. Take a deep breath in through the nose and let it go out through the mouth. Let's set our intention for the session:

We offer all the karmic fruits of our time together to the highest aspect of you, to the divine, sublime and eternal within you. We give the intention now to access your subtle anatomy and subconscious in accordance with your highest good. The fear that is blocking access to your wholeness melts away with ease and grace. And so it is. And it is so.

Take another deep breath in through the nose releasing out through the mouth with a sigh, letting go of all the effort required to bring you to this point in your day.

Let your breathing return to its own natural rhythm. Allow your body to sink even more deeply into the chair.

Let yourself be fully here in this ever present now. Just for these next few minutes everything you need resides inside this space. It is safe to be here. The world outside is packed away, just for these next few minutes.

(cont'd next page)

PART TWO

PRAXIS CONT.

Process (cont'd)

Take your attention to the centre of your chest. Feel, think, sense or imagine a spark of light at the centre of your chest.

With every breath in and out that spark of light begins to expand effortlessly outwards, until it fills your entire physical body from the top of your head to the tips of your toes, no effort required.

Your entire physical body illuminated by your light, your consciousness. And the light moves outwards further still, easily, gracefully, through all the layers of your energy body. Your entire energetic body shining in your light.

And still the light expands outwards, easily, elegantly, until it fills the entire space in which you sit. Expansive, open, this is your true nature.

The whole room now, and everything in it, bathed in your light. And the light continues to expand easily and gracefully with every breath in and out until it bathes the entire city, [town or region]. Your light bathes the entirety of _____.

With each breath the light grows, no effort required, until your light covers the entire state [or county] and then the whole country. Effortlessly, your light bathes the entire country.

Open. Expansive, the light of your consciousness moving ever outwards, across oceans and continents, no effort. Until, in the next breath your light expands to encircle the globe.

The light of your consciousness surrounding the entire planet. Take a deep breath in through the nose. Let it go out through the mouth. As we journey to meet and clear subconscious fear, know that you are very safe. I am here to guide you every step of the way.

PART TWO

STEP TWO
FEAR PROFILING &
SHADOW ARCHETYPE

PHILOSOPHY

> FEAR AS A PRODUCTIVE ILLUSION IS A METAPHYSICAL, TRANSPERSONAL AND MULTIDIMENSIONAL CONCEPT, AS IS OUR WORK AS INTUITIVE INTELLIGENCE TRAINERS. WE ARE SURRENDERING OUR HUMAN EXPERIENCE, AND IN DOING SO, WE START SEEING THINGS DIFFERENTLY, AND AS SUCH, WE CAN FACILITATE THAT FOR OUR CLIENTS. WE ARE CHANGING OUR PERCEPTION OF THINGS THAT HAVE HAPPENED TO US.
>
> AS AN INTUITIVE INTELLIGENCE TRAINER, WE ARE DOING THIS WITH AND FOR OUR CLIENTS. WE ARE INTENTIONALLY JOURNEYING TO THE DEEPEST PART OF WHO THEY ARE, THEIR SUBCONSCIOUS, TO IDENTIFY AND RELEASE THE DOMINANT FEAR PROGRAM THAT WE ARE BEST ABLE TO RELEASE WITH THEM.

Until fear clears from the subconscious, our client cannot trust their intuition, deeply heal, or find their way to an abundant and powerful life. We can support our clients to become unafraid of their fear.

We can think of the Hindu God, Ganesha. He is prayed to as the remover of obstacles. However, what few realise is that Ganesha, the elephant-headed god, is also the one who places the obstacles in the way! In another powerful parallel with our work, Ganesha's holy vehicle, which transports him through the celestial realms, is a mouse. What we know to be true about elephants is that they are terrified of mice! The only way for Ganesha to travel is to ride his fear. And so it goes with us. Meeting our fear is the only way to evolve!

Meeting our subconscious fear is ultimately a willingness to get over our littleness and see ourselves and the world with spiritual sight. It is a return to our wholeness/holiness. A Course in Miracles tells us that there is nothing to fear. It is not possible to even understand this when we are looking at the world with human sight. We cannot solve our life situation, our issues or meet our fears at the level they were created. It is simply not possible. It is our task to support our client to expand their perception of themselves and their life situation.

PART TWO

STEP TWO CONT.
FEAR PROFILING & SHADOW ARCHETYPE

Compassion

Compassion is spiritual perception. When we perceive with compassion, we see as God sees. There is nothing to heal in your client when you are witnessing them through this lens. It does not mean that there is no work to do, but we see fear as an illusion. It is not absolute; it is not insurmountable. We invite our client to change their mind about themselves through the journey we facilitate.

Compassion is a fearless state. You can only witness your client with this gaze if you are committed to your awakening journey. Otherwise, you will be 'triggered' (activated) by your unmet fear that you see in them. We must not enter into the belief that what we are witnessing is a problem. Fear is the problem, but it is also the solution.

Fear as the thread of the Method session

As we learn how to facilitate the Method, it is vital to understand that the dominant fear you identify in the subconscious is the thread you follow throughout the entire session.

Every phase of the session is designed to illuminate how the fear has been blocking the flow of life force to and from the client and causing the symptoms of their dis-ease. The journey is, as we have learnt, an intentional descent into the fear, fearlessly. We must not lose sight of this, or else we lose the thread of the session.

Client/Trainer Alchemy

Why does a specific fear present itself to you to be released in your work with the client? Is it the only dominant fear the client possesses? The answer to that is straightforward. No. The client has more than one dominant fear. This particular fear makes itself known to you because you are best equipped in every way to meet and release that fear on behalf of the client. Most often, this is because it is a match for what we also need to release. In truth, there is only one of us here, and the most powerful starting point for our work is to recall this truth. 'When I serve, I am serving myself'. It cannot be any other way. 'My service is my medicine'.

The alchemy between the client (as me) and myself, unlocks the subconscious and allows us to work together to meet and release the perfect subconscious fear for us both.

PART TWO

PRAXIS

Trainer

I will now attune to your dominant negative self-belief stored in your subconscious. The fear has layers. I will speak the layers out loud until we reach the deepest level.

> *You will hear/see/know/feel the dominant fear as a sentence stated in the first person.*
>
> *For example...*
>
> - 'I am not good enough'
> - 'I am not worthy'
> - 'I am unlovable'
> - 'I am not enough'
> - 'I deserve bad things to happen to me'
>
> *Here you will notice that the fear has 'layers'. Speak these out loud to the client. As you speak the first fear, another fear reveals itself behind it. It is the fear informing the fear. It may not happen like this but if it does feel confident to reveal it to your client.*
>
> *For example...*
>
> 'I am not worthy. Behind that is I do not deserve love. And underneath that is, I have been forsaken by God'.
>
> Conclude the layers of fear with the statement of the primary fear.

Your dominant negative self-belief is...

PART TWO

STEP TWO CONT.
SHADOW ARCHETYPE

PHILOSOPHY
Sacred 13 Shadow Archetype Overview

> "THE SHADOW IS A MORAL PROBLEM THAT CHALLENGES THE WHOLE EGO-PERSONALITY. FOR NO ONE CAN BECOME CONSCIOUS OF THE SHADOW WITHOUT CONSIDERABLE MORAL EFFORT. TO BECOME CONSCIOUS OF IT INVOLVES RECOGNIZING THE DARK ASPECTS OF THE PERSONALITY AS PRESENT AND REAL. THIS ACT IS THE ESSENTIAL CONDITION FOR ANY KIND OF SELF-KNOWLEDGE."
>
> *Carl Jung, Aion (1951)*

The "shadow" is a concept first coined by Swiss psychiatrist Carl Jung that describes those aspects of the personality that we unconsciously choose to reject and repress. It is this collection of repressed aspects of our identity that Jung referred to as our shadow self. In this section we are considering the central Sacred 13 archetypes we work with in their shadow aspect, as well as learning more about the Shadow generally. In Step Six we consider the Sacred 13 in their light aspect.

Jung states, "Unfortunately there can be no doubt that man is, on the whole, less good than he imagines himself or wants to be. Everyone carries a shadow, and the less it is embodied in the individual's conscious life, the blacker and denser it is. If an inferiority is conscious, one always has a chance to correct it. Furthermore, it is constantly in contact with other interests, so that it is continually subjected to modifications. But if it is repressed and isolated from consciousness, it never gets corrected."[20]

Shadow work, then, is the process of making the unconscious conscious. In doing so, we gain awareness of our unconscious impulses and can then choose whether and how to act on them. We begin this process when we take a step back from our normal patterns of behavior and observe what is happening within us. It is a vital phase of the Method and the work of the Intuitive Intelligence Trainer.

[20] *Carl Jung, Psychology and Religion (1938).*

PART TWO

STEP TWO CONT.
SHADOW ARCHETYPE

It is our task as Intuitive Intelligence Trainers to recognise the pattern or relationship between the dominant fear and the shadow archetype. We are seeing the impersonal or symbolic level of the fear/shadow relationship. This is something our client may not yet perceive as it is below the level of their Conscious Reasoning Mind. Caroline Myss shares the following:

"People who can recognize archetypal patterns, even to a slight degree, are at an advantage in relationships in that they are positioned to understand "what's really going on here." We often know that something unspoken is the real cause underlying ruptures in any relationships, from personal to friendships as well as relationships in the workplace. A person who is emotional and insecure will never be able to see what is actually unfolding around him or her because that individual is frozen in fear. Everything looks "personal" and frightening to someone who is terrified, angry and hurt. Examined through archetypal patterns, however, any and every situation instantly becomes "impersonal".[21]

Myss explains the importance of identifying the shadow in this way...

"When you bring your Shadow into the light, it no longer has power over you. The Shadow is that part of you that remains unknown, yet influences every part of your life. However, the Shadow isn't bad—it's just hidden. And since it's hidden, it runs around with no supervision, often wreaking havoc and causing suffering in your life.[22]"

On archetypes more generally, Myss states, "Archetypes are everywhere. We live and breathe in an archetypal universe. Every relationship we have is an archetypal connection, even with our children, beginning with the primal Mother-Child bond. Every event in society is a creation of our collective archetypal energies. Nothing, not war or peace, not disasters or global events, just "happen." We are participants in everything. We are co-creators of the events unfolding in this world, but the means through which we "co-create" is not our "will power." Co-creation occurs through our archetypal patterns and the deep-rooted stories and beliefs we cling to that are rooted in our archetypes.[23]" These beliefs are stored in our subconscious as we have learned. As we support our clients by identifying the dominant patterns in their subconscious through the fear and associated shadow archetype we are bringing them closer to their own Intuitive Intelligence by 'decluttering' or unknotting the subconscious programs.

Your client will be working from one of the following shadow archetypes as it relates to the dominant fear you have identified. In identifying the shadow archetype at play in ourselves, whenever we go into fear we can move the fear into the light very quickly, moving beyond the personal to the symbolic meaning of our fear. This is what we are helping our clients to do also.

Whilst we must be familiar with the following information, it is important to allow nonlocal intuition to illuminate the relationship between the dominant fear and the shadow. **This means allowing the interplay between the fear and how it 'acts' in the world of your client to reveal itself to you.**

---

[21] *https://www.myss.com/cmed/online-institute/series/archetypes-everywhere/*
[22 & 23] *ibid*

PART TWO

SACRED 13 ARCHETYPE CHART

ARCHETYPE	LIGHT	SHADOW
MAIDEN	INNOCENCE, OPEN HEARTED, INDEPENDENT, FULL OF WONDER, CURIOUS	SELFISH, CHILDISH, FAILURE TO MATURE, LACKING PERSONAL BOUNDARIES, DESTRUCTIVE
MOTHER	FIERCE LOVE, PROTECTOR, SUSTAINER, RESPONSIBLE, CREATOR, LIFE-GIVING	MARTYR, CONTROLLING, MANIPULATIVE, OVERBEARING, NO SENSE OF IDENTITY OUTSIDE OF RELATIONSHIPS, ABSENT
MAGA / ENCHANTRESS	WISE, FREE, SELF-ASSURED, SOVEREIGN, ENIGMATIC, UNFUCKWITHABLE	BITTER, ARID PURPOSELESS, DISAPPOINTED BY LIFE, CYNICAL, SELF-SABOTAGING, MID-LIFE CRISIS
CRONE	NON-ATTACHED, PATIENT, ALL KNOWING, DEEP INSIGHT, WISDOM KEEPER	DISENGAGED, ISOLATED, REJECTING OF SELF AND OTHERS
WILD WOMAN	SHE IS ALIVE WITH DESIRE, FULL OF CONFIDENCE AND MYSTERY, IRRESISTIBLE, REBEL, SELF-APPROVING	NEEDS CONSTANT VALIDATION FROM OTHERS, ATTENTION SEEKING, FRAGILE EGO, NARCISSISTIC, SHUT DOWN
WARRIOR	INDEPENDENT, OBJECTIVE, ACTION TAKER, RAW FEMININE POWER, SELFLESS, DISCIPLINED	FULL OF RAGE, FORCEFUL, UNCOMPROMISING, PUSHES HERSELF TOO HARD, SACRIFICES HERSELF TO HER CAUSE, OUT OF BALANCE, CRUEL
TEACHER	PROFOUND COMMUNICATION, HUMBLE, HIGHEST PURPOSE IS THE TRANSFER OF KNOWLEDGE, INSPIRER	UNFORGIVING, DISCIPLINARIAN, AUTHORITARIAN, NEVER LETTING HER STUDENTS MATURE, NOT SHOWING UP TO THE SACRED RESPONSIBILITY TO TEACH, NOT BEING THE DEMONSTRATION

PART TWO

SACRED 13 ARCHETYPE CHART

ARCHETYPE	LIGHT	SHADOW
STUDENT	EXPLORER, SEEKER, FREE SPIRIT, SELF-CONTAINED	DOUBTS HERSELF, AVOIDS TAKING ACTION BY NEVER FEELING 'READY', GIVES HER POWER TO AUTHORITY FIGURES, HIDES FROM THE WORLD IN CONSTANT STUDY WITHOUT BEING THE DEMONSTRATION
WIFE	DIPLOMAT, NEGOTIATOR, BALANCED, CO-CREATOR, THRIVES IN CONNECTION, SELF-AWARE	MANIPULATIVE, AFRAID TO BE ALONE, CODEPENDENT, SHUTS DOWN COMMUNICATION, IMMATURE
ALCHEMIST / HEALER	INTUITIVE, LIMINAL, INSIGHTFUL, TRANSFORMATIVE, MOTIVATED BY THE DESIRE TO SERVE	CODEPENDENT WITH THOSE SHE SERVES, USING HER 'MAGIC' FOR EGO GAINS OR CONVINCING OTHERS TO DO THE SAME
PRIESTESS	SELF-POSSESSED, CAN BRING THE SACRED INTO THE MUNDANE, TRANSPERSONAL, NOT DRIVEN BY EGOIC NEEDS, AUTONOMOUS, DEVOUT, MOTIVATED BY A HOLY PURPOSE	SEVERELY SELF-CRITICAL, OVERWHELMED WITH BURDEN OF 'PURPOSE', IMPOSSIBLE STANDARDS FOR OTHERS, WORKAHOLIC
QUEEN	MAGNETIC, EXPANSIVE, COURAGEOUS, JUST, RESPONSIBLE, COMMITTED TO THE GREATER GOOD, STRONG LEADER	DESTRUCTIVE, DESPOTIC, POWER OBSESSED, VAIN, COLD, TOUGH, LAZY
GODDESS	COMPASSIONATE, BOUNDLESS, INSPIRING, BALANCED, GENEROUS	WITHDRAWN FROM THE WORLD, BYPASSING OF HUMANITY, UNGROUNDED

PART TWO

PRAXIS

Trainer

You will notice one of the Sacred 13 shadow archetypes associated with the dominant fear.

The Shadow Archetype associated with the fear is...

- Maiden / Innocent
- Mother / Father
- Enchantress / Maga (no male archetype)
- Crone / Wizard
- Wild Woman / Seductress / Lover
- Alchemist Healer
- Warrior
- Teacher
- Student
- Wife / Husband
- Priestess / Priest
- Queen / King
- Goddess / God

Trainer: Next, you will communicate with your client HOW the fear and the shadow interact. The information you share here is coming from your non-local intuition. You will notice the way in which the fear is playing out through the shadow archetype. Take your time. There may be a lot or a little to share here.

In this context, the shadow archetype represents...

This archetype has a light form of _____ and in the process of our work together we restore the shadow to the light.

The fear is ready to go now. Every step of this session moves it further and further out through all the layers of consciousness until it is entirely gone.

PART TWO

STEP TWO CONT. INTEGRATIVE BREATH

(See Embodiment for philosophy)

> *Trainer – The following breath will be repeated several more times throughout the session, each time with an additional breath added. Your task is to observe your client through your intuition and determine how long to invite them to hold the breath for. You must watch your client energetically and physically and direct their breathing for maximum integration.*

We support the release of the fear from the subtle anatomy with integrative breath and tapping. Follow my instructions carefully. Begin by tapping on the side of one hand with two fingers of the other hand. Breathe in through the nose filling the belly as much as possible. Hold. Release through the mouth with an audible sigh. Let your breath return to its own natural rhythm. Return your hands to your lap.

PART TWO

FOLLOW UP TEMPLATE

Fear Profiling & Shadow Archetype

Use this phase of the Method when any new issue or life situation is raised by a client in a session. This process is used to allow the client to have direct contact with Shadow.

We explain to the client that:

- We are never afraid for the reason we think we are. We need to go beneath the known of our fears to recognise what is really going on for us, and
- That fear is a friendly ally, part of our Intuitive Intelligence letting us know when we have strayed away from our true nature.

Praxis

- Ask the client to close down their eyes
- Invite the client to hold in their mind the life situation that they have brought into this session. They don't share anything verbally with you. Just invite them to focus on it
- Lead the process as described in the Method up to but NOT including the integrative breath. **Instead of saying 'Your dominant negative self-belief' instead say, 'The dominant negative self-belief in this life situation is…'**
- Use your own words for this. The idea is that they are crossing a threshold into the sacred wisdom of their cosmic heart
- Lead them into this sacred space and invite them to find a space to be seated that feels welcoming and inviting
- Invite them to notice that approaching them now is the archetype of _____ (you can identify this archetype for the client or you can invite them to notice who is here. To do the latter, you can slowly read the list of archetypes and ask them to pay attention to which one their intuition is leading them to. If the client is familiar with the archetypes, they may not need this list to be read. Use your clinical reasoning. Alternatively, you can display the Sacred 13 cards and ask the client to notice visually which archetype is calling to them. This is most useful if you are in person).
- Invite them to notice how they are presenting themselves – age, feeling, what they are wearing etc (N.B. Whilst the archetype presented to you in their shadow form, they may be in their light or shadow OR both when they present to the client. As we have placed our conscious attention upon the shadow, it will most likely share with the client in the light form)
- The archetype sits down with them now
- Invite your client to ask the following questions of the archetype in her shadow form and to share the answers with you out loud (include any other non-leading questions that you are guided to ask):
    ◊ When did you first appear in my life?
    ◊ In which of my personal relationships are you most evident?
    ◊ Where are you located in my body?
    ◊ What emotional state do you most identify with?
    ◊ What do you want me to know right now?
- When you feel this process is complete, invite the client to return to the room with you, leading them out of the Cathedral of the heart, and invite them to share anything about that experience with you.

PART TWO

STEP THREE
CHAKRA COMMUNION

PHILOSOPHY
Communing with the subtle anatomy:
Chakra Communion[24]

Our subtle body is built by our consciousness. *Our consciousness is the collection of beliefs that we hold. Our physical body is a projection of that consciousness, and the Chakra system is the organising system of the subtle body.*

The subtle body, physical body and soul are interconnected through the portals of the Chakras. These are specific channels of energy exchange, which allows the flow of energetic information to move from one system (physical, subtle or soul) to another.

Richard Gerber describes the Chakras as specialised energy centres which connect us to the multidimensional Universe. He goes on to state, "The chakras are dimensional portals within the subtle body which take in and process energy of a higher vibrational nature so that it may be properly assimilated and used to transform the physical body"[25].

[24] *The information regarding the chakra system and subtle anatomy is drawn from Richard Gerber, Caroline Myss and Dr Joe Dispenza.*
[25] *Vibrational Medicine, pp370.*

PART TWO

STEP THREE CONT.
CHAKRA COMMUNION

How to Commune with the Chakras

Our work as the Intuitive Intelligence Trainer is to look for the fear that is knotted into the client's subtle anatomy and suppressing his or her power. In the Chakra phase, we are seeking this information as it expresses through the energy centres, known in Sanskrit as Chakras. The problem (and the answer) is always the faulty fear belief. When we clear that belief, all the systems, including the physical body, can return to optimal functioning. Communicating with the Chakras helps us do this.

What impact is my client's dominant fear having on the Chakra or Chakras? How can I communicate that in a way that illuminates how the dominant fear is interrupting the flow of life force to them?

We are going to look at the chakras from two levels for our client:

- *Soul* (Superconscious)
- *Subtle body* (Subconscious)

Each level has information for the client regarding how the fear is blocking the flow of energy. People will be out of their power if they are invested in the past or projecting into the future, carrying unmet subconscious fear and lying to themselves. We are asking where my client has broken the law?

The three immutable laws give us a shorthand to notice how our client is out of balance with their power in any or all of the chakras. The following prompts are not exhaustive by any means, but give us a guide as to how the fear can impact the flow of energy to and from the client.

All is One. All is of the Mind – where is my client living in a separation mentality, or forgotten their own creative power?

As above, so below. As within, so without – where is my client behaving as a victim to her reality, or in judgement of others?

Everything is but a vibration – where has fear concretised my client, or frozen them, or caused them to live in a chaotic frequency?

There will be at least three chakras that communicate, and it is likely that the first chakra identified will be in the lower three chakras because these are the survival chakras, most often where we store our fear stories.

Focus primarily on the subtle body and symbolic meaning of any symptom we 'see' in the chakras. It is the subtle body that contains the information that will allow the client to return to love, not in treating the symptoms of the fear. We are working first and foremost with the energy body, also known as the subtle anatomy.

Think of the Chakras as archetypes. Be present with the information you are receiving non-locally for each chakra with which you connect. We must understand the theory of the chakra system, which we will explore now, but beyond that, we must trust the non-local information we are receiving from each chakra.

---

[24] *The information regarding the chakra system and subtle anatomy is drawn from Richard Gerber, Caroline Myss and Dr Joe Dispenza.*
[25] *Vibrational Medicine, pp370.*

PART TWO

Soul *(Superconscious)* Level

*The **Soul Level** will guide you very quickly to the deepest level of meaning of the dominant fear for your client.*

Base — All is One
Sacral — Honour One Another
Solar plexus — Honour Oneself
Heart — Love is The Divine Power
Throat — Surrender Personal Will to Divine Will
Third eye — Seek Only the Truth
Crown — Live in the Present Moment[26].

Subtle Body *(Subconscious)* Level

CHAKRA	LIGHT	SHADOW
BASE	HUMILITY, COMMUNITY, PURPOSE, CHANGE	HUMILIATION, BONDAGE, SURVIVAL, CHAOS
SACRAL	RIGHT ACTION, CREATIVE, CHOICE, FLOWING	RIGHTEOUSNESS, CONTROL, VENGEANCE, UNYIELDING
SOLAR PLEXUS	SELF-ESTEEM, SURRENDER, SPIRITUAL ADULTHOOD	LOW/NO SELF-WORTH, RESISTANCE, IMMATURE,
HEART	WHOLENESS, ACCEPTANCE, FORGIVENESS, COMPASSION, ONENESS	ABANDONMENT, JEALOUS, UNFORGIVENESS, SYMPATHY, BITTERNESS
THROAT	THY WILL BE DONE, DISSOLVING INTO HOLINESS, FAITH, CHOOSING FROM LOVE	MY WILL, OVERIDENTIFICATION WITH FORM, FAITHLESSNESS, CHOOSING FROM FEAR
THIRD EYE	SPIRITUAL STAMINA, LIGHT, SYMBOLIC SIGHT	SPIRITUAL WEAKNESS, DARK, HUMAN SIGHT
CROWN	DIVINE MARRIAGE STATE OF GRACE, INTIMACY WITH GOD	LOSS OF IDENTITY, FEAR OF THE DARK NIGHT, SPIRITUAL CRISIS

---

[24] *The information regarding the chakra system and subtle anatomy is drawn from Richard Gerber, Caroline Myss and Dr Joe Dispenza.*
[25] *Vibrational Medicine, pp370.*

PART TWO

Physical Level
(endocrine system)

We are interested in the physical only as it relates to the impact on the subtle body. We focus only on the Endocrine system here. In Advanced Training we learn more about the relationship between the nervous system and the subtle body to serve our clients. In the following, Richard Gerber shares the relationship between the subtle body and the physical body:

"Subtle energies taken in by the chakras are converted to endocrine signals in a manner akin to a step-down transformer. As energy of a higher vibrational or subtle nature enters the chakras, it is stepped down and transmitted as information of a more physiological nature. Subtle energy is converted into hormonal signals from each of the major endocrine glands that are linked with the chakras"[27].

It is this level of understanding that we are interested in serving our clients – as the physical shows up through the subtle body.

Base chakra

Reproductive glands (testes in men; ovaries in women); controls sexual development and secretes sex hormones.

Sacral chakra

Adrenal glands; regulates the immune system and metabolism.

Solar Plexus chakra

Pancreas; regulates metabolism.

Heart chakra

Thymus gland; regulates the immune system.

Throat chakra

Thyroid gland; regulates body temperature and metabolism.

Third Eye chakra

Pituitary gland produces hormones and governs the function of the previous five glands; sometimes, the pineal gland is linked to the third eye chakra as well as to the crown chakra.

Crown chakra

Pineal gland; regulates biological cycles, including sleep.

---

[27] *Gerber, Vibrational Medicine p372.*

PART TWO

PRAXIS

*The dominant fear of_____
is located in the_____ Chakra.*

I am going to describe the shape, colour and the size of the chakra in the subtle anatomy where the fear is stored. I will then identify any ways in which the fear is sitting in your subtle anatomy causing real or potential issues for your physical body, emotional health and spiritual well-being.

> ### Trainer
>
> Describe exactly what you see/feel/hear/know about the chakra in terms of its appearance and feel.
>
> Then, check in at the 3 levels of physical, emotional and spiritual/soul level of the chakra as it relates to the dominant fear. Share this with your client as you receive it.

Now, I am going to take a moment to detect if any other chakras have information to communicate in regards to this subconscious fear.

> **Trainer cont'd:** Take as long as you need to identify if there are any other chakras wanting to communicate in regards to this fear. Usually there are 3 chakras or more. Share whatever else is there in as many chakras as are open to communicate.
>
> When this process is done, direct the client to breathe into the primary chakra in which you identified the fear.

We support the release of the fear from the subtle anatomy with integrative breath and gentle tapping. Follow my instructions carefully. Begin by tapping on the side of the hand with two fingers of the other hand. Keep tapping as we breathe together. Place your attention on the _____ chakra. As you breathe in through the nose filling the belly as much as possible, imagine you are breathing into the _____ chakra. Hold. Release through the mouth with an audible sigh. Again, breathe in through the nose filling the belly as much as possible, visualizing that breath travelling into the chakra. Hold. Release through the mouth with an audible sigh. Let your breath return to its own natural rhythm. Return your hands to your lap.

PART TWO

FOLLOW UP TEMPLATE

Communicating with the power centres theory

Your client doesn't need to know anything about chakras in order to be able to have an experience of direct communication with these energy centres. We are simply inviting the client to notice where it feels stuck in their body when they think about the fear or life situation you are working with together.

With this client-led practice we want them to become confident in attuning to the subtle body to notice when they have stepped out of their personal power. We are supporting the client to connect to the power centre associated with where they identify a feeling of stuckness etc.

Praxis

- Lead the client into Heart Congruence. The client keeps their eyes closed to stay out of the reasoning conscious mind
- Invite them to hold the life situation or dominant fear in their consciousness
- Ask the client to notice where in their body they can feel, see or know the fear as they tune into their life event or fearful situation
- Once they have identified their area in the body let them know the power centre associated with this area of their body.
- Ask them to describe the feeling, seeing or knowing – colours, sensations, feelings, images etc.
- Invite the client to imagine that they are walking around in this power centre. Lead them to a place in this centre where they feel to take a seat. Once settled, invite the client to ask these questions:
    ◊ What impact is the dominant fear having on this power centre? How is the dominant fear or life situation interrupting the flow of life force to me?
- Encourage the client to feel, hear, see or know the intuitive response and to share it with you out loud in whatever way it comes. Give the client time to explore what is happening for them here. Support them to make connections to the life event.
- When you feel the client is ready lead them back into the present moment
- Invite them to share anything about the experience with you
- At this point you can lead them into a deeper understanding of the chakra they connected with and the ways in which it can help them better understand their life event
- You can use the long form of the Gayatri mantra or Pranayama focussed on the specific chakra to support the return to balance for this power centre.

PART TWO

STEP THREE CONT. *KOSHAS COMMUNION*

Communicating with the Koshas (kośas) theory

According to the Taittirīya Upaniṣad, there are five layers, sheaths, or kośas, to our seemingly individual existence. Like the eight limbs of Rāja Yoga, they range from the densest part of our being (the body) to the most vast and subtle (inner joy/peace). Although presented in a linear fashion here, these layers are interconnected, and each subtle layer comprises and encompasses the layers denser than it. In becoming aware of, and examining these aspects of our being through the 8 limbs of Rāja Yoga, we can help bring our lives into balance and integration on all these levels and eventually transcend them through a deep knowing of them and rest in the Self—the loving aware presence which allows it all to be possible.

1. *Annamaya-kosha (food sheath, Earth element)*

Annamaya-kośa consists of your physical-material body, the grossest, densest part of our existence, and it is comprised of, and fuelled by, the food we eat. Annamaya-kośa is usually the sheath with which we identify the most because it is through this instrument that we sense and feel and move – it is our field of activity (kṣetra). Āsana (and prāṇāyāma) as well as a healthy diet help to keep this physical layer in optimal condition so that we can experience life through our bodies with ease, free from dis-ease.

2. *Pranamaya-kosha (vital sheath, Water element)*

This surrounds and penetrates the physical body as the vital energy that flows in and around the body. One familiar aspect of Pranāmaya-kośa is known as the aura and the life force which flows through the intricate system of nāḍis or meridians, of which there are approximately 72,000 in and around a human body. Praṇāmaya-kośa is influenced and fuelled by the prāṇa absorbed through the breath, through food, and from the cosmic Universal life-force that surrounds and permeates us. The practice of prāṇāyāma helps to keep this energy flowing freely, which also affects the health of the physical body.

INTUITIVE INTELLIGENCE TRAINER MANUAL | 112

PART TWO

3. Manomaya-kosha (mental sheath, Fire element)

Even more subtle than the first two koshas, Manomaya-kośa consists of the thinking mind and emotions and permeates the vital and food sheaths. The thoughts and emotions we experience affect the energy flow in and around us, which in turn affects our energetic and physical health. So, by becoming aware of our thoughts, judgements, and emotions as they arise and dissolve through sense-withdrawal (pratyahara) and one-pointed concentration (dhāraṇā), giving space to all of our thoughts and emotions without pushing them away and by applying this also in prāṇāyāma and āsana practice (and also in life!), we can deeply enhance the overall state of our wellbeing.

4. Vijnanamaya-kosha (intellect/intuitive sheath, Air element)

Permeating the three denser layers (manomaya, pranāmaya, and annamaya) is the home of our inner knowing and wisdom. It is this aspect of our being which knows Life intimately at the deepest level and from which we receive messages from beyond what our minds could ever understand. Within this sheath, there is still the illusion of duality, where there is a knower, the knowing, and the known. However, through the process of āsana, prāṇāyāma, dhāraṇā, and then through meditation (dhyāna), the mind becomes still and we can truly listen to the silent messages that Life speaks to us through all that exists.

It is by resting in this true nature, free from the influence of thought, emotion, and experience, that we can listen with an inner hearing that transcends what we do with our ears and hear Life's message to us, allowing this message to align itself into our thoughts (manomaya-kośa), our energy field (pranāmaya-kośa), into our field of activity, the body (annamaya-kośa), and thus into our actions and experiences. This develops into our svadharma, our deepest purpose or calling in Life.

5. Anandamaya-kossa (bliss sheath, ether/space element)

Beyond the other 4 kośas, and yet permeating and comprising them all, is the sheath of bliss. This is the aspect of our being that we recognise as a deep inner peace and joy, free from our thoughts, emotions, energy and body, and yet at the same time embracing them all. It is the sweetness of All Life that we feel when the mind is still, also known as sat-cit-ānanda—absolute truth-wisdom-bliss. It can be known as a super-conscious state of samādhi, the 8th limb of Raja Yoga, but even in this layer, there remains the duality between a knower of the sweetness and the sweetness itself.

In the study of Vedānta (Upaniṣads), they are also referred to as veils which are created for us to examine, to know and to transcend in order to lead the way back to our true nature—the Self.

The kośas are intimately related to our states of awareness (waking, dream and sleep) and our three bodies (gross, subtle and causal). As we get to know and understand each kośa from the densest to the most subtle, and how each works within our own existence, we can open each Gateway and experience the path we are treading as the road to knowing and being Oneness.

https://www.ekhartyoga.com/articles/practice/yoga-and-the-koshas-the-layers-of-being

PART TWO

The koshas are the layers of illusion concealing Atman.

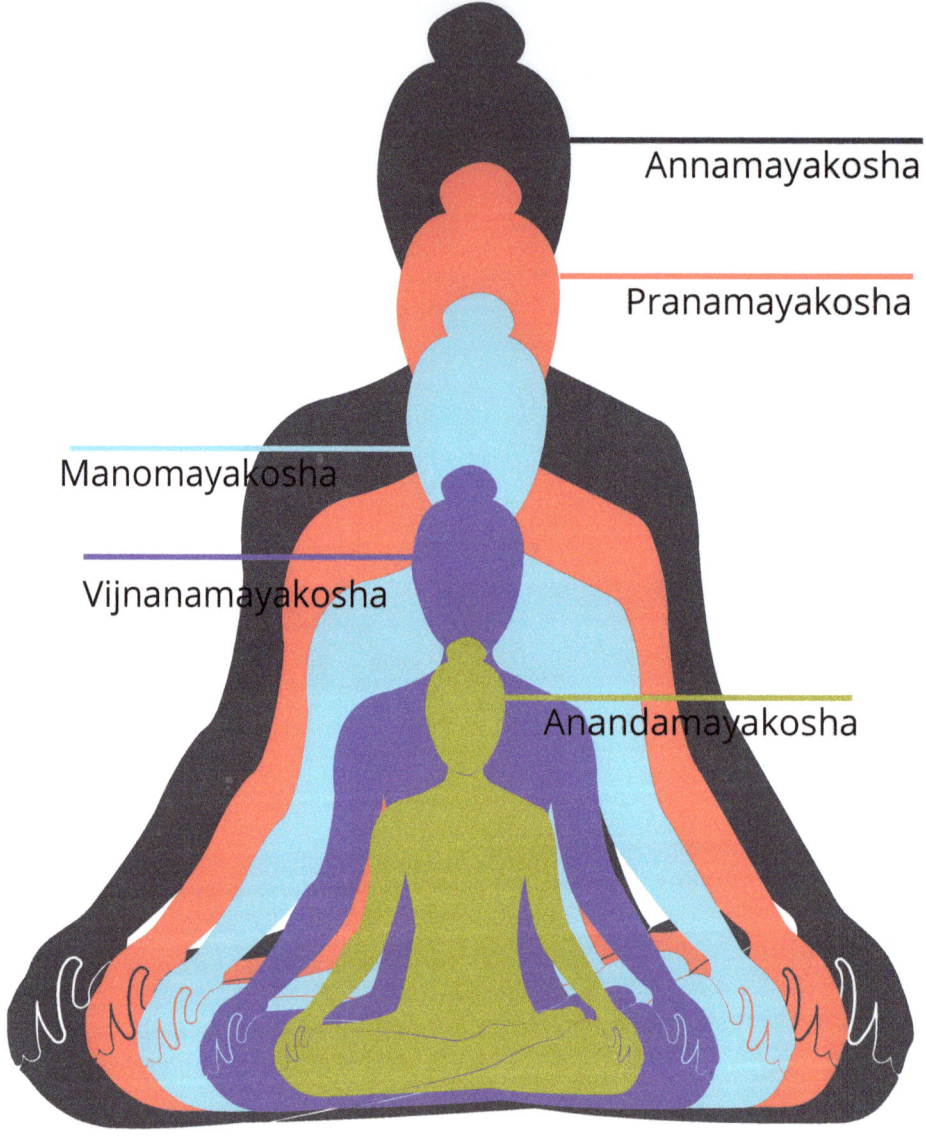

Practitioner led Process

How is fear impacting each layer?

Client led Process

Lead the client into an exploration of each kosha or identify which kosha needs attention and have a dialogue with that sheath.

Additional suggestions to work with each kosha

- Movement and what we imbibe
- Breath
- Prayer/chanting
- Meditation
- Explore the related element

PART TWO

STEP FOUR
INSTIGATING EVENT

PHILOSOPHY
The holographic nature of the cosmos
OR the end of time & space

> *"Man appears as a being whose primary level of existence is at non-space, non-time levels of the Universe, and who has placed himself in a space-time vehicle of consciousness for the purpose of growing in awareness of the True Self and generating coherence in the True Self. Our perception mechanisms at the space-time vehicle level lock us into a narrowly restricted view of reality and the Self. Disharmony created by the ego at the deeper level of self, materialises as error or disease in the space-time vehicle as an indicator that error has been created at a primary level… It teaches us that the space-time vehicle is not Life but only a simulator of Life whose only role is as a teaching tool. With our thoughts and attitudes, we continuously reprogram the simulator from the Mind level of the multidimensional universe and continuously generate our individual and collective futures by such behaviour."* [28]

The Einsteinian paradigm observes that human beings are networks of complex energy fields that interface with physical/cellular systems. Einstein proved that energy and matter are dual expressions of the same universal substance. That universal substance is a primal energy or vibration of which we are all composed. We direct this primal energy through consciousness. Gerber states that 'consciousness itself is a kind of energy that is integrally related to the cellular expression of the physical body[29]".

Joe Dispenza talks about this in terms of light and information or energy and consciousness. "Everything in our known Universe is made up or emits either light and information or energy and consciousness – which are other ways of describing electromagnetic energy… there's a sea of infinite invisible frequencies that are carrying encoded information… All frequency carries information".

This explains why we can access information about our client nonlocally and outside of time and space. And the holograph explains this even more so. What we know from understanding the science of the holographic image is every piece contains the whole. Gerber explains, "That is, one could take a hologram of an apple, cut the film into fifty pieces, and each piece, when viewed through laser light, would reveal its own miniature apple". Gerber relates the holographic principle in nature to the hermetic law of as above, so below – the law of correspondence.

---

[28] *Dr Tiller, Vibrational Medicine, p161-162.*
[29] *Richard Gerber, Vibrational Medicine, 2001.*
[30] *Dr Joe Dispenza, Becoming Supernatural, 2017.*
[31] *Richard Gerber, Vibrational Medicine, 2001.*

PART TWO

STEP FOUR CONT. INSTIGATING EVENT

Science has also demonstrated that when the image of a tiny seedling was taken using electrography, the surrounding electrical field of the seedling was the shape of the adult plant. When a leaf is photographed with the top removed, the full image of the leaf appears in the electrophotographic image. When a circular hole is cut into a leaf and then photographed, the image revealed was that of a tiny intact leaf with a similar hole in it.

Our biology is optimised at the level of the energy field to become the fullest expression of what it is. And no matter what occurs at the physical level, all we are remains whole at the energy level. What would it take for the energy field to return the material to its total health and expression?

We are optimised to become the full expression of our Soul or God nature. Anything less than that is an impediment only at the subtle anatomy level and, therefore, the physical anatomy. A correction in our perception is what makes this change possible.

As Joe Dispenza explains, what all this means for us as intuitive Intelligence Trainers is that we are simply learning to think beyond the level of form to access the information stored in the seemingly empty space around us. Dispenza states, "... you can train yourself to get a clear signal and receive information from [the field of light]. When you do this repeatedly, you tune in to a new level of light and information that you can use to influence or affect matter"[32].

> *Richard Gerber states it like this...*
>
> "EVERY PIECE OF THE UNIVERSE CONTAINS INFORMATION CONCERNING THE MAKEUP OF THE ENTIRE COSMOS. UNLIKE A STATIC HOLOGRAM, THE COSMIC HOLOGRAM IS A DYNAMICALLY MOVING SYSTEM THAT CHANGES FROM MICROSECOND TO MICROSECOND. BECAUSE WHAT HAPPENS IN JUST A SMALL FRAGMENT OF THE HOLOGRAPHIC ENERGY INTERFERENCE PATTERN AFFECTS THE ENTIRE STRUCTURE SIMULTANEOUSLY. THERE IS A TREMENDOUS INTERCONNECTIVITY RELATIONSHIP BETWEEN ALL PARTS OF THE HOLOGRAPHIC UNIVERSE. IF ONE WERE TO VIEW GOD AS "ALL THERE IS", THEN, THROUGH THE HOLOGRAPHIC INTERCONNECTIVITY OF SPACE, GOD COULD SIMULTANEOUSLY BE IN CONTACT WITH ALL CREATIONS"[33].

---

[32] Dr Joe Dispenza, *Becoming Supernatural*, 2017.
[33] *Vibrational Medicine* pp61.

PART TWO

STEP FOUR CONT. INSTIGATING EVENT

How we tap into the information, the God-consciousness enfolded into the structure of space, is to become coherent, to raise our vibration to a state in which our internal receiver is most finely tuned. Dispenza tells us that this is called a 'divergent focus'. We go from focusing on the particle to the wave (energy instead of matter, formless instead of form, nothing instead of something) to access the field of pure potential.

What this means for the Instigating event

- It is entirely possible to access the concurrent lifetimes of your client to identify where their dominant fear began because of the quantum nature of the Cosmos. All is One.
- There is a knot in the subtle body of the client that connects to the moment in the lifetime you identify on their behalf. In meeting this moment, because of the observer effect and the release of the faulty fear, we emancipate their energy trapped here.
- From the lifetime you identify, this moment could be past, parallel or future, so please be aware that it may not be a moment from 'history' as you have learned it at school. As we perceive it, there is no time and space, so we mustn't think in terms of 'past' life.
- The moment will be just that – a particular moment when the faulty fear belief entered into the client's consciousness. It is not an entire day, week, month or life.
- It must illuminate the dominant fear.
- We are most interested in identifying what the client started to believe at that moment and how it felt to them. The event itself might be quite innocuous and seemingly mundane, but the belief and associated feeling are what is essential to the disruption of life force to the client.
- Be brief, concise and unafraid of what you see. Think of the analogy of the flight attendant. If you are on a plane and it hits turbulence, and you feel fear. You look to the flight attendant's response to gauge how serious it is. If they are relaxed and getting on with the job, then you feel safe and comfortable. So it is with your client. If you describe the events, no matter how dramatic, as though we are in a soap opera, your client will go into fear.
- Remember, you are reinscribing the event by observing it from a higher level of consciousness. You are bringing a new vibration to the event and thereby altering its impact on the client. As all time and space are one, what you do in this lifetime, you do in all.

PART TWO

PRAXIS

We will now identify the instigating event, the lifetime in which the fear of _____ began. What I will describe is much like describing a scene from a movie. Some of you has been stuck in that time and space since the moment of the instigating event. We call it home now.

Let me describe what I see.

> ### Trainer
>
> Simply describe what you see. For example…
>
> 'The scene that I am seeing is when you were an initiate priestess. All the women are wearing an intense purple coloured robe. It is night. Outside. It is cold.'
>
> Describe everything you see and feel. Remember you and your client are not vulnerable to the events in this lifetime. You are simply calling the energy home through intentionally accessing the Akash. This is the most useful information to serve your client's fearlessness. Ensure you identify the FEELING state that the version of your client in this lifetime is experiencing – how do they feel as they form this fear-based belief?

This is where the fear of _____ began.

We support the release of the life event from the subtle anatomy with integrative breath. Follow my instructions carefully. Begin by tapping on the side of one hand with two fingers of the other hand. Keep tapping as we breathe together. Breathe in through the nose filling the belly as much as possible. Hold. Release through the mouth with an audible sigh. Hold. Breathe in through the nose filling the belly as much as possible. Hold. Release through the mouth with an audible sigh. Breathe in through the nose filling the belly as much as possible. Hold. Release through the mouth with an audible sigh. Let your breath return to its own natural rhythm. Return your hands to your lap.

PART TWO

FOLLOW UP TEMPLATE

Instigating Event Theory

There are unlimited opportunities to work with the instigating event in a follow up session. In my experience it can occur quite spontaneously during another process, wherein I will see the lifetime in which the presenting life issue began or was experienced.

I find this to be particularly true when I am working with tapping. In this case, I determine intuitively if it will add value to the session if I share what I am seeing/hearing/feeling/knowing with my client. Inviting the client to tap on the side of the palm as you share the event supports the release of the subconscious program, and prevents any conscious mental attachment to the event.

Praxis

- Use this practice when a client is struggling to gain perspective in regards to a particular life event. Perhaps the client is caught up in feelings of victimhood in a particular relationship, or jealousy in a professional matter, or an irrational fear for the well being of their child. Any situation in which they cannot gain perspective, and see the symbolic meaning.
- In this usage of the instigating event, we are inviting the client to see through the veils of time and space for themselves, guided by you. The intention is to show them that this fear they are carrying is part of their soul contract and that it is rising now to be cleared.
- Say something to the client such as, *"It is entirely possible to access the concurrent lifetime to identify where this fear began, because of the quantum nature of the Cosmos. All time and space is One"*.

- There is a knot in your subtle body that connects to the moment in the lifetime we will identify. In meeting this moment, we emancipate their energy that has been trapped here and bring you freedom from this fear in this moment.
- This moment from the lifetime you identify could be past, parallel or future so please be aware that it may not be a moment from 'history' as you have learnt it at school. There is no time and space, as we perceive it so it is vital we do not think in terms of 'past' life.
- The moment will be just that – a very specific moment when the faulty fear belief entered into your consciousness. It is not an entire day, week, month or life.

[Take the client into the Akash. Once in this state invite your client to connect into the life event you are working with.

Invite them to start tapping on the side of their hand. Let them know that they can continue this throughout the process or rest their hands at any time.]

PART TWO

FOLLOW UP TEMPLATE CONT.

- Notice in front of you projected on the wall of the akashic library is a scene playing as though from a movie. Describe to me what you see in as much detail as you can.

  [Give the client time to connect into the scene. If they are struggling or too caught up in trying to make sense of what they are seeing, prompt them with non-leading questions. Do you know where you are? Can you feel which person is you in this scene? How are you dressed? What time of day is it? What are you feeling here? This is a facilitated client-led experience. You must have your hands on the wheel of this practice and ensure you are aware of where the client is at in terms of their brainwave state. This can be frustrating for the client if they are trying to think their way into the experience. Keep attuned to where you feel the client is at in the experience and what you are perceiving in regards to the lifetime.. If you need to, take them out of the practice and reset with breath before entering back into the Akash (you do not need to go all the way back to the beginning of the visualisation. Just land them back at the altar).

- Stay focussed on what you feel as you watch the scene play out. This is more important than the details of the scene. Our intention is to connect to the fear non-personally. It is not specific to this lifetime. It is a soul contract that has played out over many lives. As we observe it now from this higher perspective we can release the knotted energy from your subtle body.

  [Ensure the client continues to share out loud and record anything they are communicating particularly in regards to the feelings they are experiencing].

- *When you feel the scene is complete, slowly begin to step down from the altar and make your way across the Akash floor. You notice another door and as you approach it opens effortlessly before you. As you make your way through it you find yourself in your room on this day listening to the sound of my voice. Bring some gentle movement back to your body, and when you are ready, blink open your eyes.*

  [Invite the client to share all of their experience here, including but not limited to the scene they saw playing out. Our role is to draw their attention to any ways in which this lifetime helps them understand why they are working with the current life situation and the emotions they are experiencing. As they talk through the experience and debrief, they may find parallels and insights for themselves. Don't steal their Aha moments. You may know more than they know about this situation but it is ok if it takes more time for them to understand it.]

PART TWO

STEP FIVE
AKASHIC LIBRARY

PHILOSOPHY

What are the Akashic Records?

The Akashic Records or "The Book of Life" can be equated to the Universe's supercomputer system. This system acts as the central storehouse of every individual who has ever lived upon the earth. More than just a reservoir of events, the Akashic Records contain every deed, word, feeling, thought, and intent that has ever occurred at any time in the history of the world. Much more than simply a memory storehouse, however, these Akashic Records are interactive in that they have a tremendous influence upon our everyday lives, our relationships, our feelings and belief systems, and the potential realities we draw toward us.

The Akashic Records contain the entire history of every soul since the dawn of Creation. These records connect each one of us. They include the stimulus for every archetypal symbol or mythic story, which has ever deeply touched patterns of human behaviour and experience. They have been the inspiration for dreams and invention. They draw us toward or repel us from one another.

Everything that happens in our consciousness draws from the Akash. They embody an ever-changing fluid array of possible futures that are called into potential as we humans interact and learn from the data that has already been accumulated.

How to access the Akash – the fourth dimension

Imagination is letting go of analytical and conceptual thinking. It is you, present and relaxed. The Universe wants to create something through you. You align with a mighty energy stream.

It is not fantasising, which is about escape from presence.

An anecdote about Albert Einstein can best illustrate the role of imagination in intuition.

Berlin, 1929. The poet and journalist George Sylvester Viereck has charmed an interview out of an initially reluctant superstar physicist. He asks: "How do you account for your discoveries? Through intuition or inspiration?" Albert Einstein replies:

"Both. I sometimes feel I am right, but do not know it. When two expeditions of scientists went to test my theory, I was convinced they would confirm my theory. I wasn't surprised when the results confirmed my intuition, but I would have been surprised had I been wrong. I'm enough of an artist to draw freely on my imagination, which I think is more important than knowledge. Knowledge is limited. Imagination encircles the world."[34]

The key to having confidence in your intuition is like all things outlined in this manual. It is about clearing our blocks to trust our co-creative partner, intuition, and, ergo, our imagination.

---

[34] https://neurotaylor.files.wordpress.com/2012/09/thes-for-web-ii.pdf

PART TWO

STEP FIVE CONT.
AKASHIC LIBRARY

Much is written about the intersection between scientific breakthrough and the capacities of the imagination, with good reason. The great scientists often speak of the moment of inspiration that took them from frustration at what they could not see to enlightenment about their subsequent discovery. It is with imagination and intuition. A properly prepared mind will be able to hear the imagination-fuelled language of intuition. Intuition is visual and symbolic. No wonder then that the imagination brings its insights.

When we understand and practice both the techniques of emptying our Subconscious Minds and the tools that enhance the muscle of intuition, then we can trust the imagination's offerings. Imagination is a portal. When we resist it, we impede the flow of our intuition.

We also begin to understand why we must not surrender to fantasy. We must strive to keep our imaginations pure, and we do that by staying present. Fantasy is always an attempt to escape the now. Your thoughts are the currency for your life. How do you want to spend them?

The First Hermetic law: The law of Mentalism states that all is of the Mind. Therefore all reality is an imaginative act first. This is why creativity is such a sacred and necessary aspect of human/spiritual experience.

We can also think of this in terms of dimensions. The fifth dimension is pure vibration or energy. The third dimension is matter or form.

How do we translate the vibration of the fifth dimension to the third dimension?

This happens through the fourth dimension. This dimension is ego/thinking/personality/emotion or, in other words, beliefs as they manifest as feeling. This is alchemy.

At the quantum level, we are not fixed to the third-dimensional laws of time and space, and as such, we can access all time and all space. This is how we can access the 'alternate' lifetimes of our clients. In truth, there is no past and no future, and so we are accessing what is most relevant to remove the dominant-negative fear of our client.

In entering into the Subconscious Mind and letting it reveal itself to you, you are rewriting that mind program at the same time that you are reading it. Quantum Physics tells us that there are no observers in the quantum field. All acts of observation alter the field. When you find the instigating event of a fear belief in your client, you alter it just by viewing it. Hence the reason we must be in the highest vibrational frequency when we do this work.

Imagination is a place to build reality as well as how the Quantum Field communicates back to us. Things come out of it as well as things going into it! Let the Quantum field show you through the power of your imagination the appropriate lifetime of your client.

PART TWO

STEP FIVE CONT.
AKASHIC LIBRARY

"We have so lost touch with the profundity of the imagination that the outer world seems to appear solidified in form, which is merely reflecting that our imagination is concretizing. Having lost our acquaintance with the aesthetics of the imagination, we become "an-aesthetic," numb to our feelings and cut off from the heart, anesthetized from ourselves. Disconnected from the creative organ of the imagination, we lose our sense of aesthetics and our capacity to appreciate beauty. Instead of symbolizing our experience so as to creatively express and liberate it, we become seemingly held captive by a self-reinforcing feedback loop inside of our minds which continually generates a literal, particularized, and concretized viewpoint, both towards the world and ourselves. To the extent that we lose our connection with the ever-flowing novelty and majesty of our own creative imagination, we forget our fluid nature, becoming stunned into immobilization, alienated from and a trauma to ourselves. The play of and our play with the creative imagination, however, is the very act that cultivates, empowers and transfigures the subtle body into healing nectar, which dissolves and dis-spells our seeming trauma".

God the Imagination by Paul Levy

What are we doing in the Akash?

At this phase of the Method, we are entering even more deeply into the subtle body/subconscious of the client, as we guide them to a reunion with the aspect of themselves from the instigating event.

Our task is to guide the client into a conscious reconnection to themselves in the Akash, where all lived experience is held.

We are witnessing and describing this reunion whilst also allowing the space for the client's own experience. We may see more than our nonlocal intuition guides us to explain.

There is very little that we can predict about what will happen in this space or how the reunion will take place.

We know that the client's aspect from the concurrent lifetime will appear on one side of the Akash, as the client stands at the altar in the centre of the Akash.

We do know that there will be an integration of the concurrent life with the current life.

We know that we will know when this has happened via our nonlocal intuition, and then we will also invite the client to affirm that they have identified this as having happened.

We know, and we make space because the client's experience may be different to our own.

As long as the integration occurs and the client moves further from fear to love, anything else is possible. We trust our imagination, the fourth-dimensional expression of our nonlocal intuition.

PART TWO

PRAXIS

We are going deeper now through the dimensions of time and space. Let your body sink even more deeply into your seat. We retrieve the aspect of you that has been stuck in the time and space of that lifetime.

Notice you are in front of a doorway.

Notice the colour, size and shape of the door. Walk towards it.

Knock on the door signalling your intention to go deeper.

The door opens effortlessly in front of you.

You find yourself at the beginning of a narrow bridge of light. The bridge of light leads across the endless void of pure possibility.

You feel completely held and ready. You are curious. Open.

You step onto the bridge of light, and step by step, one foot in front of the other, you cross the bridge of light, crossing over the endlessness of everything and nothing below.

You are safe and held as you make this crossing. Step by step, one foot in front of the other.

You arrive at the other side of the narrow bridge and step onto the solid earth before a vast stone wall. The wall slides back, revealing the interior of an ancient stone pyramid. You run your hand across the cool, worn stone of the pyramid wall. You feel your feet on the stone floor. As you are ready, you make your way deeper into the pyramid.

At the apex of the pyramid, there is an opening through which light streams in, illuminating this sacred space.

With curiosity and love, you walk deeper within, step by step.

The temperature here is perfect for you. The air is richly fragrant. You can feel the sacredness around you and the reverent stillness of this holy space. As you look around, you observe that across the other side of the pyramid is a person.

Trainer

Describe the person from the lifetime as you saw them before, without too much detail. It's important we don't shut down the intuition of the client. From here describe exactly what you see happen. Remember this is nonlocal intuition and you will receive this information because you have requested it.

For example...

"The Priestess stares you in the eyes, and her magnetism and power is irresistible"

"There is paper on the table and the aspect of self from the alternate lifetime is writing a message"

PART TWO

PRAXIS

> This next part of the session is fluid and open. Each client will have a different experience. Your intention is to reunite your client with the lost aspect of themselves. You cannot rush this, and you must use your intuition to know when it is done.
>
> Let the process unfold. Sometimes messages will be shared, and sometimes energy will be exchanged. Your job is to witness and hold space for what is occurring. THERE WILL BE A TRANSFORMATION FROM FEAR TO LOVE FOR ALL. When it is complete, you move to the final phase.

The aspect of you from this lifetime says to you now:

> **Trainer:** Determine via your intuition which statement to use.

We are spirit. Whole and innocent. All is forgiven and released.

OR

- *I am sorry*
- *Please forgive me*
- *Thank you*
- *I love you*

You notice that the aspect of you from this alternate life is beginning to merge with your own body.

This may feel like a physical sensation, such as a change in temperature or tingling in the body. You may see something that assures you the process is complete. Or you may simply experience a certainty.

With a nod of your head, let me know when you feel that this integration is complete. Take your time. There is no hurry.

> **Trainer:** Wait upon your client here. You may get an instant response or it may take several minutes. Stay with your client observing them energetically and physically.

PART TWO

PRAXIS

With a lightness of step and a sense of wholeness, you make your way back across the pyramid floor.

As you step across the threshold, you notice that you are once more in your own space.

We support the unification of the lifetime with integrative breath. Follow my instructions carefully. Begin by tapping on the side of one hand with two fingers of the other hand. Keep tapping as we breathe together. Breathe in through the nose filling the belly as much as possible. Hold. Release through the mouth with an audible sigh. Hold. Breathe in through the nose filling the belly as much as possible. Hold. Release through the mouth with an audible sigh. Let your breath return to its own natural rhythm. Return your hands to your lap.

Bring some gentle movement back to your fingers and toes. Deepen your breath.

When you are ready, and only when you are ready, blink open your eyes. I invite you now to share any of your experiences from the session so far if you choose to do so.

Trainer: Ask your client to share any aspect of their experience with you. Some people will be very keen to do this. Others will not. Allow time. Be gentle. Move slowly. This is an epic journey. At this point you may take notes as your client talks.

Prompt them to recall details....

'When you entered the pyramid what did you feel?'
'What did you see when we went back to your lifetime?'
'Where did you feel that subconscious fear in your body?'

These are simply suggestions. Each conversation will be different. Remind your client that they have rewired their subconscious. It is profound and life-changing work.

Be careful not to override his/her own experience. You may have seen things that the client did not or vice versa. Be sure to be a partner on the journey not the authority.

PART TWO

FOLLOW UP TEMPLATE

The Akash

The Akash, also known as Ether or the Unified Field, is the container of ALL. It is the record of your Soul's awakening journey. In the Method, we go into the Akash to retrieve that aspect of Self that has become trapped in a particular moment, frozen in space and time, because of fear. But the Akash can be utilised in any way you can imagine – to create, to call forth latent skills, to encode consciousness – for it is the record of ALL.

For this practice, we are inviting the client to create from this place. We can think of this practice as entering the field, or encoding consciousness. We use it to support our client to create a new reality from a higher plane of consciousness – beyond the known of their lives.

Theory

In the simplest terms, if we want to create change in our waking life, we must begin to create that change at the energetic level – the level of pure consciousness. Consciousness encodes reality. Energy first, physical second.

The level of change and the place we create from is the subconscious. The subconscious is not impressed by language but by symbol. The way that consciousness is communicated is via vibration, which is generated by feeling. The symbol is encoded by us through consistent use. The subconscious is able to generate that feeling state instantly when it becomes familiar with the symbol. The importance of this is that regardless of the state of our reality, we have created a greater cue to the subconscious than external evidence.

Praxis

- Lead the client into Heart Congruence
- Once in that state, invite the client to see, hear, feel or know their consciousness encoding symbol for the life event they are working with. This may be a symbol such as the first letter of a word (like Expansion, Power, Abundance, Expansion, Problessness etc) or a tree, bird, animal etc. Anything that is easy for the client to bring to mind. Ask the client to open their eyes. You can invite the client to write down, or do it for them, five feelings states associated with the symbol (i.e freedom, bliss, gratitude, joy, ease, grace) that represent the feeling states of the life they want to inhabit.

PART TWO

FOLLOW UP TEMPLATE CONT.

Praxis cont'd

- Be sure to record this list for yourself as you will use it in the process
- Invite the client to close down their eyes once more, and lead them into the Theta brainwave state through the opening of the Akashic meditation up until the arrival in the Akash.
- Invite the client to call to mind the symbol they have selected. Invite them to see it like seeing an image projected on the wall of the Akashic LIbrary.
- Now lead them into the feeling states associated with the symbol. Guide them with the following:

  As you see, hear, feel or know the symbol of [client symbol], feel the feelings of _____ (list the feeling states slowly, giving time for the client o move from one to the next) filling you up, every cell in your being. Feel the feeling state flooding your entire being. You may recall a memory in which you felt _____ Or you may imagine a future moment when these feelings are your reality. Let the feelings flood over your being and through your subtle body. Stay fully present to these feeling states as we create the new subconscious program. Let's move into silence now so you can connect even more deeply to the symbol through these feelings.

- Allow the client several minutes here to encode consciousness in the Akash.
- You can repeat the statement, stay present if you feel they may have wandered off into the reasoning mind.
- When you feel they are ready, guide them with the following:

  Now surrender the feelings and mental images to the God Mind and know that the prayer is received. Now very gently, begin to bring some gentle movement back to your body, deepen your breath, and when you are ready and only when you're ready, blink open your eyes.

Invite your client to share anything about that experience that they want to.

Encourage your client to continue working with this symbol in an ongoing way. If you are working with them over time, encourage them to journal their experience and assign a frequency of use.

PART TWO

STEP SIX
SACRED 13 ARCHETYPES

PHILOSOPHY

What is channelling?

In this phase of the Method, we are channelling archetypal energy. What is channelling? And what are archetypes?

As you train in the Third Level, channelling is the connection to a higher level of consciousness than we can currently access in our normal waking state. By this definition, the entirety of the Methodology and Praxis is channelling, and this is true. We are attuning ourselves to the highest possible vibration to serve our client.

In this phase of the Method, we are doing this in a very particularised way. We are attuning to the frequency of sacred archetypal energy. So how does this happen?

Let's review the law of Mentalism for a moment. This law states that All is One. When we channel, we are attuning to an aspect of that One-ness within ourselves. We are not 'going out to connect to something or someone. We are going within. The paradox here is that 'within' is All. We contain it all.

> 'YOU ARE NOT A DROP IN THE OCEAN. YOU ARE THE ENTIRE OCEAN IN A DROP.'
>
> *Rumi*

We must put down the idea that the energy we are connecting to is separate from us. All is One. We are at that.

As we channel the archetypes, we connect to that higher vibration within us of the priestess, or the wife or the alchemist. It is an aspect of our God nature, not our little ego-identified personality. So it takes time to work the muscle of our nonlocal consciousness to allow ourselves to open to that much higher vibration of the archetype.

So what is an archetype?

In our work, archetypes are patterns of energy that repeat. They are part of us all, contained within the collective unconscious. This pattern has been witnessed so many times before that it has been named. It has a shared meaning in our collective consciousness. It is part of the consciousness of All. In the capacity of our work as Intuitive Intelligence Trainers, we may see through form to formlessness on behalf of our client to the symbolic or spiritual dimension.

Identifying with the archetype rather than a specific historical figure, angel, master, guide etc., allows us to stay out of dogma and preconceived ideas that we or our clients may have about the 'personality' you channel. Identifying the archetype alone (for example, the alchemist/healer instead of naming Jesus) avoids the client jumping into their Reasoning Mind and out of the session (for example, 'I'm not Catholic, 'I don't believe in Jesus' etc.).

Instead, we are communing with or as the archetypal pattern and allowing the wisdom to be received by the client in an open and receptive manner.

PART TWO

How do we commune with the archetype?

Like all phases of the Method, it is our nonlocal intuition that guides us here. We are simply allowing ourselves to tune into the archetype present for the client and then to allow that energy to speak 'as us', which means we would be speaking in the first person (I am the warrior) or with us (The warrior is here).

The known of the archetypes with which we commune

The amount of theoretical information provided regarding archetypes in the next section is necessary for your work with them as part of the Method. Based on the frequency with which this particular set of archetypes showed up in my one to one work, I have curated this list of archetypes. The theory has been developed from the work of Carl Jung, Caroline Myss, Clarissa Pinkola-Estes and Sally Kempton. These all have male counterparts, but our focus is on the sacred feminine in this training.

Please note, this archetype may or may not be the same as identified at the Shadow archetype phase of the Method.

Maiden

Also known as the innocent.
Full of wonder and desire, and her desires for her own heart. She is an optimist, embodying purity and independence.

Qualities: *Innocence, open hearted, independent, full of wonder, curious*

Mother

Giver of life at the cosmic and human levels. Gentle and fierce. Lioness when required. Caregiver for all. Desires to help and protect others. She is that which sustains and nurtures.

Qualities: *Fierce love, protector, sustainer, nurturing, responsible, creator, life-giving*

Maga

Within every woman there is a wild and natural creature, a powerful force, filled with good instincts, passionate creativity, and ageless knowing. Often associated with the phase of a woman's life after child rearing and before the crone, she is free of the burdens of seeking partnership, raising children or even creating a home. As such she is untethered. Cedar Barstow states, "I have arrived at my Self in this life season. I'm not trying to prove myself and so I'm now driven by a desire to use my gifts and passions to give back. The name Maga came from one of the women in our community, Sylvia Keepersii. An apt and potent image, Maga was intended as the feminine version of Magus – the wise man, magician."[35]

Qualities: *Wise, free, self-assured, sovereign, enigmatic, unfuckwithable*

Crone

Spiritual gatekeeper. Access to the deepest mysteries of the Cosmos. Has forgone the yearnings and desires of the world, and is very close to the veil between worlds. She is mystical. She is turned completely inward. She is the weaver of the Universal energy.

Qualities: *Non-attached, patient, all knowing, deep insight, wisdom keeper*

Seductress/Wild Woman

She is alive with desire, full of confidence and mystery. She lives outside of the rules of the world. She is the dark goddess. Also thought of as a rebel, she does not adhere to expectations. She is irresistible and powerful.

Qualities: *Irresistible, rebel, self-approving*

Warrior

Assertion, control, strength, courageous, tenacious, selfless, humble, on the path of service for a greater good. She cultivates a sense of safety for others without dominating. She is efficient, clear thinking and precise. She wants to prove her worth through her deeds.

Qualities: *Independent, objective, action taker, raw feminine power, selfless, disciplined*

---

[35] http://www.moonsong.com.au/evolution-of-the-triple-goddess/

PART TWO

Teacher

Her higher purpose is mastery of the knowledge she attains so that she may communicate it to others. She is a mentor. The teacher brings an aspect of advocating "right action," dharma. The teacher observes, tracks, scans, monitors data from all sources (within and without) and channels wisdom leading to "right action."

Qualities: *Profound communication, humble, highest purpose is the transfer of knowledge, inspirer*

Student

Deep reverence for life long learning. Also known as the explorer or the seeker. The student is inspired by the attainment of the sacred mysteries and to know herself at deeper and deeper levels. She is a free spirit and does not want to be contained or remain fixed. She is self-contained.

Qualities: *Explorer, seeker, free spirit, self-contained*

Wife

Strength, compassion, partnership, co-creation and compromise are all part of the higher nature of the wife. She is willing to see from other perspectives, and to forgo her own desires to create something bigger than herself in shared partnership. She is a diplomat and a negotiator and a peacemaker.

Qualities: *Diplomat, negotiator, balanced, co-creator, thrives in connection, self-aware*

Healer/alchemist/medicine woman:

Service above all else, to ease the suffering of the world. She is intuitive, patient, otherworldly, with access to wisdom from outside of time and space. She is the embodiment of compassion. Desire to understand the fundamental laws of the Universe and the true nature of healing, can journey between the worlds to find the medicine for her clients.

Qualities: *Intuitive, liminal, insightful, transformative, motivated by the desire to serve*

Priestess

Transpersonal, both within the world and outside of it, she can occupy multiple realms of consciousness at once. She meets the needs of her community above all else. She is a connector, a facilitator between the material and the spiritual, a mediator of powerful spiritual, psychological and emotional energies that make up who we are. The Priestess calls forth and directs energies between unconscious and conscious awareness, affecting our material and spiritual sense of well being. She is also known as the Mystic.

Qualities: *Self-reliant, can bring the sacred into the mundane, transpersonal, not driven by egoic needs, autonomous, devout, motivated by a holy purpose*

Queen

A courageous and life sustaining leader, she can make the choices that others do not have the courage to make, for she can see beyond the dimensions of time and space to access the bigger picture. She is fearless, fierce and carries deep and ancient wisdom. She is uncompromising for she knows what others do not yet know, and she carries this responsibility with grace and authority. She is magnetic.

Qualities: *Magnetic, expansive, courageous, just, responsible, committed to the greater good, strong leader*

Goddess

A woman in the fullness of her Goddess archetype feels like this: She emanates dynamic energy, flowing, ever changing with boundless intuitive wisdom and creativity. Her presence is inspiring and causes one to feel renewed—stimulated and revitalized. She is "immanence" (divine presence) personified, spiritually balanced, transcendentally driven, and emanates love to all without.

Qualities: *Compassionate, boundless, inspiring, balanced, generous*

PART TWO

THE SACRED 13 *SPEAK*

Maiden

I am open and so willing. I want to fit the whole world into my being. I want to consume life without hesitation, all of it, the light and the dark. I want to taste it all. I am unafraid of the new and unknown. I am certain of my success. Even if I fall I have won, for understanding is what I seek. I bring my courage like a light to shine into the darkness. I transmute my pain with the innocence of my heart. I am a bold adventurer. Make way for me, because here I am.

Mother

I am the love that requires nothing in return. I am the giver and the sustainer of life. I seek not for return on my investment of love, for love is its own reward. I sustain my own life by nurturing the deep well of love within me. I have the strength to create life from my very being. I return to the abyss and am born anew again and again. This is my power. I cannot be destroyed. I am deeper than time, older than space. I am the cosmic container that contains all. What is greater than me?

Crone

I am not afraid of your beliefs about me. I know when the time comes, and I seep into your veins. You will understand what I know to be true – I already have all that you are seeking. I am the end result of all your fruitless longing. I have lived and died and lived again. I am the vessel and the balm that is poured within. I have danced with the Cosmos and I have peered through the veils. I am unafraid because I know who I am and I am not afraid of her. I embrace that I am outcast, as will you, for in this space of nothingness, everything belongs.

Maga /Enchantress

Without fear, I command the Universe into action. I have occupied the sidelines long enough. I have been forgotten, set aside, abandoned, and overlooked. And finally I hold a mirror up to my own glory, and witness the creatress that I am, without hesitation. For all I thought I wanted has been ripped asunder, and still I rise. I am the most dangerous force on the planet, for I do not need your approval, and yet still I have desire. And with that desire I rip away the veil of illusion and reveal life. I am unstoppable in my power.

Warrior

I am not the half-dressed woman riding bare back into battle. I am the one who casts my fear demons aside by sitting with the discomfort of my history, the agony of my pain, the emptiness of my doubt. I slay my dragons with acts of deep devotion, refusing to settle on the mediocrity of comfort. I do not fear fear. I do not wait to be consumed by unmet ancient wounds. I take out my light and search into the darkness, refusing to be silenced by other people's concern. I am the wise woman warrior, creating spaces of light in the dark night of all. I hold myself accountable to the fire of truth.

Wild woman seductress

I am not your usual kind of weary woman. I am unbridled within my being. I am not consumed by your thoughts of me. I encode my reality with the heat of my purpose. I hold space open between dimensions for fresh wonder to flood the earth. Beyond pain, beyond joy, I am love of the kind you have never met. Self-approving, boundless, untethered from ordinary life, I cast my web wide to draw the world into a new paradigm of consciousness.

PART TWO

Teacher

I am the one you have been waiting for to lead you to the new paradigm of your life. I am not content with the known. I break new ground in your mind and heart and very being to show you what else is possible. I am the flame keeper of your being for my fuel fires your soul. When hopelessness consumes you, I show you the way. I am the one who opens the door and brings in fresh air and fresh life to the weary places by saying, look again, look deeper, you do not know what you see.

Student

I am the closest thing there is to God in this dream, for I have the humility to sit in uncertainty and doubt, when all around me want the mysteries resolved. I will not stop seeking and my restless agitation scares them. But I am the one who inspires the teachers, the dreamers and the creators. My restless yearning sits inside their souls and begs them to go deeper and vaster and wider so that I may make a seat at their feet and feel the bliss of transformation that is my soul's true desire.

Wife

I am the embodiment of true partnership. I am unafraid to speak what is truth for my evolution is the evolution of all. When I rise into my gloriousness I take the world with me. I am the diplomat and the seer of both sides. I dissolve my boundaries into ecstatic union, and emerge into my holiness through my devotion to my beloved. I am not lesser than. I am the greater part because I can hold space for my own and my beloved's truth.

Alchemist Healer

In my presence you are made holy, and my holiness is the medicine. I am the vessel into which you pour yourself so that the healing may occur. My medicine is alchemical. Transmutation of fear into love through the grace of your remembered holiness. It is not magic, this medicine. It is the truth we are all here to recall. I am the medicine woman for all consciousness. I am the healing balm, for I have the willingness to make alchemy of my fear and turn it into love.

Priestess

I stand on the bridge you are yet too fearful to cross, beckoning you to come to me so you may know what I know. From where I stand I can see all time and space. I am anchored in all worlds, peeling back the veil to rearrange time and space on your behalf. I am the bridge that you stand upon to uproot your world and see it from another side. My purpose is clear – to be your guide to the world within the world, and back again, so you too may anchor the truth in the hearts and minds of all.

Queen

I can carry what you cannot yet carry on your own. I carry truth on my shoulders and in my arms and bear the heavy weight of that responsibility lightly because I can see what others cannot yet see. I can hold with grace and dignity the entire Cosmos on my crown, yet still walk with ease, for I have won the battle with the demons within, and I am not afraid of what I am being asked to do on behalf of all. I know my purpose. I know I was born to do it and I am willingness itself.

Goddess

Breathe me in, for I am in everything. I am immanence. I am beyond your ideas of me. I cannot be contained in an idea or an image. I am all. I am grace. I am not even in this world. But everything exists in this world because of me. I am not the stars and the trees and the mountains. But I am the reason they exist. I am the creative power that birthed the Cosmos, and I am bigger than that. You can see my reflection in everything that startles you awake with wonder. I am.

PART TWO

PRAXIS

For this section, you can have your eyes closed or open. Do whatever feels right for you. I will now connect to the primary archetypal energy working with you at this time in your life. As the fear is cleared we can now have a clear connection to the archetypal energy that is surrounding and supporting you. Information received from the archetypal guide always pertains to your soul path and will guide your next steps.

The archetype you are working with now is...

Trainer

As you connect to nonlocal intuition you will sense which archetypal energy is with your client. It will be one of the following...

- *Maiden / Innocent*
- *Mother / Father*
- *Maga / Enchantress (no male archetype)*
- *Crone / Wizard*
- *Wild Woman/ Seductress /Lover*
- *Alchemist Healer*
- *Warrior*
- *Teacher*
- *Student*
- *Wife / Husband*
- *Priestess / Priest*
- *Queen /King*
- *Goddess/God*
- *Wife / Husband*
- *Priestess / Priest*
- *Queen /King*
- *Goddess/God*

Allow whatever guidance arrives here to be shared with your client. Please remember that this is the Soul level of the Method. The information will not pertain to the mundane material world and it is not the time to let implicit knowledge interfere. You are channelling the *Superconscious Mind*.

The archetype is your guide. She goes with you now on the next phase of your journey. I encourage you to _____.

Trainer: Use your intuitive intelligence to identify some embodied practices that supports the client to connect to the archetype in daily life. For example...commune with her, meditate with her, ask her your questions and invite her into your life. You might find an image to place somewhere that reminds you of her.

PART TWO

FOLLOW UP TEMPLATE

Archetype Theory

In our follow up sessions with our client, we can invite the client to connect directly with an archetype to help them find the symbolic meaning of their life situation. This may or may not be a new experience for the client. Either way you can support them to have that direct connection to the archetype for themselves.

Praxis

- Take the client into the ASOC by using Heart Congruence.
- If you are working with the Sacred 13 cards then you can show these to your client and allow them to intuitively select the archetype from the cards (eyes open, looking at the images. NOT blindly choosing without looking!)
- If not working with the cards, invite the client to close their eyes and to listen as you read out the names of the archetypes. Invite the client tintuitively. Let them know that they may feel, see, know or hear the archetype for them.
- Explain to the client that they will now commune directly with the archetype, speaking out loud either as the archetype or with the archetype. Give them an example of each. i.e. With – 'The Priestess wants me to know that she is always with me'. As – I am the Priestess and I am always with you.' Don't get caught up in too much explanation. Let them get into the experience as quickly as possible to avoid them overthinking.
- Once the client has connected to the archetype they are working with in this session, invite them to close their eyes once more and to place two fingers at the centre of their chest. As they are already in congruence, simply allow them a few moments to connect and then encourage them to begin sharing out loud as quickly as possible.
- Once the information has been received and shared (you can take notes if you feel to during this process).
- Once they have opened their eyes, welcome them to share anything about the experience with you. Support the client to connect to this archetype after their session with you.

PART TWO

STEP SEVEN
THE ATONEMENT

PHILOSOPHY

What is the Atonement?

The Atonement is the most significant power we have to serve. The principle of Atonement from A Course in Miracles is that the separation from God never actually happened.

> "ATONEMENT IS THE COMPLETE FORGIVENESS OF WHAT NEVER WAS. IT IS THE FORGIVENESS, THE UNDOING OF THE SINGLE CAUSE OF THE FORM OF SUFFERING, THE ONE THE EGO APPEARED TO MAKE, WHETHER IT BE PAIN, DISEASE, CONFLICT, LOSS, SCARCITY OR EVEN DEATH. WHEN WE ACCEPT ATONEMENT FOR OUR MISTAKEN PERCEPTION OF THESE, WE ACCEPT HEALING (FORGIVENESS) OF THE SINGULAR CAUSE OF THEM ALL, WHICH IS OUR GUILT AS UNCONSCIOUS SELF-ATTACK."
>
> *Nouk Sanchez*

This phase is the final undoing of the ego and the completion of the return to love for the client. Every step of the journey has been the return to love and the release of fear. At the final stage of the session, we bless the work of fear releasing to ensure that the new subconscious program of love is restored permanently.

We have spoken on behalf of Superconsciousness and transmuted fear on behalf of our client. This is alchemy.

The Atonement is forgiveness

Forgiveness is the correction of perception – our correction to know ourselves as One with the mind of God (nondualism). Forgiveness does not mean to bypass or belittle the experience of suffering we have endured, but to change our mind about it, by recognising its higher purpose. This is our task as Intuitive Intuitive Intelligence Trainers on behalf of our clients.

"Everything in and about our lives runs off the fuel of our hearts. We will all have experiences meant to "break our hearts" – not in half but wide open. Regardless of how your heart is broken, your choice is always the same: What will you do with your pain? Will you use it as an excuse to give fear more authority over you, or can you release the authority of the physical world over you through an act of forgiveness?[36]*"*

Forgiveness begins with radical acceptance of what was/is in order to meet the fear within that situation (what will you do with your pain?). This opens us to our symbolic sight (deeper meaning) of the life event.

---

[36] *Anatomy of the Spirit*, pp 216.

PART TWO

STEP SEVEN CONT.
THE ATONEMENT

Forgiveness is the meeting point of the three immutable laws, and the most spiritually fierce practice of all. This sacred practice brings all of the laws into action. Knowing that all is one, that what is within us is reflected in the world, and that the vibration of the feeling state we carry determines the success of our lives, we can witness how invaluable it is to have a regular forgiveness practice, and to give our clients an experience of it via the Atonement, even if they do not know that is what is occurring.

Forgiveness & increasing Intuitive Intelligence

Practicing forgiveness with the same regularity as we practice gratitude takes us beyond ever feeling like we need to forgive. In other words, we stop believing that fear is even a possibility. This section on forgiveness also comes last as it will take all your spiritual fierceness to commit to forgiveness as a daily part of your life. Fear will fight for us and tell us that we need to be right, to maintain our grievances, not let others get away with things. God doesn't need us to police the world. We must forgive if we desire to meet our true nature, which is love.

Unforgiveness and love cannot co-exist – only one of them is real. So we would have to be mad to say we believe in love and then maintain unforgiveness. We must forgive as an act of self-love. When we hold unforgiveness, we poison our consciousness with this low vibration.

Forgiveness is not the same as condoning. We do not forgive so we can be permissive of bad behaviour. We use our discernment to determine where it is best to spend our time and with whom. We do not have to leave with anger and unforgiveness. We can make a choice for love – for self-love – and remove ourselves from situations, people, and places that are not in accordance with the high vibrations we want to inhabit. But we cannot argue with what has happened. Acceptance is the beginning of the forgiveness process.

But what next? How do we move from these feelings of unforgiveness? With gratitude for what has been. Yes. Forgiving is really a willingness to see that the events of our lives have been in our service. From our human perspective, it might be impossible to see how this is so. But luckily we don't need to see how in order to accept, with faith, that this is so. Remember the cornerstone of Intuitive Intelligence is the belief that I am a divine piece of God who is always working on my behalf. At times, this requires all our spiritual fierceness to remember. But it is possible, especially with regular practice. The laws are impersonal – they exist whether we can conceptually engage with them or not.

ACCEPTANCE OF WHAT IS (END OF JUDGEMENT) >>> FORGIVENESS OF WHAT IS >>> GRATITUDE FOR WHAT IS (WHAT WILL YOU DO WITH YOUR PAIN?) >>> CULTIVATION OF SYMBOLIC SIGHT >>> SERVICE (ASCENDING CONSCIOUSNESS)

PART TWO

STEP SEVEN CONT.
THE ATONEMENT

What is the intention of this phase of the Method?

- The client is being invited to the most active and participatory (at a conscious level) that they have been to date in the session
- By re-entering into fear at the final phase, we are demonstrating that there is never an end to fear, and that knowing how to work with fear productively is the key to freedom (as opposed to the end of fear, which is not possible when we are in human form)
- We are showing our client that fear is a friendly ally and not something to reject or be afraid of and that they can alter their vibrational state at will
- We are offering the client an experience of their God nature
- We are offering the client an experience of the Micro Method before we send them away with it and ask them to use it for themselves for seven days post-session
- It is offering them an energetic scaffold. Suppose you think of the analogy of a broken bone. The Method journey has reset the bone, and the Atonement (and the Micro Method) is the cast that holds the bone in place as it heals (as we adapt to the new normal of this fear being absent in our subconscious). It gives the client an energetic boost before they leave us for that reset to hold fast and 'heal' in the most expedient way.

What are we doing as the Trainer at this phase?

- We invite the client to identify a rating for how intensely the dominant fear we have been working without throughout the Method.
- We want them to have an experience of altering their vibrational state at will, so we want the number to be above an eight so that they can see the change most powerfully.
- If they are not feeling a strong fear towards the dominant fear, we invite the client to connect with any other fearful thought that rates highly for them. This is vital to allow them to witness how they can productively work with their fear.
- Our task during this phase is to be such a fierce container for them that their success in bringing that number down is inevitable.
- We do this by moving into heart congruence, guiding the client to do so, with all our fierce focus.
- We are working with more power here than at any other time during the session. This is the work of the Method – vibrational medicine.

PART TWO

PRAXIS

Every moment of this session has transformed the unmet subconscious fear stored in your subtle anatomy into love. We have journeyed to the realm of the subconscious and safely returned together at a higher state of consciousness. Now it is time to re-enter the world. Before we do that let's do a final clear of the dominant fear of _____.

- *Close your eyes and take a deep breath in through your nose, letting it go out through your mouth with an audible sigh. Maintain a slightly extended breath, breathing in for four counts and out for 6 counts*
- *Rate the fear on a scale of 1-10, 10 being the most intense. Our aim is to bring that number down*
- *Share the number with me when you have it*

> ### Trainer
> If the client is not identifying with the specific fear from the beginning of the session then ask them to notice any other stressful thoughts or fears that may have emerged. Often in the heightened state of the session the client is free of fear but it is an important step to perform the atonement. It is training their consciousness to not accept fear as a natural state, and showing them how to change it.

- *In your own way, in one or two words describe the emotion you are feeling, and also where you can feel it in your body.*
- *Place two fingers at the centre of your chest*
- *Now, turn your attention to feelings of _____ (attune to the feeling state that you intuit is the most powerful for your client. For example, gratitude, appreciation, joy and freedom. Name only one feeling). Bring to mind a specific place that you love, have been to, or desire to go to. It could be your bed, a tropical island, or anywhere else real or imagined that evokes this feeling of _____. See, feel, or know yourself in this place. Notice the scents in the air, the temperature on your skin, and the time of day. Notice what you are wearing and how your body feels in this place. Let yourself be fully present in this favourite place.*
- *You must give yourself over to this feeling of _____ with your whole being. Let it build in intensity. Allow the feeling to expand in you with as much focus as possible. As you hold these feelings I am holding you, and the Infinite is holding us both. We exponentially magnify the power of this atonement. Let's move into silence now.*

PART TWO

PRAXIS

> **Trainer:** Go into silence for at least a minute and until you feel the atonement has occurred. You and your client are both in heart congruence but you are guiding the energy.

- *Take a deep breath in and let it go out through the mouth*
- *Look around in your mind's eye for the fear of _____ that felt like _____ that you rated at _____. When you find it, if you find it, rate it again. Let me know this number.*

> **Trainer:** If the number is above 2, repeat up to two more times from the 'Place two fingers at the centre of your chest' bullet point

- *Now, take a deep breath in, and let it go. Bring some gentle movement back to your body, and when you're ready open up your eyes. You have rewired your subconscious away from this fear to a deeper connection to your intuition. Well done.*

> **Trainer – Please note:** If, for any reason you discern through your non-local intuition, your client is not able to actively participate in the Atonement, then it is appropriate for you to be the active creator of space and to allow the client to just receive. In this case use the Follow up Template – the Practitioner led Atonement. This is not the preferred way of working. We want very much for the client to be self-empowering. The option is there for you, however, if required, to invite the client to let go and allow you and the Superconscious Mind to hold that high vibration on their behalf. You may find that after even one round of this, if the number has reduced that you can invite them to actively engage with the process.

PART TWO

PRAXIS

Step 7 – CLOSING

> *Trainer:*
> - To end the session, ensure your client is grounded and fully present. You can do this by a few minutes of chatting, asking them to drink water, to walk around the room or to take some deep breaths in through the nose and out through the mouth with an audible sigh. Use your clinical reasoning to determine how much support they need to anchor back into present time.
> - Give them the Micro Method (hardcopy or explain it to them and send them the recording. You can also add the recording and explanation to a USB for them to take home). Talk them through the Micro Method step by step (draw similarities to what you just did with the Atonement).
> - Ask your client to work with the Micro Method every day for 7 days. Here's what you can say to them to explain why...

There is a good chance that in the days following our work together you may experience uncomfortable emotions. I want you to know that this is very normal, and in fact, it is a really good sign that genuine change has been made at the level of your subconscious. If you do experience discomfort, which might include being short tempered, teary, low vibing, tired, angry, impatient, questioning or even anxious, please note that this is very normal, and that you are very, very safe. In fact, you are probably in the greatest place you've ever been.

This is a positive shift– neurological, physiological, hormonal, and chemical – as your body's addiction to subconscious fear we have just released is altered, and a deeper connection to your intuition is established. When you look at it this way, you can see that this is exactly what you've been calling for. Real change. Let the process happen. Take baths, go for walks, cry, listen to music and most importantly, do the Micro Method, every day for 7 days. Even if you do not have a strong discomfort response to the session, which is also completely normal, please use this tool every day to continue the process of subconscious fear releasing we have begun together. We really don't want the old pattern to take hold, and the Micro Method will support you to keep the subconscious agile and fluid as the work is done. Ideally, we'll also get to spend more time together if that feels right to you.

PART TWO

PRAXIS

POST SESSION

Trainer:

Check in with your client 48 hours after the initial session. Do this via email. The check in is an opportunity to ensure they are using the Micro Method and that they are sitting comfortably with the new vibration they are holding. Change is registered as a danger by the ego, and so it is important to remind your client if they are experiencing fear that this is the habitual response of the ego, and that the Micro Method, journaling, walking, laughter and meditation are the best responses.

PART TWO

FOLLOW UP TEMPLATE

The Practitioner led Atonement

The Atonement in the Method is our opportunity to get our client actively participating in the process. We are holding them in the process, but we are inviting them to lead.

This Atonement, on the other hand, is a practitioner led process which can be used when:

- *Your client is overwhelmed,*
- *They can't get out of the reasoning conscious mind,*
- *They are concretised in fear.*

We step in to connect them directly to heart's Intuitive Intelligence. With this they may have an experience of their God nature, and calm the ego-identified self.

Theory

We use Intuitive intelligence Tapping for this process. Please see your Tapping manal for more on the ways we work with Tapping. In short, Intuitive Intelligence Tapping is our intention to encourage clarity, brightness and flow within the subtle anatomy to enable a stronger communion with our Soul for our client.

To clear the blocks to knowing ourselves as Light, bringing our Soul wisdom, grace and compassion to our thinking, emotions and choices.

To surrender into the I am that I am.

To increase our capacity for happiness and joy, our birthright.

The Reasoning Mind of our client can become overloaded, and confusion is often the result. Trying to think our way out of our confusion with the same mind that led us into it can take us into overwhelm.

So, how do we make Intuitively Intelligent decisions while we are in this state? How do we move into peace?

We surrender. We surrender by remembering. We remember self as God. The beauty, the power, the honesty, the unlimited wisdom, and the unconditional love that is God. Our eternal nature.

PART TWO

FOLLOW UP TEMPLATE CONT.

In this exercise our intention is to build a conscious bridge between our client's dominant human identity (with all its limiting belief systems – BS!) and their intuitive self, their gracious God nature, which is truly limitless.

Praxis

[**Practitioner:** *Connect the client with an issue they wish to address. It may be physical, emotional, mental, spiritual and anything in-between.*

Ask the client to give this issue a rating of intensity from 1-10 with 10 being the most intense.]

Read the following to your client:

- Now, gently close your eyes.
- Slow your breathing, in for 4, hold for 4. Out for 6.
- Connecting with your heart centre, place 2 fingers or your palm over the centre of your chest.
- Imagine now that your breath is moving in and out through your sacred heart centre.
- Breathing in for 4, holding for 4, breathing out for 6. Do this in your own timing.

Tapping side of hand, repeat after me:

'It is my intention to immerse myself/in my gracious God nature Energy/with all of its wisdom and love.'

'I release all of my emotional attachments/ to anything and everything/that may get in the way of this happening.'

'I let go of all resistance I may be holding/ toward connecting with my Gods' wisdom and love, as me.'

Relax your hand to your lap.

- Sense now that you are breathing into a soft, powerful ball of Golden White Light, emanating from your heart centre.
- Allow yourself to merge with this loving and nurturing Light, as it expands to enfold you completely.

PART TWO

FOLLOW UP TEMPLATE CONT.

- This is the power place that is your heart's Intuitive Intelligence.
- Feel the depth of peace here.
- Gently, peacefully, effortlessly surrendering into the deepest wisdom and Love of the Golden White Light.
- The Light is everywhere, and you are expanding effortlessly into Golden White Light.
- Here you are the Love, which is unconditional.
- Floating in this Light of unconditional Love.
- Love and forgiveness, at every level of your being.
- Forgiveness is finding every hiding place in your body.
- Every cell releases its reasons for blame and shame.
- Forgiveness of self and all else.
- Understanding, deep, deep wisdom and understanding, of all you have ever experienced.
- Surrender into this place of perfect beauty and truth.
- Everything else is a part of the dream you have dreamed.
- This place is you, the truth of you. Your eternal, Divine truth.
- Here you are connecting with your own Divine healing power as your vibrational pattern aligns with your perfect Divine blueprint.
- Be in the deep stillness now and receive from the Divine God Source you are.
- In this sacred place you might sense, hear, or feel the wisdom of your Intuitive Intelligence, sharing with you what you need to know.

[**Practitioner:** *Pause for a few minutes here to allow this process to take place.*]

- When you feel ready, become aware of your beautiful body, and thank it for all it does.
- Gently open your eyes and look around at the colours and shapes of your environment.
- Breathing with awareness now.
- Consider your initial issue and re-rate it, 1-10.
- Have a sip of water and take a moment to note your new insights.

PART TWO

FOLLOW UP TEMPLATE

The Optimise Method

- Client explains their life situation that is creating a fear response
- Open with Heart Congruence (3-minute practice to create a high vibrational feelings state)
- Lead the client into the cathedral of their heart
- Invite the client to tap on the side of their hand or through all the points as they focus on the life situation
- Identify the dominant negative self-belief of the life situation for the client (you can get them to do this if it feels right).
- Ask them to identify where in the body they can feel the fear of the life situation

Lead the client through 3 part breathing

- Let the client know that they may feel lightheaded or heat around the head. Let them know they may experience an emotional release. Advise them that the breath is intentionally disruptive and may feel irritating. This is exactly the point.

- This process can also be done lying down. Prepare them by inviting them to have tissues nearby, to take a sip of water or to apply lip balm as the mouth may become dry.

- Demonstrate the breathing technique to the client. Inhale through the mouth, exhale through the nose. Guide them for at least five rounds of breathing.

    ◊ *Inhale through the mouth into the lower belly*
    ◊ *Inhale through the mouth into the solar plexus*
    ◊ *Inhale through the mouth into the heart*
    ◊ *Hold*
    ◊ *Exhale through the nose in one slow release back to the base of the spine*

PART TWO

FOLLOW UP TEMPLATE CONT.

Invite them to continue leading themselves.

- Use a 5-minute piece of music whilst they breathe after you have instructed five rounds. Ensure to share through advanced settings in Zoom so the sound is coming through your computer when working online
- Pause the music at the end of the 5 minutes
- Let the client complete the final round, then invite them to:
    ◊ *Inhale through the nose and hold the breath*
    ◊ *Exhale with audible sounds (moan, sigh, cry, etc), releasing the energy from the part of their body holding the fear. Encourage them to move their body if this feels right*
    ◊ *Encourage the client to continue making sounds for as long as they desire*
    ◊ *Make releasing sounds alongside the client if this feels right*
- When complete, ask the client to identify how that part of their body is feeling now and the intensity of the fear or any state change
- If still intense, then do the breath for another 5-minute round

Lead the client through the Practitioner-led Atonement to complete. You can use the language the client has mentioned in the session in the Atonement.

PART THREE

TAPPING PRACTICES

PART THREE

INTUITIVE INTELLIGENCE TAPPING

What is Tapping?

Falling into the category of energy psychology, tapping is a stress reduction technique. It combines physical stimulation (tapping the fingertips on acupressure points) with remembering a traumatic event in order to release emotional attachments and restore energy flow to bring calm and clarity.

There are many versions of tapping. Clinical Emotional Freedom Techniques, developed by Gary Craig, (an adaptation of TFT), has had a great deal of research. To date there are in excess of 275 peer reviewed, published studies and 5 meta-analyses (a statistical analysis combining the results of multiple scientific studies) coming from around the world.

Dr Larry Nims tells us: "Your unconscious mind is your faithful servant and it will carry out your commands." The intentions used in tapping work are commands to your unconscious mind. It is a practical way to restore calm and clarity. This work can reconnect you to your inner resources, your confidence, and your personal power.

We can use tapping to help release attachments to past conditioning and free us to be who we are to live our own version of success, starting from where we are now.

Tapping on energy meridians while remembering an event, emotion, feeling, pain, etc. helps to release tension and the anxiety held in the body and mind. The physical tapping calms the amygdala in the midbrain, part of the limbic system (thought to be responsible for emotions, survival instincts and memory), resulting in a decrease in the output of the stress hormones, cortisol, and adrenaline.

The amygdala detects stress and instructs the hypothalamus-pituitary-adrenal axis to release cortisol into the bloodstream. Calming the ever-alert amygdala is of vital importance to our health. Recent studies are showing the potential for change with tapping.

The Journal of Evidence Based Integrative Medicine reports

Emotional Freedom Techniques improves multiple physiological markers of health:

- Cortisol down 37%
- Pain down 57%
- Depression Down 35%
- Happiness up 31%
- Food cravings down 74%
- Immune system markers up 113%
- Anxiety down 40%
- PTSD symptoms down 32%
- Blood pressure down 8%

Tapping – A Short History

Roger Callaghan, an American psychologist, had been working with Mary, who had a severe water phobia, for some time, without success.

Callahan was aware of the energy meridians that flow through the body and when Mary reported feeling uneasy in her stomach while looking at water, he decided to tap on a meridian end point under the eye, associated with the stomach. After some time, Mary was able to splash water on her face, reporting no fear!

Callaghan went on to develop a treatment procedure which he called Thought Field Therapy.

Quite a complex process, using a specific algorithm for each issue presented.

PART THREE

One of his students was a Stanford trained engineer, **Gary Craig**, who simplified the process of TFT creating **EFT, Emotional Freedom Techniques**. This is the method of tapping most widely used and researched today.

Two of Gary Craig's students of EFT were **David Lake** MD and psychologist **Steve Wells**. Together they developed **Simple Energy Techniques**, and another called Provocative Energy Techniques – SET and PET.

More recently Steve Wells has developed a technique he calls **Intention-based Energy Process** or IEP, sometimes referred to as Intention Tapping. Inspired by the work of Byron Katie, this method is getting some very good feedback from practitioners around the world who have incorporated it into their work.

Dr Dawson Church has done a great deal of research into tapping and makes that available to all via www.eftuniverse.com. He also records a lot of research by others.

Dr Peta Stapleton – Assoc Professor at Bond University is one of the world's leading researchers in the world of Clinical EFT. Working with fMRI imaging, Peta was able to show what actually happens in the brain as a result of tapping.

There are many specialty areas in the tapping world, such as anxiety, finance, performance, PTSD, trauma, abundance, weight loss, relationships, children, eating disorders, sports performance, and pain.

Although tapping is popularly known for its miracle 10-minute cures, they are not the norm. Tapping work is often effective much more quickly than talk therapy (for example) but it is important to understand that it is often an on-going process.

Intuitive Intelligence Tapping

*Intuitive Intelligence Tapping has been developed by Angelique Adams to support the work of **The Method** within the Institute of Intuitive Intelligence.*

Intuitive Intelligence Tapping is used to help people **accelerate spiritual awakening**, to connect with a deeper awareness to their Soul wisdom and to support people to move more quickly through their limiting beliefs to live optimised lives.

It supports the physical, mental, and emotional aspects to come into balance, aiding the healing process.

Intuitive Intelligence Tapping is nurturing and supportive while bringing clarity. It invites us to erase pain and self-doubt, while releasing some of the limitations that belief systems, born of that pain and self-doubt, have created.

We help to release attachments to energy we may have been connected to for lifetimes, our own and that of our lineage, clearing energy in all directions of time and space.

We give intent to separate our delicate energy field from the fears and self-doubt of the mass consciousness on this planet, in order to create our own unique path.

Intuitive Intelligence Tapping Intention Statement

It is our intention to encourage clarity, brightness, and flow within the subtle anatomy to enable a stronger communion with our Soul.

To clear the blocks to knowing ourselves as Light, bringing our Soul wisdom, grace and compassion to our thinking, emotions, and choices.

To surrender into the I am that I am.

To increase our capacity for happiness and joy, our birthright.

PART THREE

Diagram of Energy Centres

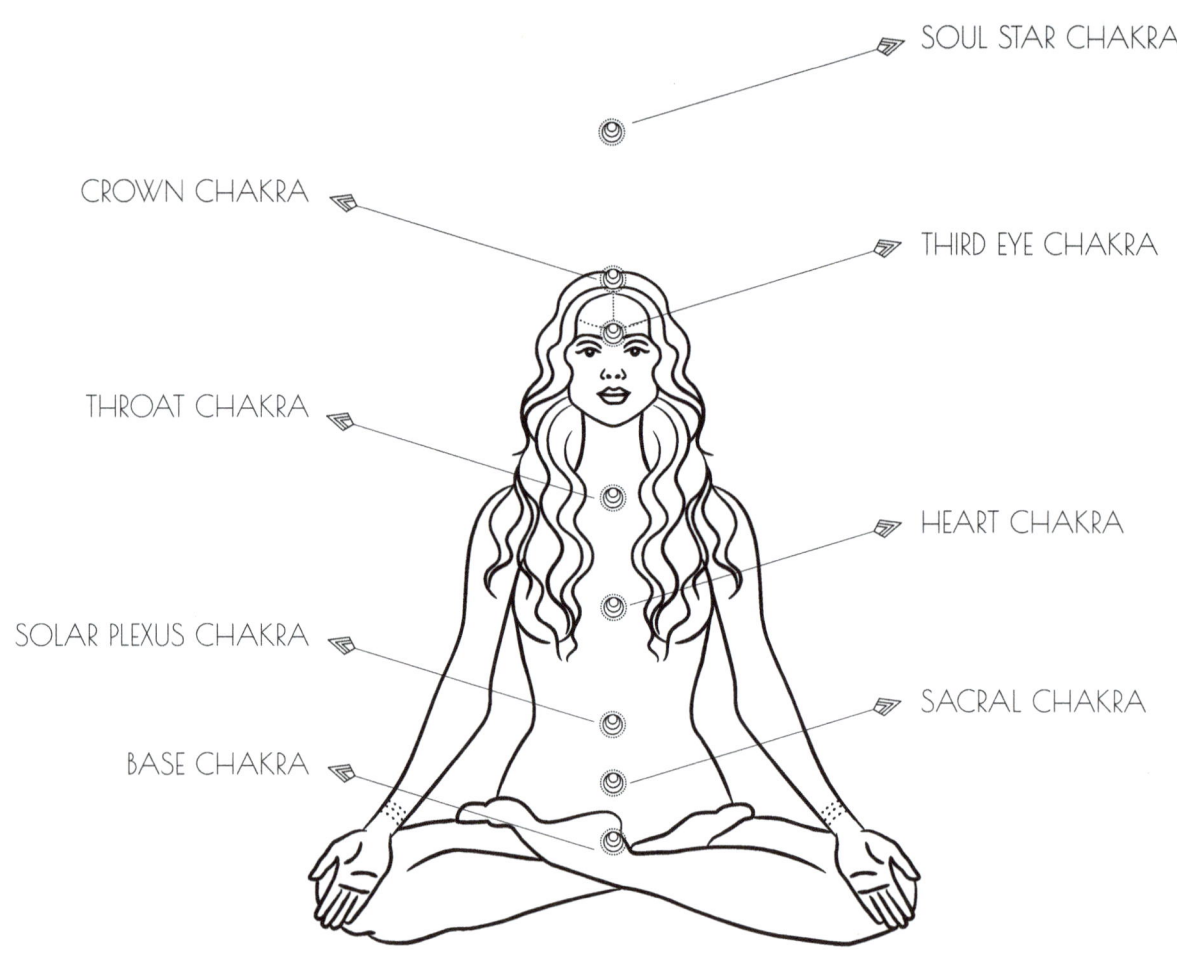

PART THREE

The Tapping Points

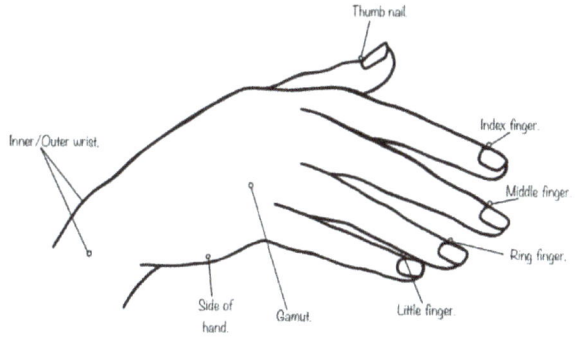

PART THREE

The Tapping Points

Head & Body

Top of head – using the flat of your hand tap lightly across the fontanelle

Eyebrow point – tapping with two fingers at the beginning of the eyebrow

Side of eye – on the bone surrounding the eye – not on the temple

Under eye – on the bone surrounding the eye – in alignment with the pupil

Under the nose – with two fingers (one hand) only

The chin – under the lip in the crease of the chin (one hand only)

Collarbone point – with two fingers on the end of the collarbone (the lumpy bits) – where you tie your tie – come down 1 inch or 2½ cms to an indentation

Underarm – 4 inches or 10 cms down from the underarm (in the middle of the bra strap)

Thymus point – middle of the chest

Hands

Wrists – inner and outer – measure two finger widths towards the elbow, from the crease. Here you can gently slap across the wrist with the fingers of the other hand. Some people like to gently slap the wrists together.

Side of hand – tap with the fingers of your dominant hand on the fleshy side of the other hand, (this was called the karate chop point and you will still see some references to this)

Finger points – tap with two fingers on the side of the thumb near the base of the nail. Go onto the pointer, middle, ring and little fingers in turn, tapping on the same place. This is useful for discrete tapping. You can also use the thumb to tap on the side of the fingers of the same hand.

Gamut point – on the back of either hand. Come down between the little finger and the ring finger until you find the valley.

You can tap with either hand or both hands. Some people feel as though they get better value with two hands, however all of the research in Clinical EFT is done using one hand. You can tap on either side and change sides at any time. Tap 7-10 times on each point, approximately. You can tap slowly or faster if it feels right for you. Tap with enough pressure to feel it but not so hard that it is uncomfortable.

PART THREE

The Primo Vascular System

There is a new biomedical theory that explains the possible existence of a previously unknown system.

Called the Primo Vascular System, it integrates the features of the cardiovascular, nervous, immune, and hormonal systems.

It provides a physical substrate for the acupuncture points and meridians.

The Primo Vascular System is a possible PHYSICAL meridian system (not energetic).

This would explain why tapping on it (or using traditional acupuncture) actually has biochemical changes, and why you need to tap the exact acupoint.

Tapping protocols may also be more easily accepted as mainstream when we use language such as Primo Vascular System and meridians or energy.

Dr Peta Stapleton

Mechanosensory Transduction

The process that converts mechanical forces into electrical signals.

When mechano receptors are stimulated, mechanically sensitive cation channels open and produce an inward transduction current that de-polarises the cell.

Cation – a positively charged ion (cat ion)

Mechanosensory transduction refers to the processes through which cells sense and respond to mechanical stimuli by converting them to biochemical signals that elicit specific cellular responses.

Dr David Feinstein:

How can tapping points send signals to the brain?

Cells can convert pressure on the skin into electrical activity. Electricity caused by pressure is piezoelectricity. Cells sense and respond to mechanical stimuli by converting them to biochemical signals that elicit specific cellular responses.

Stress Management

The most important gift tapping brings is stress reduction.

Dr Peta Stapleton, Associate Professor, Bond University:

"Tapping is very effective for reducing anxiety, stress and other emotional issues and it works on both real and imagined stressors.

Tapping significantly increases positive emotions and self-esteem and resilience and decreases negative emotional states.

Tapping appears to affect the amygdala (stress centre in the brain) and hippocampus (memory centre) and both play a role in the decision process when you decide something is a threat.

Tapping has been shown to lower cortisol levels, which is the stress hormone. Too much cortisol can result in lowered immune function and ultimately affect our physical health."

Karl Dawson, creator of Matrix Reimprinting and one of the master teachers of EFT:

"Science is proving that our body's ability to heal and repair itself is greatly affected by our beliefs, thoughts, emotions, and intentions. They have a profound vibrational effect upon our continually evolving genetic code. We are the programmers of the code. DNA activation is our software upgrade".

PART THREE

Tapping can help us to bring balance to our beliefs, thoughts, and emotions.

The wonderful Dr Bruce Lipton, cell biologist, tells us:

"The moment you change your perception is the moment you rewrite the chemistry of your body. What's interesting about EFT tapping is that it is a process which really, in some sense, engages super learning. And super learning is the equivalent of pushing the 'record button' on the subconscious mind."

With tapping we can help to change our perceptions.

Tapping helps us find and eliminate the blocks to happiness.

It is a simple method of stress relief.

It does not need us to believe in anything.

It has been called the WD40 for emotions!

Tapping is an essential component in your 'managing my life' toolkit.

The Subtle Anatomy

With Intuitive Intelligence Tapping, the intention is to create balance within the subtle anatomy, our personal energy field.

Our subtle anatomy is responsive to all of our thoughts and emotions, good and bad. It is responding within the moment to our environment, what we ingest, what we read and watch on TV, how safe we feel, the stories we tell ourselves, how others treat us, love us, accept us. How well we do those things for ourselves. It responds to movement, meditation and so on.

Our subtle anatomy is being impacted by the energy we encounter every day. Although we have a resilient energy body that works hard to neutralise the toxins that we are subjected to, it benefits from our awareness and attention to bring it back into a state of balance and beauty.

What is the purpose of the energy field/subtle anatomy?

For our purpose, suffice it to say that we are humanity wrapped in divinity. And that divine aspect of us is connected via the subtle anatomy.

I see the subtle anatomy as an interface between our temporary identification with self (our humanity) and our eternal nature (our divinity).

When the subtle anatomy is healthy, bright and beautiful, energy flows. The body knows health or can heal itself more efficiently. The mind is stable, and we are more creative. We enjoy radiant energy.

We are a healthy cell within the body of life. And a healthy cell can shine its light for other cells. A healthy cell is vibrating at a frequency that others are attracted to. A healthy cell is a healing cell.

With tapping we are supporting our vital energy within the auric field.

Often there is a more enthusiastic approach to being creatively alive.

Simple Energy Techniques

SET was developed by Australian Energy Psychology pioneers Steve Wells, Psychologist, and Dr. David Lake, medical practitioner and psychotherapist. Many of the techniques and strategies used in SET are adapted and modified from Emotional Freedom Techniques (EFT), Thought Field Therapy ™ (TFT), and other energy psychology approaches, although SET also has several elements that make it uniquely different from those approaches.

With Simple Energy Techniques:

Continual tapping is implemented throughout the entire session. Dr Lake discovered that he achieved better results when his patients had more time tapping on the meridians.

PART THREE

SET uses **finger point tapping** in addition to the head, upper body and hand points.

You tap on **whatever you are aware of**.

SET introduces an effective way of working with tapping that allows us to work where we are at.

No set-up statement is needed. This can be hugely beneficial for people who may get stuck thinking they must use the right words or it won't work! This puts stress on the process.

No reminder phrase is used.

Simple Energy Techniques information is available from:

https://www.eftdownunder.com/wp-content/uploads/2013/11/setreport.pdf

Please take the time to read this report.

Continual Tapping

Just tapping continually for 30-60 minutes a day is wonderful for **toning/tuning the energy body and the nervous system.**

Break this down into times that suit your day.

Tap anytime, any place you feel comfortable.

It is not necessary to be focused on an event, emotion or feeling.

It sidesteps the thinking mind. We just tap and see what happens.

As Steve Wells says, here we are not trying to be our own psychologists. We are not asking the client to change anything.

Because it is neutral and non-judgmental, the client's self-criticism, self-judgement and self-punishment may soften.

Steve Wells –

'Enough meridian stimulation may cause a shift in your nervous system so that negative problems cannot take hold in the same way.'

Tap this way to support your body/mind to function more smoothly, to raise your vibrational frequency. Personal Peace Procedure.

Making Peace with Your Past

The personal peace procedure is a valuable tool for you to become clearer as a person and as a practitioner. As you release your own triggers you are less likely to be caught up in the stories you will inevitably hear.

This is a very useful exercise for you to meet some of the subconscious tripping points in your own interpretation of life. It is simple to do.

If you feel unsure about approaching a memory that may overwhelm you, please seek assistance from someone trained in tapping, or a qualified therapist, (also preferably trained in tapping) to support you.

Personal Peace Procedure Recipe

Begin by making a list of 5-10 unsettling issues that have presented in your life. Things that you wish had not happened. If you were writing the book of your life these might be chapters you would like to leave out!

Work with tapping on mind (thoughts, beliefs, memories, worries) or body (feelings, intensity, physical location).

Devote time every day and be amazed at your progress.

Note that often one issue is linked to others on your list and by clearing one you may also be clearing others. This may become apparent when you move onto another issue only to find that it no longer has an emotional charge. Victory. **This is called the generalisation effect.**

PART THREE

Make another list when you feel the first one is complete.

Every aspect of your life is positively impacted by the Personal Peace Procedure and you will become clearer as a practitioner, and as a person, freeing yourself from issues that may have snagged you in the past.

You will find other parts of your life becoming easier. Life just feels better, clearer!

By adding this to the list of things you do each day for your own well-being, you will quickly notice a positive difference in many areas.

Dealing with High Emotional Intensity

Even though it is not our intention to activate deeply held memories that may cause angst, it can sometimes happen and it is necessary to have ways to deal with this.

If your client becomes emotional – **tap without words**.

Stay Calm. The most important thing here is for you to remain calm.

Use the quality of your voice to calm the situation.

Your client may access an intense/painful memory that they may not have felt in a long time.

Help your client to feel safe. Have her keep her eyes open.

Tell her that the event is in the past and that she is safe in this time.

Suggest she rest her tongue on the floor of her mouth.

Have her slow her breathing and soften her eyes.

Feel her feet on the floor.

Ask – *can you just rest into the back of your chair?*

Sometimes it is useful to have the client hold or rub a tapping point and breathe. The sore spot is a good one to use. This can be very calming.

If necessary 'break the state.' Ask your client a question about something unrelated to the event. You can ask 'tell me where you are now' or 'what colour are the walls in the room you are in' or 'what do you see through the window'?

When the client is calmer you may gently proceed.

Occasionally you may find the issue has resolved itself without words.

If it is necessary, refer the person to a qualified therapist – ideally one who uses tapping. It is a good idea to have a number of practitioners to whom you may send a client if necessary.

If **you** experience "**secondary trauma**" from working with a client be sure to tap after the session to release this. In some cases, it may be best for you to work with a mentor or support person. As Gary Craig says, 'we are never fully done.'

PART THREE

INTUITIVE INTELLIGENCE TAPPING PROCEDURES

Intuitive Intelligence Tapping – Our Intention Statement

It is our intention to encourage clarity, brightness, and flow within the subtle anatomy to enable a stronger communion with our Soul.

To clear the blocks to knowing ourselves as Light, bringing our Soul wisdom, grace and compassion to our thinking, emotions, and choices.

To surrender into the I am that I am.

To increase our capacity for happiness and joy, our birthright.

Intuitive Intelligence Tapping – The Procedures

Subtle Anatomy & The Centres of Energy

Releasing fears and self – doubts within the energy centres and subtle anatomy. This is the essence of Intuitive Intelligence Tapping. A powerful journey through the chakras so we may more clearly commune with our gracious Soul.

A Colour Meditation

Using light as colour to bring harmony and balance. Use this for a gentle yet effective realignment when a sensitive touch is needed.

Remembering Soul – A Visualisation

Creating a stronger awareness and connection to Soul Energy, Wisdom and Beauty. Intuiting Soul to guide & direct and bring magic to our everyday-ness.

The Golden Light – A Visualisation

A gentle and empowering way to complete your session or as a stand alone experience to bring an empowered sense of calm. This can be a useful way to connect with a client.

PART THREE

The Subtle Anatomy & The Centres of Energy

Bringing Balance to the Chakras with the Power of the Light

This is a journey through the centres of energy that connect us, body and mind, with our energy field, our subtle anatomy.

Here we are combining Tapping with Light and Colour, with visualisation and imagination in order to repopulate each chakra with the healing Light of Source.

We are choosing to work with vibrational frequencies to bring about a re-alignment with our Perfect Divine Blueprint within each chakra.

We are attempting the realignment of the human condition with the Divine perfection that is always available to be accessed at any moment. The perfect Divine blueprint. Using imagination in this way allows the flow of an energy that is needed to create harmony and balance'.

Our intention is to release blocks to happiness and joyfulness.

To prepare yourself before working with another:

For yourself, while tapping a few rounds:

'I release all my emotional attachments to anything and everything that would prevent me from doing my best work with...

Use your creativity here to work with however you are feeling.

Make a **heart connection** to the person you are working with. It is also wonderful to consciously connect with your own **Soul wisdom** and from there ask to serve your client via their Soul wisdom.

Do this before your session with the client.

Have a chakra chart on hand to demonstrate chakra locations.

And the tapping points chart as well.

They are both available in this manual but use your own if you prefer

It is most effective to be able to show them on your screen when working on-line.

Demonstrate the tapping points precisely. Remember it doesn't matter if the points are done in a particular order, but it is essential that the points used are accurate.

Preparation for your client

Disclaimer

Although gaining in scientific support, tapping is still considered to be experimental. It is important that you take full responsibility for your own health. Intuitive Intelligence Tapping is not a substitute for traditional medical attention, counselling, therapy or advice from a qualified health care practitioner. It is not intended to be used to treat, diagnose, cure or prevent any disease or disorder.

Intuitive Intelligence Tapping helps us release tension and anxiety held in our body and mind and is a valuable aid to stress reduction.

We use colour, light, creative visualisation, and our wonderful imagination, along with Intuitive Intelligence Tapping.

You are supported every step of the way and we will move at your own pace.

PART THREE

When this releasing process feels complete, we will restore positive energy flow to each energy centre.

We will move up through all of the major chakras aligned with the physical body and then to one more which is above the head in the energy body. We access this using our powerful imagination.

It will usually take a number of sessions to complete all of the chakras.

Intuitive Intelligence Tapping Intention Statement

It is our intention to encourage clarity, brightness and flow within the subtle anatomy to enable a stronger communion with our Soul.

To clear the blocks to knowing ourselves as Light, bringing our Soul wisdom, grace and compassion to our thinking, emotions and choices. To surrender into the I am that I am.

To increase our capacity for happiness and joy, our birthright.

Visualisation

Let's do a gentle visualisation to help us relax into the present moment.

Make yourself comfortable and ensure you won't be disturbed. Close your eyes and become aware of your breathing.

Gently breathe in for 4 seconds, hold at the top for 4 seconds, and breathe out fully for 6 seconds. Do this a few times.

Allow a little time for this.
Allow your breathing to become easy.

(Pause)

Softly place your hand over the energy centre in the middle of your chest and imagine you are breathing in and out through this chakra.

(Pause)

And as you breathe in and out through your heart centre you may feel the energy there beginning to soften and radiate in all directions.

(Pause)

Gently, softly breathing in and out through your heart centre.

(Pause)

You might feel your energy flowing throughout your energy field.

Relaxing, letting go, releasing.

(Pause)

Take a deep breath and open your eyes.

As we work together today, our intention is to release blocks to happiness and joy.

We will begin with the base chakra.

PART THREE

Base Chakra

Bringing Balance to the Chakras with the Power of the Light

Here we are combining Light and Colour with visualisation and imagination in order to repopulate each chakra with the healing Light of Source.

The Practice:

Guide your client to:

Begin tapping on the centre of your chest, your thymus point, and take a gentle breath.

(Pause)

Now tap under your nose and take a gentle breath

(Pause)

Tap under your lip in the groove of your chin and take a deep breath

(Pause)

As you tap gently and slowly on the side of either hand, place your attention and your awareness on the area of your base chakra at the bottom of your spine. This includes the area of the pelvic floor and the first 3 vertebrae.

You can tap on any of the points with a minimum of 5 different points being optimal.

Imagine, sense, or feel the energy you are holding in your base chakra at this moment.

(Pause) to allow time for this connection

What is happening here for you?

It might be just a fleeting glimpse, or it may be a full picture. It may be a sensation, a thought or a feeling. It might be an emotion. Just allow and observe.

(Pause)

If your client has difficulty connecting, we can invite them to get a little more creative. Suggest there is a cave here that they can connect into via their powerful intuitive imagination. Invite them to enter into this sacred space.

What does it look like in the cave?

This aspect of you may have a voice and may want to communicate with you. You can ask if there is anything you should know and take the time to listen.

(Pause)

If they are still stuck, ask them 'what colours do you see here, what are the walls made of, how much Light is here.'

(Allow your intuition to guide you here) Record what they share with you.

Make sure they are still tapping, side of hand and finger points...

Using a hypnotic and soothing voice –

Now from above your head imagine, sense, feel or see a powerful beam of radiant White Light flowing easily and effortlessly down and in through your crown chakra. Flowing down your spinal column and down, down, immersing your base chakra area in brilliant Light.

The White Light fully illuminates the base chakra area brilliantly. So beautiful.

You can feel any limiting energy here melting away, being dissolved by the Light. It feels very relaxing, very soothing.

The Light continues to flow effortlessly, illuminating your base chakra so brightly. Enjoy this feeling of being nurtured and harmonised and healed by the Light.

Your base chakra is releasing, relaxing, letting go of the energies that may have been keeping you caught up in the stress created by fear and anxiety and self-doubt.

Allow yourself to feel the softening here.

(Pause) here to allow a little time for this to process. At least 60 secs...

PART THREE

What is your experience in your base chakra now?

Usually the energy will be bright and feeling harmonious. If your client is still having some difficulty here we simply remind them to visualise the flow of the powerful white Light flooding the whole area, releasing and relaxing, soothing and brightening.

If necessary, introduce The Simple Energy Techniques.

Ask your client to focus on whatever their issue is at the moment while they continue tapping.

Have them notice when the issue changes as they continue tapping.

Repeat after me, I accept who I am, and I honour the way I feel right now.

At this point ask for their experience.

When you feel the time is right, move on.

Please repeat after me:

I now give myself permission / to release all the limiting vows / I have ever made / relating to my base chakra energy, / in this and all my lifetimes

You can explain that this is like a prayer to the Universe, to focus awareness on the power of these words when they put their intention behind them

(Pause)

Repeat after me:

I restore the right connection / to my perfect Divine blueprint

Share that nature abhors a vacuum, and we can infuse our magnificent Soul energy into the empty space created when we released the limiting vows

Repeat after me:

I restore the right energy flow / of radiant colour to my base chakra

Remembering that colour is one of our most powerful healing tools, it is valuable to gently encourage your client to visualise/sense/feel/ imagine this happening, and to be immersed in the wonderful power of colour. It is appropriate for any colour to present itself. It is not necessary for the known chakra colour to be used here.

Allow some time for this process

Tapping all points, beginning with the side of hand, repeat after me –

I choose a life of joyful abundance.

The energy in my base chakra flows effortlessly

I choose a strong connection to Mother Earth

Check how your client is feeling now

At the end of each chakra, invite your client to take a drink, do a little stretching, take a slow and gentle breath and now, if your client is ready, continue…

Sacral Chakra

As you tap gently and slowly on the side of either hand, place your attention and your awareness on the area of your sacral chakra, four finger widths below your belly button.

You can tap on any or all of the points. Imagine, sense, or feel the energy you are holding in your sacral chakra at this moment.

(Pause) to allow time for this connection

What is happening here for you? It might be just a fleeting glimpse, or it may be a full picture. It may be a sensation, a thought or a feeling. It might be an emotion. Just allow and observe. Pause

If your client has difficulty connecting, invite them to get a little more creative. Suggest there is a cave here your client can connect into via their powerful intuitive imagination. Invite them to enter into this sacred space.

What does it look like in the cave?

(Pause)

PART THREE

This aspect of you may have a voice and may want to communicate with you. You can ask if there is anything you should know and take the time to listen.

(Pause)

If they are still stuck, ask them

'What colours do you see here, what are the walls made of, how much Light is here?'

(Allow your intuition to guide you here) Record what they share with you.

Make sure they are still tapping, any points they prefer and using a soothing voice –

Now from above your head imagine, sense, feel or see a powerful beam of radiant White Light flowing easily and effortlessly down and in through your crown chakra. Flowing down your spinal column and down, down, immersing your sacral chakra area in brilliant Light.

The White Light fully illuminates the sacral chakra area brilliantly. Nurturing and supporting.

You can feel any limiting energies here melting away, being dissolved by the Light.

It feels very relaxing, very soothing.

The Light continues to flow effortlessly, illuminating your sacral chakra so brightly. Enjoy this feeling of being nurtured and harmonised and healed by the Light.

Releasing, relaxing, and letting go of the energies that may have been undermining your ability to create your life joyfully.

Allow yourself to feel the energy softening.

Pause here to allow a little time for this to process. At least 60 secs... time this

What are you experiencing in your sacral chakra now?

Usually the energy will be bright and feeling harmonious. If your client is still having some difficulty here we simply remind them to visualise the flow of the powerful white Light flooding the whole area, releasing and relaxing, soothing and brightening.

At this point ask for their experience.

If necessary, introduce The Simple Energy Techniques here:

Ask your client to focus on their issue, while they continue tapping.

Ask them to notice when the issue changes as they continue tapping.

When the issue is comfortably reduced:

Repeat after me, I accept who I am / and I honour the way I feel right now.

When you feel the time is right, move on.

Feel the nurturing energy of the White Light flowing through to your Sacral Chakra

Please repeat after me:

I now give myself permission / to release all the limiting vows / I have ever made / relating to my sacral chakra energy, / in this and all my lifetimes

You can explain that this is like a prayer to the Universe, to focus awareness on the power of these words when they put their intention behind them

(pause)

Repeat after me:

I restore the right connection / to my perfect Divine blueprint

Share that nature abhors a vacuum, and we can infuse our magnificent Soul energy into the empty space created when we released the limiting vows

PART THREE

Repeat after me:

I restore the right energy flow / of radiant colour to my sacral chakra

Remembering that colour is one of our most powerful healing tools, it is valuable to gently encourage your client to visualise/sense/feel/imagine this happening, and to be immersed in the wonderful power of colour. It is appropriate for any colour to present itself. It is not necessary for the known chakra colour to be used here.

Allow some time for this process

Tapping all points, beginning with the side of hand, repeat after me -

I choose to be joyfully creative

I can choose to create my life with ease and grace

My creative energy flows effortlessly

Check how your client is feeling now

At the end of each chakra, invite your client to take a drink, do a little stretching, take a slow and gentle breath and continue…

Solar Plexus Chakra

Tapping all points, beginning with the side of the hand, repeat after me…

As you tap gently and slowly, place your attention and your awareness on the area of your solar plexus chakra, four finger widths above your belly button.

You can tap on any or all of the points.

Imagine, sense, or feel the energy you are holding in your solar plexus chakra at this moment.

(Pause) to allow time for this connection.

What is happening here for you?

It might be just a fleeting glimpse, or it may be a full picture. It may be a sensation, a thought, or a feeling. It might be an emotion. Just allow and observe.

(Pause)

If your client has difficulty connecting, invite them to get a little more creative. Suggest there is a cave here that they can connect into via their powerful intuitive imagination. Invite them to enter into this sacred space.

What does it look like in the cave?

(Pause)

This aspect of you may have a voice and may want to communicate with you. You can ask if there is anything you should know and take the time to listen.

(Pause)

If they are still stuck, ask them 'what colours do you see here, what are the walls made of, how much Light is here. (Allow your intuition to guide you here) Record what they share with you.

Make sure they are still tapping, any points they prefer. Using a hypnotic and soothing voice –

Now from above your head imagine, sense, feel or see a powerful beam of radiant White Light flowing easily and effortlessly down and in through your crown chakra. Flowing down your spinal column and down, down, immersing your solar plexus chakra area in brilliant Light.

The White Light fully illuminates the solar plexus chakra area brilliantly. Nurturing and supporting. You can feel any limiting energies here melting away, being dissolved by the Light. It feels very relaxing, very soothing.

The Light continues to flow effortlessly, illuminating your solar plexus chakra so brightly. Enjoy this feeling of being nurtured and healed by the Light.

Releasing, relaxing, and letting go of the energies that may have been undermining your ability to create joyfully.

Allow yourself to feel the energy softening.

(Pause) here to allow a little time for this to process. At least 60 secs…

PART THREE

What are you experiencing in your solar plexus chakra now?

Usually the energy will be bright and feeling harmonious. If your client is still having some difficulty here, simply remind them to visualise the flow of the powerful White Light flooding the whole area, releasing, and relaxing, soothing and brightening.

At this point ask for their experience.

If necessary, introduce The Simple Energy Techniques.

Ask your client to focus on whatever their issue is at the moment while they continue tapping.

Have them notice when the issue changes as they continue tapping.

When this issue is resolved:

Repeat after me, I accept who I am, and I honour the way I feel right now.

At this point ask for their experience.

When you feel the time is right, move on.

Please repeat after me:

I now give myself permission / to release all the limiting vows / I have ever made / relating to my solar plexus chakra energy, / in this and all my lifetimes

You can explain that this is like a prayer to the Universe, to focus awareness on the power of these words when they put their intention behind them

(Pause)

Repeat after me:

I restore the right connection / to my perfect Divine blueprint

Share that nature abhors a vacuum, and we can infuse our magnificent Soul energy into the empty space created when we released the limiting vows

(Pause)

Repeat after me, I restore the right energy flow / of colour to my solar plexus

Remembering that colour is one of our most powerful healing tools, it is valuable to gently encourage your client to visualise/sense/feel/ imagine this happening, and to be immersed in the wonderful power of colour. It is appropriate for any colour to present itself. It is not necessary for the known chakra colour to be used here.

Allow some time for this process

Now tapping side of hand:

I choose to live life as my unlimited Self

I choose to radiate my Light into every aspect of my life

I choose to love the unlimited me

Radiant me

Brilliant me

Check how your client is feeling now

At the end of each chakra, invite your client to take a drink, do a little stretch, take a slow and gentle breath and continue...

Heart Chakra

As you tap gently and slowly on the side of either hand, place your attention and your awareness on the area of your heart chakra, in the centre of your chest.

You can tap on any or all of the points.

Imagine, sense, or feel the energy you are holding in your heart chakra at this moment.

(Pause) to allow time for this connection

What is happening here for you?

It might be just a fleeting glimpse, or it may be a full picture. It may be a sensation, a thought, or a feeling. It might be an emotion. Just allow and observe.

(Pause)

If your client has difficulty connecting, invite them to get a little more creative. Suggest there is a cave here that they can connect into via their powerful intuitive imagination.

PART THREE

Invite them to enter into this sacred space.

What does it look like in the cave?

(Pause)

This aspect of you may have a voice and may want to communicate with you. You can ask if there is anything you should know and take the time to listen.

(Pause)

If they are still stuck, ask them – what colours do you see here, what are the walls made of, how much Light is here?

(Allow your intuition to guide you here) Record what they share with you.

Make sure they are still tapping, any points they prefer...

Using a hypnotic and soothing voice –

Now from above your head imagine, sense, feel, or see a powerful beam of radiant White Light flowing easily and effortlessly down and in through your crown chakra. Flowing down your spinal column and down, down, immersing your heart chakra area in brilliant Light.

The White Light fully illuminates the heart centre area brilliantly. Nurturing and supporting.

You can feel any limiting energies here melting away, being dissolved by the Light.

It feels very relaxing, very soothing.

The Light continues to flow effortlessly, illuminating your heart centre so brightly. Enjoy this feeling of being nurtured and harmonised and healed by the Light.

Releasing, relaxing, and letting go of the energies that may have been undermining your ability to joyfully give and receive love in ease and grace.

Allow yourself to feel the energy softening.

(Pause) here to allow a little time for this to process. At least 60 secs... time this

What are you experiencing in your heart chakra now?

Usually the energy will be bright and feeling harmonious. If your client is still having some difficulty here, we simply remind them to visualise the flow of the powerful white Light flooding the whole area, releasing, and relaxing, soothing and brightening.

At this point ask for their experience.

If necessary, introduce The Simple Energy Techniques.

Ask your client to focus on whatever their issue is at the moment while they continue tapping.

Have them notice when the issue changes as they continue tapping.

When this issue is resolved:

Repeat after me, I accept who I am, and I honour the way I feel right now.

I now give myself permission / to release all the limiting vows / I have ever made / relating to my heart chakra energy, / in this and all my lifetimes.

You can explain that this is like a prayer to the Universe, to focus awareness on the power of these words when they put their intention behind them

(Pause)

Repeat after me:

I restore the right connection / to my perfect Divine blueprint

Share that nature abhors a vacuum, and we can infuse our magnificent Soul energy into the empty space created when we released the limiting vows

Repeat after me:

I restore the right energy flow / of radiant colour to my heart chakra

PART THREE

Remembering that colour is one of our most powerful healing tools, it is valuable to gently encourage your client to visualise/sense/feel/imagine this happening, and to be immersed in the wonderful power of colour. It is appropriate for any colour to present itself. It is not necessary for the known chakra colour to be used here.

Allow some time for this process

Continue to tap and repeat after me:

I choose to joyfully love and accept love

I choose to experience the energy of my heart as unconfined and unlimited

My loving energy flows effortlessly

This grace and beauty of my heart

Check how your client is feeling now

At the end of each chakra, invite your client to take a drink, do a little stretch, take a slow and gentle breath and continue...

Throat Chakra

As you tap gently and slowly on the side of either hand, place your attention and your awareness on the area of your throat chakra.

You can tap on any or all of the points.

Imagine, sense, or feel the energy you are holding in your throat chakra at this moment.

(Pause) to allow time for this connection

What is happening here for you?

It might be just a fleeting glimpse, or it may be a full picture. It may be a sensation, a thought, or a feeling. It might be an emotion. Just allow and observe.

(Pause)

If your client has difficulty connecting, invite them to get a little more creative. Suggest there is a cave here that they can connect into via their powerful intuitive imagination. Invite them to enter into this sacred space.

What does it look like in the cave?

(Pause)

This aspect of you may have a voice and may want to communicate with you. You can ask if there is anything you should know and take the time to listen.

(Pause)

If they are still stuck, ask them 'what colours do you see here, what are the walls made of, how much Light is here.'

(Allow your intuition to guide you here) Record what they share with you.

Make sure they are still tapping, any points they prefer...

Using a hypnotic and soothing voice –

Now from above your head imagine, sense, feel or see a powerful beam of radiant White Light flowing easily and effortlessly down and in through your crown chakra. Flowing down your spinal column and down, down, immersing your throat chakra area in brilliant Light.

The White Light fully illuminates the throat centre area brilliantly. Nurturing and supporting.

You can feel any limiting energies here melting away, dissolved by the Light.

It feels very relaxing, very soothing.

The Light continues to flow effortlessly, illuminating your throat centre so brightly. Enjoy this feeling of being nurtured and harmonised and healed by the Light.

Softening, relaxing, and releasing anything that may have been limiting the flow of Light energy through your gracious throat centre.

Allow yourself to feel the energy softening.

(Pause) here to allow a little time for this to process. At least 60 secs... time this

What are you experiencing in your throat chakra now?

PART THREE

Usually the energy will be bright and feeling harmonious. If your client is still having some difficulty here, we simply remind them to visualise the flow of the powerful white Light flooding the whole area, releasing, and relaxing, soothing and brightening.

At this point ask for their experience.

If necessary, introduce The Simple Energy Technique.

Ask your client to focus on whatever their issue is at the moment while they continue tapping.

Have them notice when the issue changes, as they continue tapping.

When this issue is resolved:

Repeat after me, I accept who I am, and I honour the way I feel right now.

At this point ask for their experience. When you feel the time is right, move on.

Please repeat after me:

I now give myself permission / to release all the limiting vows / I have ever made / relating to my throat chakra energy, / in this and all my lifetimes.

You can explain that this is like a prayer to the Universe, to focus awareness on the power of these words when they put their intention behind them.

(Pause)

Repeat after me:

I restore the right connection / to my perfect Divine blueprint

Share that nature abhors a vacuum, and we can infuse our magnificent Soul energy into the empty space created when we released the limiting vows.

Repeat after me:

I restore the right energy flow / of radiant colour to my throat chakra

Remembering that colour is one of our most powerful healing tools, it is valuable to gently encourage your client to visualise/sense/feel/imagine this happening, and to be immersed in the wonderful power of colour. It is appropriate for any colour to present itself. It is not necessary for the known chakra colour to be used here.

Allow some time for this process

Continue tapping and repeat after me:

I choose to safely express my truth / with confidence and compassion

I can speak my truth with love

I choose to speak with clarity and compassion

Check how your client is feeling now

At the end of each chakra, invite your client to take a drink, do a little stretch, take a slow and gentle breath and continue...

Third Eye Chakra

As you tap gently and slowly on the side of either hand, place your attention and your awareness on the area of your third eye chakra, in the centre of your forehead.

You can tap on any or all of the points.

Imagine, sense, or feel the energy you are holding in your third eye chakra at this moment.

(Pause) to allow time for this connection

What is happening here for you?

It might be just a fleeting glimpse, or it may be a full picture. It may be a sensation, a thought, or a feeling. It might be an emotion. Just allow and observe.

(Pause)

If your client has difficulty connecting, invite them to get a little more creative. Suggest there is a cave here that they can connect into via their powerful intuitive imagination. Invite them to enter into this sacred space.

What does it look like in the cave?

PART THREE

(Pause)

This aspect of you may have a voice and may want to communicate with you. You can ask if there is anything you should know and take the time to listen.

(Pause)

If they are still stuck, ask them

What colours do you see here, what are the walls made of, how much Light is here?

(Allow your intuition to guide you here) Record what they share with you.

Make sure they are still tapping, any points they prefer...

Using a hypnotic and soothing voice –

Now from above your head imagine, sense, feel or see a powerful beam of radiant White Light flowing easily and effortlessly through your crown chakra to your third eye.

The White Light fully illuminates your third eye centre area brilliantly. Radiant Light shining in all directions.

You can feel any limiting energies here melting away, being dissolved by the Light.

It feels very invigorating.

The Light continues to flow effortlessly, illuminating this centre so brightly. Enjoy this feeling of being harmonised and healed by the Light.

Releasing, relaxing, and letting go of the energies that may have been limiting your ability to see clearly.

Allow yourself to feel this energy softening.

(Pause) here to allow a little time for this to process. At least 60 secs...

What are you experiencing in your third eye chakra now?

Usually the energy will be bright and feeling harmonious. If your client is still having some difficulty here, we simply remind them to visualise the flow of the powerful white Light flooding the whole area, releasing, and relaxing, soothing and brightening.

At this point ask for their experience. If necessary, introduce The Simple Energy Technique. Ask your client to focus on whatever their issue is at the moment while they continue tapping. Have them notice when the issue changes, as they continue tapping. When you feel the time is right, move on.

Please repeat after me:

I now give myself permission / to release all the limiting vows / I have ever made / relating to my third eye energy, / in this and all my lifetimes.

You can explain that this is like a prayer to the Universe, to focus awareness on the power of these words when they put their intention behind them.

(Pause)

Repeat after me :

I restore the right connection / to my perfect Divine blueprint

Share that nature abhors a vacuum, and we can infuse our magnificent Soul energy into the empty space created when we released the limiting vows

Repeat after me:

I restore the right energy flow / of radiant colour to my third eye chakra.

Remembering that colour is one of our most powerful healing tools, it is valuable to gently encourage your client to visualise/sense/feel/ imagine this happening, and to be immersed in the wonderful power of colour. It is appropriate for any colour to present itself. It is not necessary for the known chakra colour to be used here.

Allow some time for this process.

PART THREE

Continue tapping and repeat after me:

I choose to see clearly and confidently as my third eye opens joyfully.

I am safe and in control. It is safe for me to see clearly.

Check how your client is feeling now.

At the end of each chakra, invite your client to take a drink, do a little stretch, take a slow and gentle breath and continue...

Crown Chakra

As you tap gently and slowly on the side of either hand, place your attention and your awareness on the area of your crown chakra, on the top of your head.

You can tap on any or all of the points.

Imagine, sense, or feel the energy you are holding in crown chakra at this moment.

(Pause) to allow time for this connection

What is happening here for you?

It might be just a fleeting glimpse, or it may be a full picture. It may be a sensation, a thought, or a feeling. It might be an emotion. Just allow and observe.

(Pause)

If your client has difficulty connecting, invite them to get a little more creative. Suggest there is a cave here that they can connect into via their powerful intuitive imagination. Invite them to enter into this sacred space.

What does it look like in the cave?

(Pause)

This aspect of you may have a voice and may want to communicate with you. You can ask if there is anything you should know and take the time to listen.

(Pause)

If they are still stuck, ask 'what colours do you see here, what are the walls made of, how much Light is here.'

(Allow your intuition to guide you here) Record what they share with you. Make sure they are still tapping, any points they prefer...

Using a hypnotic and soothing voice –

Now from above your head imagine, sense, feel or see a powerful beam of radiant White Light flowing easily and effortlessly into your crown chakra.

The White Light fully illuminates your crown centre area brilliantly. Radiant Light shining in all directions.

You can feel any limiting energies here melting away, being dissolved by the Light. It feels very enlightening.

The Light continues to flow effortlessly, illuminating this centre so brightly. Enjoy this feeling of being nurtured and harmonised and healed by the Light.

Releasing, relaxing, and letting go of the energies that may have been limiting your ability to commune clearly with your own Divine Soul wisdom and love.

Allow yourself to feel this energy softening.

(Pause) here to allow a little time for this to process. At least 60 secs... time this

What are you experiencing at your crown chakra now?

Usually the energy will be bright and feeling harmonious. If your client is still having some difficulty here, we simply remind them to visualise the flow of the powerful white Light flooding the whole area, releasing, and relaxing, soothing and brightening.

At this point ask for their experience. If necessary, introduce The Simple Energy Techniques.

PART THREE

Ask your client to focus on whatever their issue is at the moment while they continue tapping.

Have them notice when the issue changes as they continue tapping.

When this issue is resolved:

Repeat after me:

I accept who I am, / and I honour the way I feel right now.

At this point ask for their experience. When you feel the time is right, move on.

Please repeat after me:

I now give myself permission / to release all the limiting vows / I have ever made / relating to my third eye energy, / in this and all my lifetimes.

You can explain that this is like a prayer to the Universe, to focus awareness on the power of these words when they put their intention behind them. (Pause)

Repeat after me:

I restore the right connection / to my perfect Divine blueprint

Share that nature abhors a vacuum, and we can infuse our magnificent Soul energy into the empty space created when we released the limiting vows

Repeat after me:

I restore the right energy flow / of radiant colour to my crown chakra.

Remembering that colour is one of our most powerful healing tools, it is valuable to gently encourage your client to visualise/sense/feel/ imagine this happening, and to be immersed in the wonderful power of colour. It is appropriate for any colour to present itself. It is not necessary for the known chakra colour to be used here.

Allow some time for this process

Tapping all points, beginning with the eyebrow, repeat after me:

I choose joyful and unlimited communion with my Souls wisdom.

I choose joyful communion with the unconditional love of my Soul.

I celebrate this amazing Soul connection.

The beauty of my Soul.

Check how your client is feeling now

At the end of each chakra, invite your client to take a drink, do a little stretch, take a slow and gentle breath and continue...

Soul Star Chakra

(non-physical approx. 30-60cms above the Crown Chakra)

Have your client sense/imagine/feel this beautiful energy centre. Ask her to use her wonderful imagination as you guide her through this visualisation.

Tapping all points,

It is most important to allow the time for visualisation, pausing between each instruction...

In my soul star chakra, I throw open the doors to my highest wisdom.

The frequency of Divine Love flows in bringing joy and beauty.

I sense this energy as sparkling and radiant diamond light.

I am grateful. I am blessed.

(Pause)

I sense this radiant diamond Light flowing down and into my crown chakra, awakening the energy here more brilliantly. I imagine the petals of the lotus opening to invite a greater flow of the diamond light.

(Pause)

PART THREE

The diamond light is illuminating and radiating from my third eye. I allow myself to sense an opening to a greater awareness of all that is. It feels safe to see a more expansive vision of my life.

(Pause)

As the light continues to flow, I feel it softening my throat energy. I can visualise the energy here radiating gently in all directions, easily and effortlessly. I can express myself with kindness and love.

(Pause)

The diamond light flowing from my Soul Star Chakra is pouring into my beautiful heart. I can feel a great expansion of love emanating from my heart in all directions, as my heart is healed. I am blessed. I am grateful.

(Pause)

As the flow of the diamond light continues, it illuminates my solar plexus. I can imagine/feel/sense my solar plexus glowing as the diamond light heals and releases all blocks to my personal power. Radiating brilliantly.

(Pause)

The magical, mystical diamond light flows in to nurture the energies in my sacral chakra. This sacred area is held lovingly in the light, healing with Divine Love. Releasing everything that limits my power to be a creative God.

(Pause)

And as it reaches down to strengthen my base chakra, I feel, sense the power of the diamond light illuminating my connection to Gaia,

(Pause)

flowing down into the crystalline core of Mother Earth

(Pause)

I am the bridge of Divine Light between Heaven and Earth.

Continue tapping all points...

I restore the perfect flow of Light to all of my energy centres.

Vibrant energy flows in perfect communion with my subtle anatomy and with my Soul Light, always for my highest good and the highest good of all.

Allow a little time for this to quietly percolate through. This is the end of this cleanse and re-connection.

Allow your client to sit with this quietly for a little while you note anything you thought to be note-worthy.

Discuss what your client experienced and take notes.

Advise this work will continue energetically for some time.

Advise staying hydrated and being quiet and gentle with themselves.

If they are in a position to take a 15-minute nap that would be excellent.

PART THREE

A Colour Meditation

Why we work with Colour

The work we do on clearing the energies within the subtle anatomy has a more profound effect than the reasoning mind can encompass.

Energetic blocks are removed or dissipated from the auric field.

As a result, you may feel differently because energies that were helping to define you are now released. Although much finer than the physical, the subtle anatomy is still a dense matter body. In order to fully integrate with the fine energy of the Soul we will use the energy of colour, as an aspect of Light.

We will use tapping to infuse the vibrations of colour where they are needed in order to re-align the frequency of the whole being.

We are all Light beings vibrating at our own unique frequency. Introducing colour as an aspect of Light takes us to the next level of possibility.

Colour brings balance, harmony and joy to the individual, be that a cell, a muscle, an organ, a chakra, a person or a planetary system!

When colour is out of balance, life is out of balance and you are seeing this now at a planetary level. And when the entire planet seems to be out of alignment it is so much more important for the individual to be aware of and attend to their own field of energy and influence.

Colour is free health care and maintenance. As you are aware, illness can be seen in the subtle anatomy before it manifests in the body. Using colour to return the energy field to balance will help to support a healthy you. Attend daily to this aspect of you. It can be likened to a life support system for your physical, emotional and mental bodies.

In this time of our rapid evolution of consciousness, colours in the energy field may look different. This is because we are raising our vibration. We can now begin to see colour at a heightened vibrational frequency. Raising our own frequency gives us access to a new level of sight! You may or may not sense a difference, but I mention this because some people are having this experience. It is commonly reported in NDE's and heightened meditative states.

Intuitive Intelligence Tapping – A Colour Meditation

In this gentle tapping meditation, we present self, as vibrational frequency, to The Light of All. We surrender all into this communion. Every aspect of self, flowing, merging and being in The Light. Allowing the Light. Remembering Light. Remembering the perfect vibrational frequency of self as Light. And in the remembering, aligning every aspect of Self with its own divine perfection, with its perfect Divine blueprint. This is true healing.

Let us begin - *using a gentle, soft, hypnotic voice...*

Let's tap a few rounds together, beginning with the eyebrow point. As we move through the points you may feel a sense of relaxation as your breathing becomes easier.

Tap two rounds, then continuing tapping –

Now slow your breathing. Breathe in for the count of 4, hold for 4 and breathe out for the count of 6. Allow your breathing to carry you into your sacred space, deep within your gracious heart.

PART THREE

And as you tap, imagine you are breathing in through your heart centre and breathing out through your heart centre.

Allow yourself to feel, as your heart centre releases, relaxes, expands. Becoming soft, flowing effortlessly. The energy that is your radiant heart, radiating effortlessly. Letting go, letting God.

Because you can. And it feels so good. This is so easy. Your heart Light is glowing, radiating. Now place your hands in your lap as you enjoy this experience.

Stop speaking here for a moment to allow this direction to land.

A ball of delicate Golden Light, immersed in a soft cloud of White Light emerges from the centre of your heart-space.

This gentle and powerful energy embraces every aspect of you, body and mind. And every part of you aligns with the Golden Light.

Take a few moments here to feel the alignment, with all the gifts it brings. At every level. Surrender everything you are into this Light.

(Pause)

Tapping again, side of hand. Relaxing more deeply now, effortlessly. Letting go. Letting go and floating in the Light.

The Light is alive and vibrant. It is Life itself. Surrendering into this delicate cloud of Golden Light.

Dissolving into The Light. Oneness. No beginning, no end. Becoming the Light.

(Pause)

From deep within the Light that you are, emerges a colour that is perfect for you in this moment.

Observe this colour as it expands. Like Angel wings it wraps you in its powerful energy, bringing to you what you most need.

Just let yourself be in this magical space, created for you. Perfect for you.

(Pause)

Know that a powerful alignment is taking place. Drawing back all of the scattered aspects of you.

And you are becoming stronger in your wholeness.

You may experience greater clarity of mind.

Integrating all of you into the Light, the truth of you reclaiming its place in your life.

Sit within this energy of alignment while I am silent.

(Pause) for 2 minutes – more if you feel it is right for your client.

Breathe gently with awareness. And as you come back into awareness of your body and the place you are in, allow the Light to stay present, to be with you all of the time.

Stretch your body a little and take a few minutes to record your unique experience.

Know that you are the Light and it is always there for you to connect into with greater awareness.

PART THREE

Remembering Soul – A Visualisation

*Please become familiar with this
process before presenting it.*

Use these ideas (in your own words) to prepare your client for the work...

*We are so much more than our physical/emotional/
mental bodies, remarkable as they are. We are Soul.
We are Light. This is our eternal nature.*

*We know that a small portion of our great Soul Light is temporarily
inhabiting a human body. Eternally we are Soul in all its wisdom
and grace. This is our divine nature, the truth of us. We are Soul.*

*In this exercise, Remembering Soul, we use tapping with
visualisation to invite a more intimate awareness of communing
with our magnificent Soul. It is in this conscious re-connection
with our Soul wisdom and love that we can free ourselves,
support ourselves to become the best version of SELF.*

*We can learn to run all of our ideas and thoughts, our intentions
and our desires, our hopes, dreams and wishes through the wisdom
and love of the Soul. We can connect into the wisdom of the sage.*

*And it is here that we find the love and support we may have been
looking for all of our lives. It is here in this sacred space of us that
we will know we are loved, loving, loveable, that we are love.*

*In this visualisation it is our intention to expand our consciousness
to allow a greater flow of Light to transport us to a feeling of deep
connection, of reconnection to all that we can be, to all that we are.*

*Nothing here is new, we are simply opening the door to
remembering SELF in all its powerful beauty and truth.*

PART THREE

Let's begin with a visualisation.

Describe here the power of imagination, of visualisation. When we take the time to go within and to visualise something that may be dear to us, we begin the process of drawing that imagined thing closer. We are creating cords of energy that we send out into the universe.

The universe responds energetically, and we begin to see clues supporting our intention begin to manifest in our lives. Soooo exciting.... so practise this often with a clear intention in mind. The clear intention to remember and to immerse yourself in your gracious Soul.

Shall we begin? ...

Tapping all points beginning with the side of hand, for one round, saying out loud...

It is my intention now to immerse myself / in my gracious Soul Light / with all of its many gifts...

I release all my emotional attachments / to anything and everything / that may get in the way of this happening.

Remember to leave time after each instruction

Relax your hands

Close your eyes now and place 2 fingers on your heart chakra in the centre of your chest. Slow your breathing, softly and gently now.

(Pause)

Imagine you are breathing into a ball of golden light in your heart centre.

Observe as this radiant light begins to expand to include all of you, with each breath you take.

Until you are completely immersed in a cloud of brilliant golden light.

(Pause)

Guide your client (slowly) to:

Visualise, sense, imagine or feel a pathway of light emerging from your heart, moving upwards through your throat, your third eye and your crown, going higher and higher.

This pathway of Light flows effortlessly up and into your Soul Star chakra, approximately 30-60cms above your head. Remember, imagination is a powerful gift for creating a new reality.

And you sense your Soul Star chakra becoming more active and vibrant as you place your attention here. You find it easy to sense this powerful energy centre.

As your Soul Star chakra begins to radiate even more brightly than usual, the Light flows, expanding in all directions.

And this Light becomes even finer and more delicate, as it reaches to meet your incredible Soul Essence.

Spend a little time here immersing yourself in this feeling.

(Pause) here to allow the imagination time to do its work.

Here we are working with **The ESSENCE of Soul**

Tapping side of hand, repeat after me –

I restore the right energy flow and balance / with the essence of my Soul.

(Pause)

I choose to immerse myself in deep awareness / and in communion with my Soul.

(Pause)

PART THREE

I allow it to be easy to merge with / and remember this eternal part of me.

Take time here to allow this communication.

Here we are working with **The LOVE of Soul**

I restore the right energy flow and balance / with the love that is my Soul.

(Pause)

I choose to embrace this deep luscious love / as the very essence of me.

(Pause)

I allow this Divine love to flow easily / for me and through me, to all else.

Take time here to allow this experience

Here we are working on the **WISDOM of Soul**

I restore the right energy flow and connection / with the wisdom of my Soul.

(Pause)

I choose to know that this wisdom is there for me always.

(Pause)

And I make the choice to allow this connection with my Soul Wisdom to be easy.

(Pause)

Relax your hands now and enjoy a little precious time immersed in Soul energy while I am quiet.

Allow maybe 2 minutes of quiet time here – time this and mute your microphone

Tapping all points beginning with the side of hand, repeat after me.

I choose to live with ease / in the grace and beauty of my Soul

I choose to know that I am eternally one with the power and joy of my Soul

(Pause)

Here you might give yourself permission to relax even more deeply, while you luxuriate in your Soul's mystical, magical beauty.

Let her enfold you in your own divine perfection, healing, balancing, nurturing and loving you, all of you.

And you just know that everything you have been searching for is here.

Surrender into deep communion.

There is healing occurring at every amazing level of you.

Relax your hands.

Now just be quietly present for a few minutes to receive easily and effortlessly.

Allow 2-3 minutes of quiet time here. Remember to time this and to mute your mic.

You may choose to give a clear intention to remember your Soul connection every day, until it is ever-present in your awareness of self.

Gently bring them back and ask about their experience and make a record.

And so it is, and it is so!

PART THREE

The Golden Light – A Visualisation

In this tapping sequence, we immerse ourselves in Golden Light.

You will experience the Golden Light in your own unique way.

The words open you to opportunities to connect with The Light and enjoy your own mystical experience.

Letting in The Golden Light can feel magical.

Activate your powerful imagination here to maximise the potential of this process.

Slow your breathing now, in for the count of four, hold for four, breathe out for 6.

Or if you have a favourite breathing method, use that.

Repeat this as you imagine breathing into and out from your own sacred heart centre.

Feel yourself relaxing, releasing, letting go.

Feel the energy in your heart centre beginning to flow softly, gently.

Close your eyes and, tapping on the side of your hand, repeat after me...

I choose to feel relaxed and quiet / all of me / my breathing is easy / a fine mist of Golden Light surrounds me / nurturing me, softly, gently.

(Pause) to allow the visualisation to happen – approximately 1 minute

This is a command to every level of your being, which often responds very quickly. This is about the power of choice to influence your body.

Tapping on your Eyebrow Point

My heart energy softens / as the Golden Light flows in / sparkling, radiant.

(Pause) here for approx 1 minute

Here we are giving the command to release and relax. We are activating our 40,000 heart neurons, enhancing the communication between heart and head.

Tapping on the Side of your Eye

I am unlimited / Golden Light showers over me / it flows through me / I release my energy into The Golden Light.

(Pause) to allow the visualisation

Fear, anxiety, stress and self-doubt can be challenged and replaced by a more joyful choice. And by recognising the power of choice, it might be applied to other aspects of your life.

Tapping under the Eye now

I can create miracles / I am the architect of my life / re-building, rejuvenating / merging with Golden Light

(Pause)

I can create miracles – suggesting you are Divine energy made manifest, so why not make the choice to move into your Divine power right now. Changing up your energy – it is all so do-able. Every miracle is based on unconditional love. We are Soul – unconditional love, therefore we can create miracles!

Tapping Under Nose

In this sacred space that I am, I choose love / I sense my innocence / I sense my purity / Golden Light illuminates every cell.

(Pause) for at least 1 minute here

PART THREE

You are a sacred being of Divine energy, right here, right now. This is sending your prayer to the universe. 'I sense my innocence' is inviting us to remember that we are always a perfect child of God. Sensing our innocence is a challenge, but in truth we are eternal Soul.

We are innocent and pure and our Divine nature cannot be damaged.

Tapping on the Chin

Immersed in Golden Light / I am nurtured, loved and whole / I am blessed

(Pause) for 1 minute

Golden Light will always hold us as we remember and become more of our truth, our innocence, our purity, our sacred nature, our great Soul Self.

Collarbone Point

I am a divine gift to planet Earth / I surrender into this perfect love of The Golden Light.

(Pause)

You are an essential and wondrous gift to Planet Earth. You made the choice to be here now, to gift your presence, regardless of what your mind may tell you. Let the Golden Light be your support system until you can truly know 'I am the Light'.

Under Arm Point

I can create a magical life / I can choose to colour my life in beauty and joy

(Pause)

The potential for us to re-invent our lives is huge.

Choosing a new attitude is just a thought away from where we are at this moment.

And a new attitude brings a new feeling state.

Magical. Choosing joy is our super power. We can practise choosing joy.

Heart Centre – Thymus

I choose love and joy to colour my thoughts / to colour my words / and to colour my deeds / as I breathe into the Golden Light.

(Pause)

This is moving into mastery.

Every aspect of your life is returned to love.

Merging with the Golden Christ Light.

Moving into your own Christhood.

Blessed.

Now breathe yourself back into a gentle awareness of your body, and when you feel ready, open your eyes.

Sense the Golden Light all around you.

Repeat this visualisation often.

Each experience will guide you closer to your unlimited potential towards mastery of self.

The Golden Light is always present, just choose to tune in at any time to enhance your awareness of the beauty and joy in your life at any moment.

PART FOUR

FULL METHOD

PART FOUR

THE METHOD PROCESS

For accredited Intuitive Intelligence Method & Trainer Practitioners

DISCLAIMER

The theory and praxis included in this text are for use by qualified Intuitive Intelligence® Method practitioners who graduated from the Institute for Intuitive Intelligence. Intuitive Intelligence ® is a registered trademark. For your reading convenience, we do not repeat ® throughout the text.

The theory and praxis in this text are for professional use by registered Intuitive Intelligence Method Practitioners and Trainers in one-to-one settings.

Overview of the Intuitive Intelligence Method Session

1. Welcome and prepare the client
2. Opening & ASOC
3. Fear Profiling & Shadow
4. Chakra Diagnosis
5. Instigating event
6. Journey to Akashic Library
7. Archetype
8. Atonement & Closing

PART FOUR

THE FULL METHOD SESSION

Pre-client preparation

Praxis

Give yourself around 20-30 minutes before your client's arrival to prepare vibrationally. Move into extended heart congruence for up to 20 minutes, or utilise any other devotional practice. Notice if you have any fear or discomfort and use the Micro Method or Intuitive Intelligence Tapping to meet and clear that fear. Your priority is to hold the highest vibration possible. Do whatever you need to do to ensure this is the case.

> **Understand that everything that happens in the session with you is sacred, from the moment that your client makes the appointment with you to the final goodbye.**
>
> You have entered a sacred contract to perform the divine task of' orienting our consciousness towards a loving investigation in this mysterious, subtle space of our spiritual heart'.
>
> Our work is not the work of the gross, material plane.
>
> We are transpersonal guides, remote viewing through the dimensions of time and space to locate and clear subconscious fear. We are traversing consciousness to return our client to the no-space no-time state of unified, infinite God Self.

Step One – Opening & Asoc

> *Trainer:* When your client arrives or the online session begins ensure:
>
> - Phone is off or out of the room
> - Disclaimer has been read and signed
> - They will not be disturbed
> - No children are present in the room
> - They have water
> - Ask the client where they are located
>
> **Then, prepare them by explaining the process.**

We are now going on an intentional descent to the underworld of your subconscious to clear a specific dominant fear and, in so doing, return you to your true state, which is wholeness. In this state, your innate intuition is optimised, and we accelerate the awakening of your consciousness.

There are reasons that have brought you to this session, yet I do not need to know them. My role is to go beyond the known of your fears to the root of the issues and to rewire your subconscious at this deepest level. Meeting and releasing subconscious fear is the only way to return to wholeness. You are very safe to meet and release your fear in this space with me.

On the journey we are about to take, we are reprogramming your subtle anatomy and your neural pathways so that you can make the permanent shift from fear to love. You will have your eyes closed for the majority of the session. I will guide you into an altered consciousness so you are in the brainwave state that allows the deepest possible reprogramming.

PART FOUR

Let's begin. Close your eyes. Take a deep breath through the nose and let it go out through the mouth. Let's set our intention for the session:

We offer all the karmic fruits of our time together to the highest aspect of you, to the divine, sublime and eternal within you. We give the intention now to access your subtle anatomy and subconscious in accordance with your highest good. The fear that is blocking access to your wholeness melts away with ease and grace. And so it is. And it is so.

Take another deep breath in through the nose, releasing out through the mouth with a sigh, letting go of all the effort required to bring you to this point in your day.

Let your breathing return to its own natural rhythm. Allow your body to sink even more deeply into the seat.

Let yourself be fully here in this ever-present now. Just for these next few minutes, everything you need resides inside this space. It is safe to be here. The world outside is packed away, just for the next few minutes.

Take your attention to the centre of your chest. Feel, think, sense or imagine a spark of light at the centre of your chest.

With every breath in and out, that spark of light begins to expand effortlessly outwards until it fills your entire physical body from the top of your head to the tips of your toes, no effort required.

Your entire physical body is illuminated by your light, your consciousness. And the light moves outwards further still, easily, gracefully, through all the layers of your energy body. Your entire energetic body shines in your light.

And still, the light expands outwards, easily, elegantly, until it fills the entire space in which you sit. Expansive and open, this is your true nature.

The whole room now, and everything in it, bathed in your light. And the light continues to expand easily and gracefully with every breath in and out until it bathes the entire city, *[name the place that they live, town or region]*. Your light bathes the entire _____.

With each breath, the light grows. No effort is required until your light covers the entire state *[or county]* and then the whole country. Effortlessly, your light bathes the entire country.

Open. Expansive, the light of your consciousness moving ever outwards with no effort, across oceans and continents until, in the next breath, your light expands to encircle the globe.

The light of your consciousness surrounds the entire planet. Take a deep breath in through the nose. Let it go out through the mouth. As we journey to meet and clear subconscious fear, know that you are very safe. I am here to guide you every step of the way.

Step Two – Fear Profiling & Shadow Archetype

I will now attune to your dominant negative self-belief stored in your subconscious. The fear has layers. I will speak the layers out loud until we reach the deepest level.

> **Trainer:** You will hear/see/know/feel the dominant fear as a sentence stated in the first person.
>
> *For example...*
> - 'I am not good enough'
> - 'I am not worthy'
> - 'I am unlovable'
> - 'I am not enough'
> - 'I deserve bad things to happen to me'

INTUITIVE INTELLIGENCE TRAINER MANUAL | 184

PART FOUR

Here you will notice that the fear has 'layers'. Speak these out loud to the client. As you speak the first fear, another fear reveals itself behind it. It is the fear informing the fear. It may not happen like this but if it does feel confident to reveal it to your client.

For example...

'I am not worthy. I do not deserve love. I am not worthy or deserving of anyone's love. I am not worthy of God's love'.

Conclude the layers of fear with the statement of the primary fear.

Your dominant negative self-belief is...

Step Two cont. – Shadow Archetype

Trainer: You will notice one of the Sacred 13 shadow archetypes associated with the dominant fear.

The Shadow Archetype associated with the fear is...

- Maiden / Innocent
- Mother / Father
- Enchantress / Maga (no male archetype)
- Crone / Wizard
- Wild Woman/Seductress/lover
- Alchemist Healer
- Warrior
- Teacher
- Student
- Wife / Husband
- Priestess / Priest
- Queen /King
- Goddess/God

Trainer: Next, you will communicate with your client HOW the fear and the shadow interact. The information you share here is coming from your non-local intuition. You will notice the way in which the fear is playing out through the shadow archetype. Take your time. There may be a lot or a little to share here.

In this context, the shadow archetype represents _____.

This archetype has a light form of _____ _____ and in the process of our work together we restore the shadow to the light.

The fear is ready to go now. Every step of this session moves it further and further out through all the layers of consciousness until it is entirely gone.

Step Two cont. – Integrative Breath

Trainer: The following breath will be repeated several more times throughout the session, each time with an additional breath added. Your task is to observe your client through your intuition and determine how long to invite them to hold their breath. You must watch your client energetically and physically and direct their breathing for maximum integration.

We support the release of the fear from the subtle anatomy with integrative breath and gentle tapping. Follow my instructions carefully. Begin by tapping on the side of one hand with two fingers of the other hand. Keep tapping as we breathe together. Breathe in through the nose filling the belly as much as possible. Hold. Release through the mouth with an audible sigh. Let your breath return to its own natural rhythm. Return your hands to your lap.

PART FOUR

Step Three – Chakra Communion

The dominant fear of _____ is located in the _____ Chakra.

I will describe the shape, colour and size of the chakra in the subtle anatomy where the fear is stored. I will then identify how the fear is sitting in your subtle anatomy causing real or potential issues for your physical body, emotional health and spiritual well-being.

> *Trainer:* Describe exactly what you see/feel/hear/know about the chakra in terms of its appearance and feel.
>
> Then, check-in at the three levels of physical, emotional and spiritual/soul level of the chakra as it relates to the dominant fear. Share this with your client as you receive it.

Now, I am going to take a moment to detect if any other chakras have information to communicate in regards to this subconscious fear.

> *Trainer cont'd:* Take as long as you need to identify if there are any other chakras wanting to communicate in regards to this fear. Usually, there are 3 chakras or more. Share whatever else is there in as many chakras as are open to communicating.
>
> When this process is done, direct the client to breathe into the primary chakra in which you identified the fear.

We support the release of the fear from the chakras with integrative breath. Follow my instructions carefully. **Begin by tapping on the side of one hand with two fingers of the other hand. Keep tapping as we breathe together.** Place your attention on the _____ _____ chakra. Imagine you are breathing into the _____ chakra as you breathe in through the nose filling the chakra as much as possible. Hold. Release through the mouth with an audible sigh. Again, breathe in through the nose filling the belly as much as possible, visualising that breath travelling into the _____ chakra. Hold. Release through the mouth with an audible sigh. Let your breath return to its own natural rhythm. Return your hands to your lap.

Step Four – Instigating Event

We will now identify the instigating event, the lifetime in which the fear of _____ began.

What I will describe is much like describing a scene from a movie. Some of you has been stuck in that time and space since the moment of the instigating event. We call it home now.

Let me describe what I see.

> *Trainer:* Simply describe what you see. For example…
>
> 'The scene that I am seeing is when you were an initiate priestess. All the women are wearing an intense purple coloured robe. It is night. Outside. It is cold.'
>
> Describe everything you see and feel. Remember you and your client are not vulnerable to the events in this lifetime. You are simply calling the energy home through intentionally accessing the Akash. This is the most useful information to serve your client's fearlessness.

PART FOUR

> Ensure you identify the FEELING state that the version of your client in this lifetime is experiencing - how do they feel as they form this fear-base belief?

This is where the fear of _____ began.

We support the release of the life event from the subtle anatomy with integrative breath. Follow my instructions carefully. **Begin by tapping on the side of one hand with two fingers of the other hand. Keep tapping as we breathe together.** Breathe in through the nose filling the belly as much as possible. Hold. Release through the mouth with an audible sigh. Hold. Breathe in through the nose filling the belly as much as possible. Hold. Release through the mouth with an audible sigh. Breathe in through the nose filling the belly as much as possible. Hold. Release through the mouth with an audible sigh. Let your breath return to its own natural rhythm. Return your hands to your lap.

Step Five – Akashic Library

We are going deeper now through the dimensions of time and space. Let your body sink even more deeply into your seat. We retrieve the aspect of you that has been stuck in the time and space of that lifetime.

Notice you are in front of a doorway.

Notice the colour, size and shape of the door. Walk towards it.

Knock on the door signalling your intention to go deeper.

The door opens effortlessly in front of you.

You find yourself at the beginning of a narrow bridge of light. The bridge of light leads across the endless void of pure possibility.

You feel completely held and ready. You are curious. Open.

You step onto the bridge of light, and step by step, one foot in front of the other, you cross the bridge of light, crossing over the endlessness of everything and nothing below.

You are safe and held as you make this crossing. Step by step, one foot in front of the other.

You arrive at the other side of the narrow bridge and step onto the solid earth before a vast stone wall. The wall slides back, revealing the interior of an ancient stone pyramid. You run your hand across the cool, worn stone of the pyramid wall. You feel your feet on the stone floor. As you are ready, you make your way deeper into the pyramid.

At the apex of the pyramid, there is an opening through which light streams in, illuminating this sacred space.

With curiosity and love, you walk deeper within, step by step.

The temperature here is perfect for you. The air is richly fragrant. You can feel the sacredness around you and the reverent stillness of this holy space. As you look around, you observe that across the other side of the pyramid is a person.

You instantly know that this is you from the life we just identified. I will describe to you what I see. Be conscious of your own experience, too.

> **Trainer:** Describe the person from the lifetime as you saw them before, without too much detail. It's important we don't shut down the intuition of the client. From here, describe exactly what you see happen. Remember this is nonlocal intuition and you will receive this information because you have requested it.
>
> *For example...*
> "The Priestess stares you in the eyes, and her magnetism and power is irresistible" "There is paper on a table and the aspect of self from the alternate lifetime is writing a message."

PART FOUR

> This next part of the session is fluid and open. Each client will have a different experience. Your intention is to reunite your client with the lost aspect of themselves. You cannot rush this, and you must use your intuition to know when it is done.
>
> Let the process unfold. Sometimes messages will be shared, and sometimes energy will be exchanged. Your job is to witness and hold space for what is occurring. THERE WILL BE A TRANSFORMATION FROM FEAR TO LOVE FOR ALL. When it is complete, you move to the final phase.

The aspect of you from this lifetime says to you now:

> *Trainer:* Determine via your intuition which statement to use.

We are spirit. Whole and innocent. All is forgiven and released.

OR

- I am sorry
- Please forgive me
- Thank you
- I love you

You notice that the aspect of you from this alternate life is beginning to merge with your own body. This may feel like a physical sensation, such as a change in temperature or tingling in the body. You may see something that assures you the process is complete. Or you may simply feel a certainty.

With a nod of your head, let me know when you feel that this integration is complete. Take your time. There is no hurry.

> *Trainer:* Wait upon your client here. You may get an instant response, or it may take several minutes. Stay with your client observing them energetically and physically.

With a lightness of step and a sense of wholeness, you make your way back across the pyramid floor.

As you arrive at the threshold, you notice that you are once more in your own space.

You notice that you are in your seat now, opposite me, listening to the sound of my voice.

We support the unification of the lifetime with integrative breath. Follow my instructions carefully. **Begin by tapping on the side of one hand with two fingers of the other hand. Keep tapping as we breathe together.** Breathe in through the nose filling the belly as much as possible. Hold. Release through the mouth with an audible sigh. Hold. Breathe in through the nose filling the belly as much as possible. Hold. Release through the mouth with an audible sigh. Let your breath return to its own natural rhythm. Return your hands to your lap.

Bring some gentle movement back to your fingers and toes. Deepen your breath.

When you are ready, and only when you are ready, blink open your eyes. I invite you now to share any of your experiences from the session so far if you choose to do so.

> *Trainer:* Ask your client to share any aspect of their experience with you. Some people will be very keen to do this. Others will not. Allow time. Be gentle. Move slowly. This is an epic journey. At this point, you may take notes as your client talks.

PART FOUR

Prompt them to recall details....

'When you entered the pyramid what did you feel?'

'What did you see when we went back to your lifetime?'

'Where did you feel that subconscious fear in your body?'

These are simply suggestions. Each conversation will be different. Remind your client that they have rewired their subconscious. It is profound and life-changing work.

Be careful not to override his/her own experience. You may have seen things that the client did not or vice versa. Be sure to be a partner on the journey, not the authority.

Step Six – Sacred 13 Archetypes

For this section, you can have your eyes closed or open. Do whatever feels right for you. I will now connect to the primary archetypal energy working with you at this time in your life. As the fear is cleared, we can now have a clear connection to the archetypal energy that surrounds and supports you. Information from the archetypal guide always pertains to your soul path and will guide your next steps.

The archetype you are working with now is...

Trainer: As you connect to nonlocal intuition, you will sense which archetypal energy is with your client. It will be one of the following...

- Maiden / Innocent
- Mother / Father
- Maga / Enchantress (no male archetype)
- Crone / Wizard
- Wild Woman/Seductress /Lover
- Alchemist Healer
- Warrior
- Teacher
- Student
- Wife / Husband
- Priestess / Priest
- Queen /King
- Goddess/God
- Wife / Husband
- Priestess / Priest
- Queen /King
- Goddess/God

Allow whatever guidance arrives here to be shared with your client. Please remember that this is the Soul level of the Method. The information will not pertain to the mundane material world, and it is not the time to let implicit knowledge interfere. You are channelling the **Superconscious Mind**.

The archetype is your guide. She goes with you now on the next phase of your journey. I encourage you to _____.

Trainer: Use your intuitive intelligence to identify some embodied practices that supports the client to connect to the archetype in daily life. For example... commune with her, meditate with her, ask her your questions and invite her into your life. You might find an image to place somewhere that reminds you of her.

PART FOUR

Step Seven – The Atonement

Every moment of this session has transformed the unmet subconscious fear stored in your subtle anatomy into love. We have journeyed to the subconscious realm and safely returned together at a higher state of consciousness. Now it is time to re-enter the world. Before we do that, let's do a final clear of the dominant fear of _____.

- Close your eyes and take a deep breath in through your nose, letting it go out through your mouth with an audible sigh. Maintain a slightly extended breath, breathing in for four counts and out for six counts
- Rate the fear on a scale of 1-10, 10 being the most intense. Our aim is to bring that number down
- Share the number with me when you have it.

> **Trainer:** If the client is not identifying with the specific fear from the beginning of the session, then ask them to notice any other stressful thoughts or fears that may have emerged. Often in the heightened state of the session, the client is free of fear, but it is an important step to perform the atonement. It is training their consciousness not to accept fear as a natural state, and showing them how to change it.

- In your own way, in one or two words, describe the emotion you are feeling and also where you can feel it in your body.
- Place two fingers at the centre of your chest
- Now, turn your attention to the feeling of _____ (**Trainer:** attune to the feeling state that you intuit is the most powerful for your client. For example, gratitude, appreciation, joy and freedom. Name only one feeling).
- Bring to mind a specific place that you love, have been to, or desire to go to. It could be your bed, a tropical island, or anywhere else real or imagined that evokes this feeling of _____. See, feel, or know yourself in this place. Notice the scents in the air, the temperature on your skin, and the time of day. Notice what you are wearing and how your body feels in this place. Let yourself be fully present in this favourite place.
- You must give yourself over to this feeling of _____ with your whole being. Let it build in intensity. Allow the feeling to expand in you with as much focus as possible. As you hold these feelings, I am holding you, and the Infinite is holding us both. We exponentially magnify the power of this atonement. Let's move into silence now.

> **Trainer:** Go into silence for at least a minute and until you feel the atonement has occurred. You and your client are both in heart congruence, but you are guiding the energy.

- Take a deep breath in and let it go out through the mouth
- Look around in your mind's eye for the fear of _____ that felt like _____ that you rated at _____. When you find it, if you find it, rate it again. Let me know this number.

> **Trainer:** If the number is above 2, repeat up to two more times from the 'Place two fingers at the centre of your chest' bullet point – only evoking the positive feeling.

- Now, take a deep breath in, and let it go. Bring some gentle movement back to your body, and when you're ready, open up your eyes. You have rewired your subconscious away from this fear to love. Well done.

PART FOUR

Trainer – Please note: If, for any reason, you discern through your non-local intuition your client is not able to actively participate in the Atonement, then it is appropriate for you to be the active creator of space and to allow the client just to receive. We want very much for the client to be self-empowering. The option is there for you, however, if required, to invite the client to let go and allow you and the Superconscious Mind to hold that high vibration on their behalf. You may find that after even one round of this if the number has reduced, you can invite them to actively engage with the process.

Step 7 cont. – CLOSING

Trainer:

- To end the session, ensure your client is grounded and fully present. You can do this by a few minutes of chatting, asking them to drink water, to walk around the room or to take some deep breaths in through the nose and out through the mouth with an audible sigh. Use your clinical reasoning to determine how much support they need to anchor back into present time.
- Give them the Micro Method – you can share a link to your recording of it. Talk them through the Micro Method step by step (draw similarities to what you just did with the Atonement).
- Ask your client to work with the Micro Method every day for seven days. Here's what you can say to them to explain why...

There is a good chance that in the days following our work together, you may experience uncomfortable emotions. I want you to know that this is very normal, and in fact, it is a really good sign that genuine change has been made at the level of your subconscious.

If you do experience discomfort, which might include being short-tempered, teary, low vibing, tired, angry, impatient, questioning or even anxious, please note that this is very normal and that you are very, very safe. In fact, you are probably in the greatest place you've ever been. This is a positive shift– neurological, physiological, hormonal, and chemical – as your body's addiction to subconscious fear we have just released is altered, and a deeper connection to your intuition is established. Looking at it this way, you can see that this is exactly what you've been calling for. Real change. Let the process happen. Take baths, go for walks, cry, listen to music and most importantly, do the Micro Method every day for seven days. Even if you do not have a strong discomfort response to the session, which is also completely normal, please use this tool daily to continue the process of subconscious fear releasing we have begun together. We really don't want the old pattern to take hold, and the Micro Method will support you to keep the subconscious agile and fluid as the work is done. Ideally, we'll also get to spend more time together if that feels right to you.

POST SESSION

Trainer: Check in with your client 48 hours after the initial session. Do this via email. The check in is an opportunity to ensure they are using the Micro Method and that they are sitting comfortably with the new vibration they are holding. Change is registered as a danger by the ego, and so it is important to remind your client if they are experiencing fear that this is the habitual response of the ego, and that the Micro Method, journaling, walking, laughter and meditation are the best responses.

PART FOUR

THE MICRO METHOD

The Intuitive Intelligence Micro Method

The Intuitive Intelligence Micro Method is a simplified version of the full Method that allows whoever uses it to access the Method's power for themselves and have a robust tool to meet his or her fear every day. We must meet our fear every day, and when we apply the Micro Method to our fearful beliefs and physical symptoms, we can quickly move the fear block out of our consciousness.

The Methodology and Praxis work with subconscious fear, for as A Course in Miracles tells us, we are never afraid for the reason we think we are. Our true fear sits beneath the surface of our Conscious Reasoning Minds. We apply the Micro Method to any stressful thought and, as such, release the layers of the fear. The Micro Method moves us beyond self-awareness. We move directly from recognition of the fear into providing the exact conditions required to release that fear. This is a profoundly elegant and straightforward process. It can be done anywhere and at any time. The more often we do it, the more efficient we become in the process. We are building the muscle of our Intuitive Intelligence with spiritual fierceness by being willing to meet our fear every day.

The Micro Method is an advanced practice of Intuitive Intelligence. It will work most powerfully for us when we have trained ourselves with techniques such as Heart Congruence. It is direct and straightforward but requires a commitment to live from the heart's Intuitive Intelligence. It is premised on the three immutable laws. The One Mind is waiting in every moment to guide us back to love. As such, the answers to show us how are always available when we create the optimal conditions for hearing that guidance. Practice the Micro Method with blissipline and be generously rewarded with the exact information required to be fearless. We are learning that we can consciously redirect our feeling states. This is particularly important when we remember that feeling is the language of God Consciousness.

PART FOUR

THE MICRO METHOD CONT.

Here's how to use the Micro Method:

1. Notice the stressful thought or physical symptom

2. Rate the stressful thought or physical symptom on a scale of 1-10, 10 being the most intense. Our aim is to bring that number down with the Micro Method

3. Close your eyes and take a deep breath in through your nose, letting it go out through your mouth with an audible sigh. Maintain a slightly extended breath, breathing in for four counts and out for 6 counts

4. Place two fingers at the centre of your chest

5. Ask silently or out loud, what is the dominant fear in this situation?

The answer will be brief and succinct and will make itself known to you through your dominant clair (clairsentience, clairaudience, claircognisance or clairvoyance). You will see, hear, feel or know the answer. It will be as brief as one word, image, sound or short phrase. Intuition is instant and precise.

6. Now, there are two choices:

    a. If you are still in a state of fear, turn your attention to feelings of compassion for your fear. See it like a hurt little child who is begging for love. Imagine yourself embracing your fear and being deeply compassionate to it. You must give yourself over to this feeling with your whole being. Let it build for around one minute. Allow the feeling to expand in you with as much intensity as possible. Now let go of the feelings of compassion

    b. If you are seasoned in this practice, focus on mental images and thoughts that invoke feelings of deep gratitude. It may be the smile of your child, the sun on your back, or the memory of a holiday. It must bring up for you only the high vibrational feeling of gratitude. You must give yourself over to this feeling with your whole being. Let it build for around one minute. Allow the feeling to expand in you with as much intensity as possible. Now let go of the feelings of gratitude

7. Take a deep breath in and let it go out through the mouth

8. Look around for the stressful thought or physical symptom that you rated on a scale of 1-10. When you find it, rate it again. If the number is above 2, repeat Step (6) up to two more times.

PART FOUR

CLIENT *DISCLAIMER*

[Graduate's Name] is a certified Intuitive Intelligence Method Practitioner/Trainer, authorised to use the methodology and praxis of Intuitive Intelligence®. As an Intuitive Intelligence Method Practitioner/Trainer, she is dedicated to assisting and supporting people in positively changing their lives by meeting and releasing subconscious fear programs in order to increase their innate Intuitive Intelligence.

The work of an Intuitive Intelligence Method Practitioner is designed to meet the needs of women and men who are awake or awakening to the path of spiritual service and seeking metaphysical and transpersonal guidance to scaffold their lives. You must be 18 years or older. If you have a known mental or physical health condition, you must be in the care of a medical health professional before you will be seen by your Intuitive Intelligence Method Practitioner.

The advice and information offered in your session are based exclusively on the impressions and experiences of your Intuitive Intelligence Method Practitioner. She makes no promises regarding the accuracy, relevance and quality of the information and the methods used in her work. She is not a medical or health practitioner. She offers her clients a spiritual, metaphysical and transpersonal perspective to aid them in their self-healing and self-empowerment. There are currently no known side effects or detrimental results when energy-oriented treatments are properly administered by a qualified, experienced practitioner. Because these methods are relatively new, the extent and breadth of their effectiveness, including benefits and risks, are not yet fully known. We encourage you to conduct your own research so you can make an informed decision before proceeding and to be honest with your Intuitive Intelligence Method Practitioner if you have any concerns during your session.

As a Client, you understand that you should never use the information provided by your Intuitive Intelligence Method Practitioner in any way that contradicts, conflicts, or opposes a course of treatment or plan of action recommended by a primary professional provider such as your licensed medical doctor, lawyer or financial adviser. If you ever perceive or feel that information given by your Intuitive Intelligence Method Practitioner opposes a primary professional provider's treatment plan or recommendations, you are strongly advised to follow the advice and instructions of your primary professional provider. If you have any concerns or feel that you do not fully understand the implications of a particular course of action in your situation, you are advised to consult your primary professional adviser before taking action.

CLIENT DISCLAIMER CONT.

It is a condition of working with your Intuitive Intelligence Method Practitioner that you exercise your own personal authority. Your choice to act on any of the information provided in the session is solely your responsibility. By signing this Disclaimer, you confirm your understanding that your Intuitive Intelligence Method Practitioner does not claim to heal or treat your physical, mental or psychological conditions. She simply offers education, physical modalities, health and spiritual guidance to allow people the opportunity to experience and access their optimal selves.

You must not be under the influence of alcohol or drugs when participating in the session, and you must disclose any mental health issues that may impact the ability of your Intuitive Intelligence Method Practitioner to safely work metaphysically with you prior to the commencement of the session. This includes but is not limited to schizophrenia and bipolar. You must be in a clear and balanced state of mind to participate in this work. The work of the Intuitive Intelligence Method Practitioner is not counselling or therapy. It is not a medical technique and does not replace the need for medical care.

Your Intuitive Intelligence Method Practitioner holds her own professional indemnity insurance and offers to work with you as an independent contractor. While the Institute for Intuitive Intelligence developed the Intuitive Intelligence Method Practitioner tools including the Intuitive Intelligence Method and Intuitive Intelligence Tapping, and has every faith in your Intuitive Intelligence Method Practitioner's abilities, the Institute for Intuitive Intelligence takes no responsibility and has no liability for the actions of individual Intuitive Intelligence Method Practitioners. If you have any questions, please discuss them with your Intuitive Intelligence Method Practitioner or email the Institute for Intuitive Intelligence before signing this disclaimer: hello@instituteforintuitiveintelligence.com.

The information that you provide as a Client is confidential and will not be disclosed to any third party at any stage unless required by law or for the specific purpose consented to below.

I agree with and understand the above statements.

Name: _____

Signature: _____

Date: _____

ACKNOWLEDGEMENTS

The work represented in this book emerges from praxis – it has been developed over the many intakes of the Intuitive Intelligence Method and Trainer programs since their inception in 2016. Each group has inspired the theory and praxis of Intuitive Intelligence to grow and expand, to this place now wherein we have created the second edition of our bible.

Born of a yearning to take spiritual development, and in particular intuition, beyond the trinkets and superstitions of the new age, I sought to create a learning environment that I craved on my journey but could not find.

Each person who came into the Institute advanced the theory and praxis of Intuitive Intelligence even more. The willingness, the deep questions, the challenges and even the rejections of the work have inspired me to go deeper, and to create something truly useful on this path of awakening.

I will never stop being the researcher, and so I know that there will inevitably be future editions of this text. But I do know that for now, it is enough. It is more than enough. Those who go forth in the Institute's name deserve this text, and my eternal gratitude.

Intuitive Intelligence is an extraordinary philosophical approach to living a deep faith, and a series of practices that represent deep work. For that is what we stand for. The deep work of a deep faith.

My deepest thanks to the hundreds who have been part of the professional Intuitive Intelligence programs.

Angelique Adams, thank you for bringing Intuitive Intelligence Tapping to the Institute and the world. It has brought so much power to the work of the Institute.

Our mission from the beginning has been to lead the revolution in the intuitive sciences. As the work has evolved and gained in its potency, we know that we do this through disrupting intuition education. And we do that best by qualifying spiritually fierce people globally as Intuitive Intelligence Trainers, socially conscious Leaders, new paradigm Priestesses & contemporary Mystics.

Our intention is to shake things up and to shake off the immature, superficial and downright incorrect myths about intuition that keep all of us from living in an intuitively intelligent world. Now is the time of the reclamation of our highest form of intelligence, and it is the students and graduates of the Institute who lead this way.

We do not do this work for ourselves alone.

It is my privilege, as always, to be in service to this cause.

ABOUT

The Author

Ricci-Jane Adams, Ph.D. is the principal of the Institute for Intuitive Intelligence ®. She trains women globally as new paradigm priestesses, socially conscious leaders and profound mystics, who graduate as clinically qualified Intuitive Intelligence Trainers. Ricci-Jane is author of bestselling *Spiritually Fierce*, a guide to developing intuition beyond the trinkets and superstitions of the new age, *Superconscious Intuition* and *Love Notes to the Divine*. Ricci-Jane has a doctorate from the University of Melbourne in magical realism. She has spent over thirty years devoted to her spiritual awakening and is a qualified Transpersonal Counsellor.

The Institute for Intuitive Intelligence

Founded in 2014 by Ricci-Jane Adams, Ph.D., the Institute for Intuitive Intelligence is a training hub for the greatest spiritual superpower we possess: Intuitive Intelligence®.

Providing short and long form programs in the development of Intuitive Intelligence®, contemporary mysticism and spiritual leadership, we serve people around the globe with online and live training, books and resources for the advancement of the intuitive sciences.

Our focus is on excellence and ethics to bring about a revolution in the perception of intuition on a global scale. We aim to mainstream the intuitive sciences to reunite people with their spiritual self-esteem.

We offer both professional and non-professional pathways. Whether you want to train your Intuitive Intelligence to optimise your life, or to increase your power to serve your community, there is a pathway for you.

https://instituteforintuitiveintelligence.com/

www.ingramcontent.com/pod-product-compliance
Lightning Source LLC
Chambersburg PA
CBHW041712290426
44109CB00029B/2858